Real
South Bank

For Sarah and Pavel, who also love the South Bank

Real
South Bank

Chris McCabe

SERIES EDITOR: PETER FINCH

Seren is the book imprint of
Poetry Wales Press Ltd
Nolton Street, Bridgend, Wales

www.serenbooks.com
facebook.com/SerenBooks
Twitter: @SerenBooks

ISBN 978-1-78172-314-2

A CIP record for this title is available from
the British Library

The publisher works with the financial assistance
of the Welsh Books Council

Printed by 4Edge Ltd, Essex

CONTENTS

EAST

SOUTH

NORTH

BEYOND

Walkt forth to ease my payne
Along the shoare of siluer streaming *Themmes*,
Whose rutty Bancke, the which his Riuer hemmes,
Was paynted all with variable flowers ...
Sweete *Themmes* runne softly, till I end my Song.

Edmund Spenser, 'Prothalamion' (1596)

Glide gently, thus for ever glide,
O Thames! that other bards may see
As lovely visions by thy side
As now, fair river! come to me.
O glide, fair stream! for ever so,
Thy quiet soul on all bestowing,
Till all our minds for ever flow
As thy deep waters now are flowing.

William Wordsworth, 'Remembrance of Collins,
Composed upon the Thames near Richmond' (1790)

The river's tent is broken; the last fingers of leaf
Clutch and sink into the wet bank. The wind
Crosses the brown land, unheard. The nymphs are departed.
Sweet Thames, run softly, till I end my song.

T.S. Eliot, *The Waste Land* (1922)

SERIES EDITOR'S INTRODUCTION

The South Bank, south of the ever-flowing river, a fluctuating two square miles of what was once Lambeth Marsh now turned into an arts and entertainment centreland by the post-war arrival of the Festival of Britain. Is that what this place is? Not quite.

The plan was to tour it all in a single day. It could be done. Like almost everyone I'd been to parts of the South Bank before, I'd seen them on TV, talked about them with others. Famous London. On this occasion to be experienced at speed but the trouble is the place turns out to be so beguiling. It's two days since I started and I'm still here. I'm tracking the crowds along the riverside. If this were the Seine I'd be strolling the Left Bank among the writers and the painters. But it's the Thames and it snakes like a devil. The South Bank. Actually it's just as much a bohemian place as the one in Paris. There they do it with Gauloises. Here we vape. Our poets and our painters are just as good. Our buildings are better.

The South Bank is a part of London that lies on the Thames' southern shore. It's watched over by the Houses of Parliament and stared down by Big Ben. It has the Southbank Centre complex of Festival Hall, Queen Elizabeth Hall and the Hayward Gallery at its centre. Most of it is in the Borough of Lambeth with parts of Southwark to the east. To the west, beyond Vauxhall Bridge is Wandsworth. Another land.

The South Bank's name was adopted during the 1951 Festival of Britain when the country desperately needed a post-war boost and a whole brutalist entertainment and exhibition complex was developed on what was once waterlogged land. The refurbishment of the district had begun earlier in 1911 with the building of what became Ken Livingstone's County Hall. The Red Lion Brewery, on the site of the present Festival Hall, was demolished in 1948. The brewery's symbol, a smiling lion in Coade stone, has been preserved and stands on a plinth gazed at by tourists using Westminster Bridge.

Today I'm following the ghost of William Blake. He wrote *Songs of Experience* here in his house on Hercules Road. The house has long gone, marked by a plaque on the side of the flats which have replaced it. You can find traces of both of them in the underpasses and walkways where memorial, celebratory mosaics have been installed by local artists. Fifty years after Blake Arthur Rimbaud

briefly lived here too, in a house he shared with poet Germain
Nouveau on Stamford Street. Demolished in the fifties. *The
Illuminations* were finished there. Today there's a Poetry Library as
part of the Southbank Centre. It gives verse a legitimacy it has
lacked for centuries. Barry MacSweeney, Alice Notley, Charles
Olson, Bob Cobbing and other boundary-pushers take centre stage.
There is even a Finch selection, all vispo and experiment. In his day
Blake would have been out along the river hand-selling his
self-published books to strangers. He did his own illustrations and
made his own inks. Mrs Blake sewed on the covers.

Along the elevated and pedestrianised The Queen's Walk, raised
to protect the former marshes from Thames flood, are tourists in
full spate. Here stands the carefully renamed Coca Cola London
Eye. County Hall has been converted into a hotel with the Sea Life
London Aquarium, the London Dungeon and Shrek's Adventure!
housed in its extensive basements. The new Skylon, taller than the
Festival of Britain original, illuminated and spinning, is a fairground
ride. If you are going to also use the South Bank put on the whole
of the Ring Cycle or celebrate the tonal music of Alban Berg then
there needs to be an antidote.

Inland from the river are multiple top-end housing developments
– apartment life, in sight of water, and with a price to match. The
streets here have more hard-hats and yellow hi-vis on them than
I've seen since the early nineties boom. In Bernie Spain Gardens
(named after local community activist Bernadette Spain) they are
protesting about the forthcoming arrival of a new Thames
Footbridge. Do we need more ways to cross the river?

Chris McCabe, whose *Real South Bank* this is, has given me a list
of things the district has to offer. He has suggested roads I might
care to walk down. I do but I deviate. Behind the wedge-shaped
sprawl of Waterloo Station with its statue of Britannia welcoming
commuters and its bike racks as big as a battleship the atmosphere
changes. Lower Marsh, a street that hangs on to the old name,
could be in any working class district right across Britain. It's
slightly down at heel with Cuban bars, street art, gable ends gaily
painted, job centre with can-holding hoodies lounging on the kerbs
outside, a train spotter's bookshop, Steve's Bed and Breakfast, fast
food cafes. Outside the community arts centre there's a wall plaque
to Dave Squires 1949-2009 Much Loved Street Sweeper. Just as
well-known as Blake round here.

Beyond the Marsh is The Cut with the Old Vic theatre and John

Calder's Bookshop. Pepys came here and drank at a pub nearby that once stood on the site of the present day stage door. From the Young Vic the road piles on down to the Oxo Tower (one time power station, later factory producing the then ubiquitous meat cube and now restaurant and art gallery complex). If you use your Oyster card you can cross the river here to the place where the lost River Fleet still enters the Thames. You do it via the new Blackfriars Station, a facility built right across the water. The London Overground offers its users magnificent London views.

Facing the Fleet the South Bank has two rivers lost to pipes and sewage systems running under it – the Neckinger and the Effra. Chris McCabe finds both of them in *Real South Bank*. You can't see them but you can sense them. Rivers rarely abandon their power.

I head back along the Thames riverfront to walk the whole of the southern bank as far as Vauxhall. The architecture is London cliché – Tower Bridge, Big Ben, London Eye, Battersea Power Station, the Shard, Tate Modern, St Paul's. As the river bends viewpoint changes as if the writer William Burroughs were cutting it up. I pass St Thomas' Hospital and the Florence Nightingale Museum both sitting in sight of the Houses of Parliament. St Thomas' is an NHS architectural melee with its extant buildings, extensions, demolitions and rooftop additions having their origins in any one of the past three centuries. The complex was founded in medieval times and named after Thomas à Becket although most of its present structure is considerably more recent. Its grounds, with their offer of glimpses into partial demolitions, gothic corridors and abandoned light wells, are worth rambling. Centrepiece is a statue of Sir Robert Clayton (1629-1707), scrivener, Whig MP and hospital president. He stands half covered with ivy against a partially wrecked wall looking as if this were Rome and his relic had only just been uncovered.

Beyond Lambeth Palace with its bridge that allows the Archbishop to cross to the Lords without getting wet on a day that's raining is the Vauxhall Cross MI6 building. Standing in what were once Vauxhall Pleasure Gardens this Mayan temple-cum-power station lookalike exudes secrecy. It is unlabelled, triple fenced and trembles with power. If you could buy an apartment here you could rule the world.

The river here is dotted with boats that double as bars and cafés, Thames floating adds value. Drink and slightly bob, this river is tidal. The slipway below the bridge lets me get Thames mud onto my shoes. The low-tide beach has imported sand on its upper reaches and an out pipe cover with the words 'Life's a Beach' chalked onto it. A riverside café housed in a nearby caravan has "The best coffee is like the perfect man. Rich, hot ... and keeps you awake all night!!!" on a chalk board outside.

The do-it-yourself theme reaches full strength back towards Waterloo Station where a pedestrian underpass, the Leake Street Tunnel, has been given over entirely to graffiti. Renamed The Banksy Tunnel in 2008 after a competition the walls, roof and everything else are day glo, soft glo, bright glo spray painted in a tumultuous rolling swirl. It's a site for photographers who are everywhere photographing their models up against the overpowering urban technicolour scrawls.

Back where I started, at the Southbank Centre itself, the theme is summer of love, doused slightly by the prevalent drizzle. The Banksy graffiti rolls on and the sound systems play. Outside the National Theatre there's a live laser disco and an open-air bar. Under Waterloo Bridge are the bookseller's stalls, locked and stored now that dusk is upon us. Round the back of the Festival Hall is a multi-racial food market flogging unexpected foods to dazzled tourists. The area is alive.

Chris McCabe's *Real South Bank* will take you through all this and so much more in both depth and style. He balances the well-known (Southbank Centre, Waterloo Station, Westminster Bridge) with the offbeat, (the site of the bear pit, the Poetry School, pubs built into holes in the wall) and makes one of London's best known districts much realer than you might have thought it could be. It takes a poet to do that. And Chris McCabe is certainly one of those.

Peter Finch

INTRODUCTION

PLACING IMAGES ON PAPER:
MY REAL SOUTH BANK

My intentions for this book can little improve upon Ford Madox
Ford's 1905 introduction to *The Soul of London: A Survey of a
Modern City*. There, he says, 'I have tried to "get the atmosphere"
of modern London – of the town in which I have passed so many
days ... A really ideal book of the kind would not contain "writing
about" a town: it would throw a personal image of the place on to
the paper.'[1]

What follows in *Real South Bank* are many such personal images
on paper. Ford suggests that rather than providing statistics for
'19,000' hat operatives the author should show a picture of one of
them: 'And there would be conveyed the idea that all these human
beings melt, as it were, into the tide of humanity as all these vapours
melt into the overcast skies.'[2] True to my experience of moving
through London at speed I have been drawn to snippets of language
(overheard and seen on walls) as well as the random glimpses of
passing strangers. This book can be read at points as a document
capturing the fleeting thousands I share the city with – fellow
travellers to the grave, to paraphrase one of Dickens's characters –
that I might only have witnessed via a passing shoe or the glance of
an eye on a packed bus. When walking across the South Bank this
impressionistic décollage of fragments becomes the reality and it is,
perhaps, the writer's role to try and piece these together in an
attempt to create a holistic impression of this complicated city.

There are poems here too. These have been written with the
intention of taking the reader to the places that the prose can't
reach. The poems allow for quicker travel and connection-making
between ideas and historical periods and aim to capture the
atmospherics of the South Bank. When read in tandem with the
prose this book aims to offer a complete 360 degree perspective of
the area which I hope is informative – being full of historical facts
and the words of writers across many centuries – as well as
containing observations which are intuitive and instinctive. But I
couldn't have written this book without getting out and walking the
South Bank: this area of just a few square miles on the southern

banks of the river Thames, facing Westminster and other iconic 'central' London landmarks such as The Strand. I've lost count of the many times I've got wet in writing this book, either from the London rain or from the Thames lapping onto my shoes. The *Real* in this book means 'my take' and has been formed over nearly fifteen years of writing, walking, working, thinking and socialising in this part of London.

This book is a book of two boroughs, Lambeth and Southwark, though most of today's South Bank falls under Lambeth Council. The name Lambeth was first recorded in 1255 and possibly fuses 'lamb' and 'hyth' to literally mean 'landing place for lambs'.[3] This is fitting given Blake's residence here and the writing of his *Songs of Innocence* – a year before he migrated from Soho – in which 'The Lamb' is perhaps the most famous poem. Until as late as the nineteenth century Lambeth was defined by its marshes: a riverside purgatorio. In this strange, liminal space, nothingness and power loomed above the river. Lambeth Palace – home to the Archbishop of Canterbury for 800 years (owner of this land with the Duke of Cornwall) – has medieval origins and was built imperiously close to the river in the shadow of what would later become the Houses of Parliament on the opposite bank.

Over ninety per cent of the area I'll be covering falls under today's Lambeth, with the Southwark border being positioned just a hundred yards or so west from Blackfriars Bridge. Yet the two boroughs are intricately linked. For those who experience this part of London – the residents, commuters, artists and corporates – there is considerable overspill between the two boroughs: the essence of the city doesn't change in line with a shift in headed paper. When passing the hinge between the boroughs at Hatfields the division is invisible to the senses and – in the mind of the walker – unrealised: physical borders blur within the atmosphere of experience.

When it comes to the presentation of historic facts I would again echo Ford: 'This author's treatment of historic matters must again be "presentations"; and he must select only such broad tendencies, or such minute historic charters as bear straight upon some aspect of his subject. The historic facts must illustrate, must cast a light upon modern London.'[4] The *Real* in the title also means *now*. I've remained focussed on the current mood and pathways of this ever-changing place and tried to present what I think you need to know when you arrive here, in contemporary times. At many stages of this book I have found that it has only proved possible to give the reader a sense of the significance of where they are through presenting some historical facts relating to the specific location being looked at. Knowing that others have been here, staking their claim on these spaces as independently as we stake ours, plays a massive part in how we make sense of the South Bank. History is a malleable, unfinished business: the fresh matter of this moment is as sharp to our senses, if we stop for a moment to take it in, as it was to the Romans, the Jacobeans and the Victorians. We're cut from the same mould. Take it all in. The South Bank won't look like this tomorrow.

Are we being mudlarked from the viaducts
        fished from concrete
Liquid City grows on the hosepipe ban
        calculates its tidetables
  by the acoustics of the ATM
 O Rimbaud   Gascoyne   Dickens
   all nightwalking chums who slipped the fishooks
where else would you have gone but here?
        Threadneedle St   King William St   Mayfair
where people hide from urgency
    wearing brown & black
cravats   claypipes   pinched sackcloth
    the tides wash against the levelling industries
beer   stone   timber   vinegar
     heartburn & architecture
  in Liquid City a quill won't do
    that bucket of water
Dickens dunked his head in for respite
           before writing on
     you have to touch & lift text
on the dérive to the powerstation
   touch & lift text
I've seen men casting hooks above commuters' heads
    a snagged ear is a portent
  but fails as bait
         O o O O o   it hears
in the wherrying stream
       these nightwalkers are the fished

touched & lifted into text

MAPPING THE SOUTH BANK:
A NURCERY OF NAUGHTY AND LEWD PEOPLE

The River Thames divides the notorious South Bank from its more sober cousin, the Thames Embankment, on the north side. The river has attracted outsiders and radicals throughout its history, creating a mythology of arrival, departure, rebellion and artistic possibility. Here the river changes from saltwater to fresh but the flow towards refinement leaves traces of indigestible grit.

I'll begin by putting my flags into the mud – at risk of watching them sink – and marking out the South Bank area that this book will cover. On the east side I'll begin at Blackfriars Bridge, which marks the point at which Bankside begins. On the west side of the South Bank I'll go as far as Vauxhall Bridge. In between these points I'll cover over two of miles of riverfront, six bridges and two underground rivers: the Neckinger and the Effra. Books need parameters but London – by its nature – seems to defy them. Which is why I have also traversed across the boundaries of the South Bank towards Shakespeare's real Globe on Bankside and the house of Apollinaire's mistress in Stockwell. I will be taking every opportunity to get off the well-trodden tourist path and drift beyond the parameters I've set – in keeping with the South Bank's reputation for not doing as it's told. The South Bank has always proved to be a fixation for me – ever since I arrived with a day return from Liverpool in 2000 – and this book is something of a paean to this fixation.

The best way to get a sense of the growth of the South Bank through the different stages of its history is to look at the maps[5]. The Agas Map of 1561 – one of the earliest true maps of London and printed from woodcut blocks – shows sheep covering the southern shore. In Frederick de Wit's map of 1666 the only architectural building along the shore is a windmill and the area is sectioned into controlled areas of arable land above which the cartographer has added the word SOUTH. By 1746 John Rocque's map shows that streets have formed with names that describe what would be for sale (Pickle Herrings) and buildings – like Tetris-blocks – have started to appear. But it's not until John Tallis's map of 1851 (produced for the Great Exhibition[6]) that the exponential growth of the modern South Bank, Southwark, and the riverside parts of Lambeth can be seen. Today the South Bank now appears in any *A-Z Street Atlas* or on Google Maps, as part of the sprawling amoeba of London, as if the whole city – north and south – has become one concentration spreading across a glass plate, with the accidental crack of the Thames running through it.

Although the South Bank has developed in just a few centuries the neighbouring environs of Bankside and Borough are built above the remains of Roman settlements, evidence of which has also been found on the South Bank.[7] The Romans built their first docks on the north side of the Thames, capitalising on the potential for the flow of goods by boat through Essex to the coast. The Strand, which runs parallel to the South Bank on the north side, is the site of the Lundenwic dock which was on the fringes of what had been the Roman centre of international trade. The river was narrow enough to be crossed by boat and bridge but deep enough for traffic to pass along. The Romans connected to the south by a bridge which was near to today's Hay's Galleria, off Tooley Street. Modern South Bank has been built up around these Roman origins although the real commercial heart of the Thames – the Pool of London, between London Bridge and Limehouse – was a few miles further east.

Southwark was known in King Alfred's time as 'suth weorc' or 'southern fort'.[8] Peter Ackroyd gleans another meaning as 'south work', which hints at the idea of ongoing development in view of the more developed north. As the city grew through the medieval period the South Bank provided an ample natural defence to potential attackers. The area also became a liberty: a place where excess and libidinousness could take place outside of the jurisdiction of the law. Southwark was under the control of the Bishops of Winchester who had a reputation for being corrupt, therefore giving the name Winchester Geese to the prostitutes who lived here.[9]

Matthew Beaumont in *Nightwalking: A Nocturnal History of London, Chaucer to Dickens* talks of how the deprivation of the area in the early modern period became associated with this lawless activity:

> Some of the suburbs to the south of the River Thames, particularly Southwark ... rivalled the reputations of inner-city slums. These areas consisted of 'small and strait rooms and habitations' crammed with 'idle, indigent, dissolute and dangerous persons', as a parliamentary stricture from 1603 put it. Collectively, Sir Stephen Soame condemned them in 1601 as 'the nurcery of a naughty and lewd people, the harbour of rogues, theeves and beggars, and maintainers of idle persons.'[10]

It was Henry VIII who first tried to clean up Southwark by ordering the closure of the brothels, or 'stews', in 1546, but the custom had stuck until Covent Garden stole the mantle with Hogarthian levels of deprivation in the seventeenth century. Southwark was later given the name of Bridge Ward Without which suggests that strong element of *other* which gives the area its distinct character.

The small physical area that Southwark retains in today's South Bank – between Hatfields and Blackfriars Bridge – is of huge significance. This is the site of Paris Garden (and a street there still has that name today) which, in the Elizabethan era, achieved notoriety as a site of bear-baiting, prostitution and secret assignations. Paris Garden was cited as having a few different locations but if we follow John Stow's description from 1598 we'll find that this notorious Bear-pit was located exactly on the border between today's two boroughs.[11] It was described by William Fleetwood, a Recorder of London, as a place where foreign ambassadors met their spies and agents; it was so dark at night that a man needed 'cat's eyes' to see.[12] It is tempting to see the marshes of Lambeth as the *momento mori* which has given the urgency to Southwark's Danse Macabre.

DEATH, STENCH, POWER:
THE ATMOSPHERICS OF THE SOUTH BANK

It's important to know what you're walking above, before you take a step: beneath the pavements and cobbled avenues of the South Bank are the concentrated remains of an avalanche of lived human experience. Like bone collectors, those wanting to understand this part of London listen for the hints given by the dead, the whispers of outsiders.

In the early modern period Southwark drew a crowd from across the complete social spectrum. Stephen Inwood, author of *A History of London*, talks of the 'economically sophisticated alien communities' of Flemings, Germans, Italians, Jews and Portugese that made up a high concentration of the borough.[13] Many of the hostelries that sold beer were owned by bishops: power sugars the palette of the working class. There was a royal ordinance of 1161 that allowed the licensing of prostitutes; in the 1990s, just beyond the western border of the South Bank – at the intersection of Union Street and Redcross Way – hundreds of female skeletons were found on a forgotten burial site. Commuters now leave flowers and ribbons at the gates.

I like to picture the Lambeth marshes as the site of hidden dissent and night-time illegalities. A kind of Dantean no man's land that has lured those who fell from wayward heights into its landscape. The marshes become the platform for personal crises. Eliot's depleted landscapes in *The Waste Land* can easily be applied to the pre-modern South Bank:

> Who are those hooded hordes swarming
> Over endless plains, stumbling in cracked earth
> Ringed by the flat horizon ...[14]

Through urgency, despair and the quick struggle of desperate lives, the city would expel its citizens to the marshes where anything goes – the inhabitants become anonymous and secure in a pre-GPS era: 'White bodies naked on the low damp ground.'[15] In the early modern period Lambeth provided the off-centre wings for Bankside's main stage.

The period of mass bridge-building from the mid-eighteenth century began to transform the South Bank. The north of the city acknowledged, if reluctantly, that the south could be more than a playground and began to send traffic – business, money, people – its way. That's not to say that the South Bank's notorious reputation was eroded. With the building of Westminster Bridge in 1750 (which replaced the ancient Lambeth Ferry) and Blackfriars Bridge in 1769 came the first stages of a more unified London.[16] Written into this architectural history is the sense of the north *giving* to the south: a sense which has never quite gone away, with the looming presence of the Houses of Parliament overlooking the area.

Following the building of the bridges came the arrival of trains, with a new line coming through to Charing Cross in the 1860s. Even this shuttling-in of new life is related to the miasma of death that saturates the area. In 1854 The London Necropolis was opened at Brookwood Cemetery in Surrey as an attempt to solve the problem of burial in London – the new cemetery offered over 2000 acres of land for the city's future dead.[17] These corpses were couriered towards the afterlife by novel means: train. Bodies departed from a private station established at Waterloo. As Catherine Arnold points out in *Necropolis*, the class-division of life was written-in to this rail dispatch service: 'a first class corpse received a higher level of customer care and a nicely decorated carriage.'[18] There was disapproval from the locals who disliked a new station for the pampered deceased being created on their doorstep.

Where the South Bank had fared well in the Great Fire of London – due to the impossibility of fire making it across London Bridge – it became unbearable in the summer of 1858 due to the stench.[19] Schadenfreude carried the stink: the politicians who hadn't listened to the warnings from people like Faraday fled from the Houses pressing handkerchiefs like submission flags to their faces. The Great Stink, as it became known, came about through an overload of human excrement and industrial effluent being pumped into the Thames. This contributed to epidemics of cholera as the private water companies were then drawing water from the river to drinking fountains: bacteria born of gestation was pumped back into the stomach of the original life-givers – whom it then killed. Two of these private water companies were in spitting distance from the South Bank: the Southwark Water Company and the Lambeth Water Works Company. One of the supporting cases made by cholera campaigner Dr John Simon was based on the Lambeth Water Company. He showed that the customers of the Lambeth Water Company (whose water came from the purer Ditton source) had a death rate in 1854 of 37 per 10,000 but those using the Southwark and Vauxhall supplies had a rate of 130 per 10,000. Before the Lambeth Company had moved its source upstream to Ditton there was little disparity between them. It took ten years for Simon to persuade the medical community that cholera was water-borne in this way.[20]

Joseph Bazalgette's new sewerage system – which pumped London's waste away from the river and out east – led to a major transformation in what can be seen from the South Bank: the

building of the Thames Embankment on the north bank. Opened in 1870 this runs from Westminster to Blackfriars Bridge and contains complex systems of effluent pumping beneath its masses of pedestrianised concrete. A large amount of expensive property was destroyed to make the embankment and the whole process – including the creation of a new embankment in the place of mud – would have been viewable from the South Bank. What people come to the South Bank for today – walking, meeting and river-watching – happened in Victorian times on the north side. The industrial workers on the South Bank would have seen, from 1878, this new embankment lit with a string of low white bulbs: this was the first street in Britain to be lit with electric lights. The darkness of the south side would have seemed denser.

Death is written deeply into the area. As Ford Madox Ford writes in *The Soul of London*: 'little by little, the Londoner comes to forget that [their] London is built upon real earth: [they] forget … that under the pavements there are hills, forgotten water courses, springs, and marshes.'[21] The Romans had only two cemeteries and – laying down the later idea for the rethinking of London burial – located both of these cemeteries outside the city's boundary. One was in Smithfield and the other in Southwark. It was customary for the Romans to bury curios and relics with the dead; as Fiona Rule tells us in *London's Docklands*: 'these items could range from personal possessions such as jewellery, toys or favourite drinking flagons to the downright obscure. Excavations ... revealed bodies buried with a bell, a comb and a chicken.'[22] The Romans also held the belief that those disturbed in death would return as 'shades' – it's impossible to ignore the continuous reminders of previous human life whilst walking the South Bank.[23]

Artists have been drawn to the pulsing anima of the South Bank and felt at home here. The radical French poet Arthur Rimbaud lived briefly in 1874 on Stamford Street, which runs a few roads back from the river, between today's Southbank Centre and Tate Modern. Turner painted the river and its industrial landscape in *The Thames Above Waterloo Bridge*. Gustav Metzger used the Queen's Walk to realise his auto-destructive happening in 1961. Three nylon canvases in white, red and black were sprayed with acid and sent up in flames. In 2013 Yoko Ono curated Meltdown and a troupe of left-field poets took to the stage under the title *Future Exiles*. The South Bank has been, and remains, a centre of urgent artistic action.

This has also been a place where journeys begin and end. I do it most days of the week, along with hundreds and thousands of Londoners. Wake up, dress and head to work. The area thrills with activity as the thousands arrive, compelled by the magnetic pull of history, necessity and artistic possibility. On the buses and incoming trains at Waterloo commuters of every shoe-size jostle for seats: staring at phones, tangled in the wires of earphones.

In these times of hyper-security, in the high-end of 'severe' possibilities of terrorist attacks, the South Bank is an exposed, vulnerable target. The surveillance – and the tension that comes with that – is extreme. This reality comes at the end of long line of attacks, with Southwark in particular being historically used as a position from which to mount an attack on the city. In 1066 William of Normandy isolated London by devastating Southwark and its surrounding countryside. Jack Cade, who led the 1450 uprising from Kent also occupied Southwark, looting the houses of the establishment while he was here.

Significant journeys begin and end here. We won't wend as far as modern day Borough to the site of the beginning of Chaucer's pilgrimage, but the linguistic capturing of the period – in cadenced, compacted consonants – steers us on our way towards an area rich with journeys of significance:

Bifel that in that sesoun on a day,
In Southwerk at the Tabard as I lay,
Redy to wenden on my pilgrimage
To Caunterbury with ful devout corage,
At night was come into the hostelrye
Wel nine and twenty in a compaignye
Of sundry folk, by aventure yfalle
In felaweshipe, and pilgrimes were they alle,
That toward Caunterbury wolden ride[24]

There is no modern day equivalent for the Middle English word 'aventure' – which means both chance and adventure – and this word fits the South Bank perfectly: the unexpected arises daily here to confirm and shatter expectations.

The South Bank has existed in a complex power relationship with the rest of the city. The whole of the western side of the area is overlooked by the Houses of Parliament. It would be a mistake, despite the swelling crowds, to try to become anonymous here: to become a living shade. When the foundations for County Hall were built, remains of a third century Roman merchant ship was found. Photographs show it as a flattened half-ribcage – the long beams pocked with the rivets of civilised craftsmanship. It was found near Westminster Bridge and gives a reminder that not all power has passed through the debating chamber of the Houses of Parliament.[25]

I walked along the Albert Embankment today, facing the Houses of Parliament (a month after the Conservative win in the 2015 election) and saw a man spray-painting lines from Dylan Thomas's 'Do not go gentle into that good night' onto the embankment wall. The South Bank is barbed with protest and poetics, twisted together in a complicated double helix. You don't have to look far to find people raging against the dying of the light.

LIVING IN A FLICKER:
LONDON'S NORTH-SOUTH DIVIDE

When I first moved to London, in 2000, I found it hard to understand the rivalry between north and south Londoners. A friend was spun into a tortuous state of indecision over whether to move from the north he'd been brought up in to the other side of the river. Years later another friend announced – after months of Hamlet-like indecision – that he was, after all, making the move to the north of the Thames. Fifteen years later I understand it. This tension between the two sides of the river is stitched into the history's fabric and is as real as the division of the river itself.

The south is the viewing platform to the north but until the 1950s was very much below the built-up platform of the opposite bank. The development of the south was initially opposed with vitriol from those on the other side. When Westminster Bridge was proposed in the mid-eighteenth century (to be the second central bridge after Waterloo) city bankers feared it would take away their business; the bridge itself was sabotaged by the watermen who feared that their diminishing incomes would be wiped-out by the new option to hoof across the water using the bridge.[26]

To reinforce this sense of the north as overseer to the south, many of London's prisons have been established on the South Bank. When the Fleet Prison was burned down in 1666 it was temporarily relocated to Caron House in Lambeth.[27] The King's Bench Prison had also been close to St George's Fields. One of its inmates was the dramatist and London prose writer Thomas Dekker, who was imprisoned there for not paying a debt of £40 to the father of fellow playwright John Webster – a reminder that poets should never involve themselves in the business of money. Marshalsea Prison, where Charles Dickens' father John was imprisoned for debt – and which influenced his son's novel *Little Dorrit* – was just beyond the parameters of this book in Southwark. Within and around the South Bank both liberty and incarceration have existed in a very close, symbiotic relationship – like the bear that is baited by the human hand.

Perhaps I've felt kinship with the south of London because its reputation has always been one projected *onto* it from the other side – from the vantage of class and money – which reminds me of my home city, Liverpool. Stereotype and discrimination have pervaded the south. Charles Booth, in *Life and Labour of the London Poor* – a series of surveys undertaken between 1886 and 1903 – found that the worst areas of poverty were in the riverside parts of south

London, particularly between Borough and Blackfriars Road.[28] In the early nineteenth century Bethlehem Hospital for mental patients was relocated to St George's Fields to its current site which houses the Imperial War Museum. The area had also housed the Lambeth Asylum for Orphaned Girls and Hanway's Magdalen House for 'penitent prostitutes'. All of the city's broken children were coming home at once. I have met many people – and no shortage of poets – who, in the extremities of mental strife, have felt most able to be themselves, or at least publicly dissolve, on the South Bank. In the 1930s the poet David Gascoyne, torn with mental strife, walked the area of a night time.

In the 1950s boys from Southwark and Lambeth took to wearing exaggerated Edwardian style dress including 'very long velvet-collared jackets, bootlace ties, tapered trousers, suede shoes with thick crepe souls, and elaborate Brylcreemed quiffs, instead of the cloth caps and second-hand clothes they would have worn a few years earlier.'[29] Teddy Boys hung around the area edges of the South Bank – at Vauxhall and Elephant & Castle – like revenants of the Jacobean playwrights in their ruffs and tight trousers: 'comical and slightly menacing'.[30] There was, however – as T.R. Fyvel points out – a 'peculiar, nasty viciousness in Teddy Boy assaults.'[31] The real threat of Teddy Boys was no doubt exaggerated by the media and through urban myth, but it is telling that the surrounding South Bank became the playground for this. Forty years later, in the 1990s, both Lambeth and Southwark were amongst the areas of England with the highest unemployment levels; many of these people were men between twenty and thirty-four, and Afro-Caribbean. There is a long history of London's young men finding themselves rooted and displaced here.

This book takes up the spirit of outsiderness that this history invites and, through doing so, offers walks and detours into the current reality of London's South Bank. When the Situationist writer Guy Debord developed the idea of psychogeography he argued that cities have atmospheres and environments that we can experience through the *dérive*: the drift. This term is often overused today, and with little reference to its genesis. We could do a lot worse before setting off than listening to what Debord said about this in his 'Theory of the Dérive' written in 1956:

> *Dérive* ... a technique of transient passage through varied ambiances. The dérive entails playful-constructive behaviour and

awareness of psychogeographical effects; which completely distinguishes it from the classical notions of the journey and the stroll. Wandering in subterranean catacombs forbidden to the public etc – are expressions of a more general sensibility which is nothing other than the dérive. Written descriptions can be no more than passwords to this great game.[32]

I have always felt that there is something missing in this argument: that we all bring with us that which we wish to seek. You will no doubt find aspects of South Bank that you relate to in your own way and I will also be bringing my own guides from the past to help navigate the current atmospherics of the area. These are my ghosts, those I wish to see and hear: spoors of atomised DNA that give us the city's codes through their remaining words. These are guides that I can follow with confidence because I truly believe in them. They will offer only the most revealing passwords to this landscape – a landscape that I've walked through, thought in, and become lost within over the past fourteen years. I've made friends here, walked with people now dead and made life-changing personal discoveries. The South Bank has become a part of who I am, or more to the point: has been a place that has allowed me to *become*.

Over a decade ago Peter Ackroyd wrote that south London 'has been underdeveloped in past centuries, but this neglect has allowed it effortlessly to reinvent itself.'[33] He writes that, compared to London's north, 'the relatively underdeveloped tracts south of the Thames are in contrast available for a spirited and imaginative transformation.'[34] At the time of writing this transformation is taking place at an accelerated pace and often with the danger of rational forces – to use the language of Blake – overpowering the imaginative ones. Ackroyd is right that this part of London is one of the 'most vigorous and varied, not to say popular' of current London, but as further corporatisation takes effect the South Bank should preserve a balance between sudden dead-ends, open space and temporary structures – amidst the need to build and develop new places for people to live. When all the possibilities are used up the area will cease to inspire the imagination.

In his book *Urban Theory a Critical Asessment,* John Rennie Short offers five possible kinds of future city: The Vulnerable City, The Globalising City, Liquid City, The City of Light and Dark and The Contaminated City.[35] He argues that we are midway through a third urban revolution (the first being the building of the mega-industrialised cities of the nineteenth century and the second being the emergence of the postmodern city based not on industry but on the collection of information and knowledge and the production of commodities) that is changing city landscapes. It is the description of The Liquid City which best describes the South Bank's fluid, sprawling landscape and geographic and cultural resistance to being bound at its edges and easily understood as a place:

> Metropolitan growth has a liquid quality; it is constantly moving over the landscape, here in torrents, there in rivulets, elsewhere in steady drips, but always in the viscous manner of a semisolid, semiliquid, half-permanent, yet constantly changing phenomenon. Metropolitan growth possesses an unstable quality that flows over political boundaries, seeps across borders and transcends tight spatial demarcation; it is a process not a culmination, always in motion, rarely at rest ... Fixity and flow in a constant dialectic as flows produce new places of fixed investment and concentration that in turn are undermined by new flows. Structure and process, solid and liquid, stasis and flow in a constant interconnected reality. The term *liquid* is used to highlight the more dynamic element of the dialectic.[36]

Much of the architecture in this part of the South Bank has been built with its relation to water in mind. Hugh Casson, Director of Architecture of the Festival of Britain, invited the water into the experience of the South Bank Exhibition: 'the water had to be part of the architecture ... Water became part of the show.'[37] Later,

Denys Lasdun – architect of the National Theatre – said that he wanted to create the feeling that 'the audience – like the tides of the river – flow into the auditoriums. Then the tide ebbs and they come out into the creeks of the small spaces that are made by all these terraces.'[38] These flows and ebbing tides will lead us where they will.

Notes

1. Ford Madox Ford, *The Soul of London: A Survey of a Modern City*.
2. Ibid.
3. There are a number of differing views on the etymology of Lambeth but I am going here with Peter Ackroyd's – the connection with lambs is too irresistible.
4. Ford Madox Ford, *The Soul of London: A Survey of a Modern City* Op. Cit.
5. Maps of the area through history can be access from the Southwark Council website at www.southwark.gov.uk/info/200212/egovernment/1370/southwark_maps
6. The Great Exhibition of Industry of all Nations took place in Hyde Park in 1851 and the building built to house the show – The Crystal Palace – was later relocated to Sydenham where it later burned down. Items on show included the worlds largest diamond and a device called The Tempest Prognosticator that forecasted a pending storm using leeches. Six million people attended the exhibition and the surplus funds were used to create the V&A, the Science Musuem and the Natural History Musuem.
7. Historical facts in this chapter have been sourced from Stephen Inwood, Peter Ackroyd and Fiona Rule. See Works Consulted for full bibliographic details.
8. Peter Ackroyd, *London: The Biography*, Op.cit.
9. Ibid.
10. Matthew Beaumont *Nightwalking: A Nocturnal History of London, Chaucer to Dickens*, Op.cit.
11. John Stow, *A Survey of London Written in the Year 1598 (with an introduction by Antonia Fraser)*; Stroud, Gloucestershire: The History Press, 2009
12. Walter Thornbury and Edward Walford, Southwark: Bankside, in *Old and New London*: Volume 6 (London, 1878), pp. 45-57 http://www.british-history.ac.uk/old-new-london/vol 6/pp45-57
13. Stephen Inwood, *A History of London* Op.cit.
14. T.S. Eliot, *Collected Poems 1909-1962* Op.cit.
15. Ibid.
16. Inwood, Op.cit.
17. I have written extensively about the creation of London's suburban cemeteries in my book *In the Catacombs: A Summer Among the Dead Poets of West Norwood Cemetery*; Penned in the Margins, 2014. The next book in this series, *Cenotaph South*, which is about Nunhead Cemetery, will be published in November 2016, These books are part of a series of books written about The Magnificent Seven Cemeteries: West Norwood, Nunhead, Brompton, Kensal Green, Tower Hamlets, Abney Park and Highgate. I am indebted to Catharine Arnold's *Necropolis*, Op.cit., for facts about Brookwood here.
18. Catharine Arnold, *Necropolis*, Op.cit.
19. Although the south side did suffer its own fire in 1676 when Southwark High Street was burned down due to a fire that began in an oil shop.
20. Indebted to Stephen Inwood, Op.cit, for much of the factual information in this chapter His one-thousand-page-plus *A History of London* is to be recommended for its detail and research – and brilliant readability.

21. Ford Madox Ford, *The Soul of London: A Survey of a Modern City* Op.cit.

22. Fiona Rule, *London's Docklands: A History of the Lost Quarter* Op.cit.

23. Although there is evidence to suggest that due to a lack of archaeological finds that Southwark was deserted between 400 and 850: a short hiatus in the ongoing attrition of burials.

24. Geoffrey Chaucer, *The Canterbury Tales* Op.cit.

25. The remains of the ship is now in the Museum of London. Indebted to Peter Ackroyd's *Thames: Sacred River* Op. cit. which shows a photograph of the remains.

26. Inwood, Op.cit.

27. One of the Fleet's most notable inmates was John Donne who was imprisoned there for marrying a lock keepers daughter, Ann More. The river, as many found before and since, spells danger.

28. Charles Booth, in *Life and Labour of the London Poor*, Op.cit.

29. Stephen Inwood Op.cit.

30. Ibid

31. Quoted in Inwood, Ibid

32. Guy Debord in Theory of the Dérive, 1956 in *Situationist International Anthology* Op.cit.

33. Ackroyd, *London: The Biography*, Op.cit.

34. Ibid.

35. John Rennie Short, *Urban Theory: a Critical Asessment* Op.cit.

36. Ibid.

37. Charlotte Mullins, *A Festival on the River* Op.cit.

38. Patrick Dillon & Jake Tilson, *Concrete Reality: Denys Lasdun and the National Theatre* Op.cit.

And time will give us goitres
　　dry as turkey wattle
　　　　blackouts & astonishments
drillholes in glass　　the worms bring light
　can you see the burials in the skies?
　　This is where celebrities age from public view
rising in a botox eclipse　　　Stringfellow
like a tigerworm banded by sunbeds
　　Archer in aquariums of light
after the tides
　　citadels of sheetmetal & embankments
sweetmeats & accidents
　　　careers ringed in eyeliner
　　as a record of the years
Liquid City puts a castle
　　on the elephant's back
paints it red　　facing the temple
　　calls it the blacking factory
　what was good for Dickens
　　　will be good for us
After Charing X is bumped for Embankment
　　we ask all the watermen & dredgers
　　　the wharfers & dockers
　　if when they're done

our imprisoned fathers can come back to us

CENTRAL

SOUTHBANK CENTRE:
A VIEW FROM HEIGHT

I'm standing, at height, inside the Royal Festival Hall.

If I'd been standing here two hundred years ago I'd be knee-deep in the mudflats bordering the marshlands that swept over the area. Mud and marsh: not the most auspicious of natural elements to build a Victorian industry upon and – more recently – London's largest cultural centre. Even from as late as the mid-eighteenth century the maps show little sign of human industry and occupation. Open fields. A solitary windmill. A sheep. Rocque's map of 1746 shows the area along the river as nothing but timber yards wallowing in empty space. As recently as 1951 *Punch* described the Thames as 'the most one-sided river in Europe'.[1] In contrast, the facing north side was being developed with architectural gravitas: the Savoy, the American Embassy, Embankment Station. The refinement of London – the London of business and dignified pleasure – was reserved for the north side.

If I were standing here a hundred years ago I'd be inside a brewery and there would be a stone lion above me. The lion was the emblem of the Red Lion Brewery, built in 1836, which now stands Aslan-like on the south side of Westminster Bridge.[2] The brewery was the site of a murder of one if its workers, George Merrett, in 1872 by a mentally ill American surgeon called William Minor who had arrived here after the American Civil War and – drawn to the promiscuity of Lambeth – had shot the worker in the night, believing he was an Irishman who had tried to steal his belongings as he slept. Simon Winchester tells the story in *The Surgeon of Crowthorne: A Tale of Murder, Madness and the Oxford English Dictionary*. Winchester depicts the marshland that the brewery – and now the Festival Hall – stands on, with the kind of relish usually reserved for evoking the Jacobean playhouses:

> Lambeth Marsh was also, as it happened, just beyond the legal jurisdiction of both the cities of London and Westminster. It belonged administratively, at least until 1888, to the county of Surrey – meaning that the relatively strict laws that applied to the capital's citizens did not apply to anyone who ventured, via one of the new bridges like Waterloo, Blackfriars, Westminster or Hungerford, into the wen of Lambeth. The village thus became fast known as a site of revelry and abandon, a place where public houses and brothels and lewd theatres abandoned, and where a man could find entertainment of all kinds – and disease of all varieties – for no more than a handful of pennies. To see a play that would not pass muster with the London censors, or to be able to drink absinthe into the small hours of the morning, or to buy the choicest of pornography newly smuggled from Paris … you 'went Surreyside', as they said, to Lambeth.[3]

That Minor was an aspiring artist, who'd visited John Ruskin on arriving in London and later contributed to the *Oxford English Dictionary* from his cell in Broadmoor, suggests how the South Bank – for its Surreyside licentiousness and gloomy marshland – attracted the artistic and deranged to its borders.

The brewery, like much of the South Bank of the time, was destroyed in the Blitz and finally demolished in 1948. When the lion was removed it was discovered that it had a recess in the tail-end of its back with a removable slate covering its contents; on opening it was found to contain two William IV coins, a green bottle containing an advertisement from the company who made the lion and a note from the artist's maker, stating that the lion was finished on Queen Victoria's birthday in 1837 – the year she took the throne.[4]

The industries that were built on the South Bank were largely functional: vinegar, bullets, stone and beer. Coade's Artificial Stone Manufactory – which made weatherproof stone until 1840 – was based here, as was the famous Doulton company, which made thirteen miles of drainpipes a week from their factory on Lambeth High Street. Simon Winchester describes it as:

> a place of warehouses and tenant shacks, and miserable rows of ill-built houses. There were blacking factories and soap-boilers, small firms of dyers and lime-burners, and tanning yards where the leather-workers used a substance for darkening skins that was known as "pure" and that was gathered from the streets each night by the filthiest of the local indigents – "pure" being a Victorian term for dog turds.[5]

Doulton's also created some of the most beautiful ceramics of the period which can be seen in many of London's still extant cemeteries, including West Norwood – where Doulton is buried. Maudslay's marine engineers created steam engines for ships and was based on Westminster Bridge Road until 1900. For over a hundred years a shot tower looms in every lithograph and photograph taken of the area, appearing like a windmill that's lost its blades: a landlocked lighthouse. The landscape was rickety with wood and there was no embankment wall to hold back the Thames. Boats lay mounted on mounds of mud. Victorian terraces were laid out in symmetrical rows around the smoking factories. During World War Two many of these houses along Commercial Road – on what is now the arcadian leisure strip housing the BFI, National Theatre and ITV studios – were bombed and then abandoned.

If I'd have been standing here sixty-four years ago I'd have been standing in the middle (slightly eastern side) of the twenty-seven acre South Bank Exhibition. I would have been in an area called 'The People'. Between this building – and the river beneath me – Lowryesque figures would have been walking with sticks of rock as children lolled on the backs of donkeys. To my left would have been the Skylon exhibit: a deflated zeppelin in a geometric tangle.

The South Bank Exhibition of 1951 attracted around eight and a half million people and gave thousands of school children their first experience of London. The Festival had been spearheaded by Herbert Morrison who was Deputy Prime Minister of the Labour Government and Leader of the House of Commons. There had been some stalling as to which site would be used for the exhibition but it was this bombed and still un-banked part of the river that was settled on, as it offered the potential to stretch across twenty-eight acres of land. As Stephen Inwood puts it in his *A History of London*: 'Long before the war was over, and even before the victory was assured, it was understood by politicians of all parties that the British people would not be satisfied with a return to the world they had known before 1939.'[6] The South Bank had been devastated through the Blitz, particularly the area between Waterloo Bridge and County Hall and – in an attempt to give an extra 5,428 acres of public land back to the public – a festival was announced to take place in 1951: a century after the Great Exhibition of 1851. Morrison said: 'I want everyone to see it, to take part in it, to enjoy it. I want to see the people happy. I want to hear the people sing.'[7]

Sixty-five years ago I might have had little joy in accessing the inside of the building I'm standing in as the concert hall was accessible for ticket owners only. As Charlotte Mullins states in *A Festival on the River*, many of the men who had worked on building the exhibition site had been invited to the opening but many couldn't go as they didn't own jackets. The Festival was not without controversy: some claimed that overcrowding would lead to fatalities. Sir Thomas Beecham said it was 'a monumental piece of imbecility' and – it was rumoured – the person on the switchboard answered the phone with 'Festering Britain here'.[8] Somewhere between the building's naming after royalty and its moniker as 'The People's Palace', The Royal Festival Hall has since been loved, contested and reinvented by hundreds of thousands of people. It belongs to all of us and each of us individually: its blank, open spaces invite people to fill them with their own imaginations and passions.

The South Bank Exhibition was put together by a team of architects who were not only young – most under the age of 45 – but also immigrants from other countries. Against the tide of a male-dominated profession there were many women involved too. Ursula Owen designed the Sports Pavilion of the Festival site saying that: 'We were building a new world. We were seeing a glimpse of the future.'[9]

This place ripples through popular culture, refracted and oblique, providing a backdrop that seems uncannily familiar to those who have never even been here. The film *84 Charing Cross Road* is a dramatisation of the relationship between an American writer and a bookshop owner on Charing Cross Road over a twenty year period. The film also focuses on the bookshop assistant (played by Anthony Hopkins) and his wife (played by Julie Andrews) who are a quiet, complimentary couple; respectful of each other and content with slightly more than just enough – wary of anything approaching excess. Halfway through the film a big event takes place: they go on a night out together. We follow them out into London as the camera pans down to the South Bank alongside Jubilee Gardens. Then they are dancing outside, swaying to a Swing Time rhythm; red, white and red balloons float patriotically next to the flowing river. The camera hovers across the Festival logo – a centurion's head on a star – offering striking design against the dropshadowed sign: *1951 Festival*. They dance distantly, their minds in other worlds. Here they are, living, their daughters tucked-up in bed at home. Their dance is the slow impossible-to-believe dance of two people who love each other, realising that they've arrived on the other side of war. She asks 'are you enjoying yourself Fred?' and he responds: 'Yes – when did we last.....?'. She says: 'I can't remember?' Fred turns her around as the dance ends. They take a break, leaning over the rails looking northwards downriver towards the Savoy. A conga is announced across a tannoy. 'Oh come on,' she says, 'it's been a long time since you've done that'. 'Okay,' he says, 'once more', and they join the back of the winding line of bodies. The camera pans out and we see them now for what they are: two people amidst a whole generation not completely undone by war and learning how to live again.

I've taken a seat in the Festival Hall now and I'm watching a film. Chief architect of the South Bank Exhibition, Hugh Casson, is leading Patrick O'Donovan of *The Observer* through the Festival site, a year after it was dismantled. The film, *Brief City*, is narrated by Casson himself. We are told that, of the two men we can see, that it's Casson – in his long mac and rain hat – who is 'the smaller of the two'. As they walk at speed away from us they skip over a NO ADMISSION sign laying flat on the ground. 'We came here when it was over' he says with poised austerity. The present we're going towards is already in the unreachable past. A newspaper blows into a puddle and tables with umbrellas lie across each other like fancy-dressed drunks. A willowing flute provides the soundtrack: the perfect note for this winter scene of near-apocalypse.

The scene moves forward to the summer before; the summer of the festival itself. Our guides are now beyond us, existing only as voices. 'We built it as a place to walk about in, a place if you like for pleasure.' The word 'pleasure' is said as if it carries an element of risk. Casson tries to assure us that the festival was meant to be 'temporary and perhaps experimental'. The camera pans across the blackened Victorian streets as a train pumps smoke into a grey sheet of sky. I have to believe – no, *want* to believe – that what we are looking at 'blazed with bright nursery colours', as we are told – though the reds and blues of the Festival logo reach me on screen in greyscale and chrome. The Dome of Discovery, like a flattened upside-down wok, clearly shows its later influence on the Millennium Dome. A pivoted UFO rigged with scaffold. The Dome, we are told, was actually built to move so that it could roll with the thumps and buffets of the wind over the Thames. This isn't a 'giant mushroom' but a considered work of art: an achievement in engineering. Next we see the Skylon: a gargantuan fishing quill, an aerodynamic suppository hovering mysteriously before the river. 'A clear statement in steel and aluminium and wire.' Someone asks the rhetorical question of what it was meant to do? 'Why simply to hang upright in the air, and astonish.'[10]

We are now walking through the crowds, past stalls, kiosks, games: we have arrived at a metropolitan Butlins. A man peers inside a viewing booth called WHAT THE BUTLER SAW ON HIS HOLIDAYS. The great British art of barely suppressed flirtation is never far away. The poet Angela Kirby once gave a talk at The Poetry Library in which she described the roundabouts she went on with her friends as the young men hawked the fringes, asking for kisses. As Casson puts it here, this is: 'That brief forgetting of the factory and the office which happens when the British go to the seaside for their holidays.'

We hear the word 'temporary' again: a transient place for

transient people, those who spend a day and depart. This time Casson uses it about the awnings. In his repetition of the word we sense that although he liked the idea of impermanence – its auto-destructive modernity – there is something regretful in the scale of the dismantled exhibition. Too much has been lost too quickly. The eight and a half million visitors have passed through the site so quickly they have barely been attached to celluloid.

In the crowd the men are wearing suits, the women dresses: nightwear in the daytime. They glare at the water, amused; ponder the home-made bars of rock. A child looks confusedly at one of the wooden characters as another sits sternly atop a donkey. These children, born just before the end of the war, have had to learn the happiness that has slowly become available to them. None of the children hold hands with their fathers – they have to learn to keep in step. The boys, we are told, 'have their secret purposes'. Happiness appears like a national project, part of a 65-year plan that we are at the current end-point of. Did it work? Casson draws us towards the bigger city, before we have time to answer: 'This exhibition was meant to be a part of London'. Dark clouds pass along the long glass windows and an albumen of a sun disappears into the matter. People run for cover. The screen shows Big Ben in the distance: 'There are no resounding proud messages here ... in a bad year in the world's history it had a spiritual quality worth remembering.'

Dylan Thomas might seem like an unlikely ghost to be rising like a fleshy-decked Jacob Marley – rattling his chains of the sea – but this is no more unlikely as him being the experimentalist who was to become a regular on BBC radio after the end of the Second World War. In fact it was the BBC who first sent him here, to report on the Festival for a piece to be broadcast on the radio. His 'The Festival Exhibition, 1951' is still the finest piece of writing about Southbank Centre. His rhapsodic prose captures the delirium and chaos of the site – past and present – in a way that couldn't have been handled by a Londoner. As with Iain Sinclair, there is something about the roving eye of the Welshman that brings a sense of clarity to Albion's metropolis. What is so engaging about Thomas's piece is that he puts the people at the centre of the exhibition; these blundering masses who can make neither head nor tail of the experience that they've become a part of. Thomas, admittedly 'speaking under the influence of the strong pink', allows his prose to hit the cadences of his poetry as the festival site fuses with the alcohol:

And other visitors begin, of course, at the end. They are the people without whom the exhibition could not exist, nor the country it trombones and floats in with its lions and unicorns made of ears of wheat, its birds that sing to the push of a button, its flaming water, and its raspberry fountains. They are the suspicious people over whose eyes no coloured Festival wool can possibly be pulled, the great undiddleable; they are the women who will not queue on any account and who smuggle in dyspeptic dogs; the strangely calculating men who think that the last pavilion must be first because it is number twenty-two; the people who believe they are somewhere else, and never find out if they are not ... old scaly sneezing men, born of lizards in a snuff-bin, who read, wherever they go, from books in tiny print, and who never look up, even at the tureen-lid of the just-tethered dome or the shining skylon, the skygoing nylon, the cylindrical leg-of-the-future jetting, almost, to the exhibition of stars; real eccentrics: people who have come to the South Bank to study the growth and development of Britain from the Iron Age till now...[11]

'The shining skylon, the skygoing nylon': in this sonic chiasmus Thomas is never anything but a poet in prose-gathering fur. Thomas's broadcast still captures the Southbank Centre's mix of personality and class and I'd stand by his advice on the best time to visit:

Go to the South Bank first by day; the rest of your times at night. Sit at a café table in the night of musical lights, by the radiant river, the glittering skylon above you rearing to be off, the lit pavilion, white, black, and silver in sweeps of stone and feathery steel, transplendant around you as you sip and think.[12]

This is Thomas's London, the London that he'd have to invent if it didn't exist – the London of a poet and a drinker – which more often than not appears through the kaleidoscopic brainfreeze of alcohol. Thomas's writing also suggests that there was an architectural fault in the original plan for the festival: Barry's decision to separate 'The Land' from 'The People'. It is the people in the space that make it what it is.

Ten years ago a bust of Thomas was found in the basement of the Royal Festival Hall, one of only two made from him in life. There is only one piece of surviving archival footage of Thomas in life, very little given the magnitude of his short life and the movements and

gestures of his rubbery, expressive face. In this sculpture his head rests wittily on a tattered scarf, a cigarette unendingly smouldering from a taboo-raising smirk. This is the Dylan looking ahead to America, before the final burn-out. The doughy folds of his flesh compacting into itself. The quote on the wall suggests the paradox of the man behind the itinerant celebrity: 'O make me a mask and a wall to shut from your spies / Of the sharp, enamelled eyes and the spectacled claws.'[13]

I look up at the roof of the Festival Hall and remember something from around eight years ago: the rooftop beehive. One afternoon I looked across at the Queen Elizabeth Hall and watched a moving black mass shift from a semi-colon, to a colon, to a sphere: bees. Mikey Tomkins, the beekeeper at the time, has since written an account of this project which appeared in Craig Taylor's book *Londoners*, giving us a rare sense of the Royal Festival Hall in relation to the London around it:

> People say to me, how can they have anything to forage on, we're in the middle of the South Bank? And you say, if you look quite closely there's Temple Gardens and there's lots of houses with green areas, and then you start to notice lots of undeveloped areas which are quite overgrown and you start to see how you might make connections across the green sites but also how a bee might be able to make those connections as well.[14]

I watched the beekeeper climb on the roof and lay out a huge net to tease the bees back to safety. That spot to my right, above the roof of the Queen Elizabeth Hall, is now a rooftop garden which heaves in the summer with hundreds of Londoners making their way up there to enjoy the herbs and wildflowers – and the carafes of mojitos. The staircase rises from the walkway in a twist of thick concrete: the levels hover in air like the serifs of a future typeface. I have often thought that the raw, clean surfaces of concrete here allow artists to feel they can perform and create here as if on *tabula rasa*; no previous artist leaves a trace of what they've done before: the slate is wiped clean for each new performance.

A BAUHAUS ON THE RUTTY BANKS:
INSIDE THE ROYAL FESTIVAL HALL

I'm sitting at the main bar on Level 2 of the Royal Festival Hall. A bar for occasional drinkers, not those in need of drink. From here you can see the clean classical lines of the inside of the building and also the slight curves to the hard white edges which lend the building warmth. If you look at the front of the building from the side you can see that its front curves outwards suggesting a Bauhaus physique fed more on currywurst than krautrock. On the

inside these curves soften the endless edges. Columns rise imperiously from floor to ceiling which lead to rows of circular lights directing the eyes towards the open spaces. Slants and angles give perspective. The design of the building, a structure that Charlotte Mullins describes as 'in keeping with the rigorous ideals of modernism and its eschewing of ornament' has parallels with the more formal strand of poetic Modernism: it is more *The Four Quartets* than *The Waste Land*.[15] Classical form sweeps away chaos: English internationalism. This is Modernism with a reserved, minimal finish. It takes some effort to completely believe that the building is built upon the ancient bone and brick of a barely drained marshland. Ernest Bean, the Royal Festival Hall's first general manager aptly described the building as 'a giant, lone tree amid the waste'.[16]

From where I am sitting the building appears to have two hearts: the ballroom floor, in front of me, and the main hall which floats above it. Or perhaps it might be best described as a building with a set of lungs and a heart: a complete cardiothoracic experience. The floating auditorium of the main hall is known as the 'egg in the box': a sonic crucible that seems to hover in space. Due to space restrictions the venue was designed to be suspended in the middle of the hall, although – as is the way with great inventions – this also helped to protect the venue from outside sound. The box for the egg wasn't fortified with polystyrene but with double layers of concrete, with a layer of air between them.

The ballroom is where people meet the unexpected and make themselves seen amongst the thing that they've come to see: a poetry or music recital, an installation or a debating chamber, a series of films or, if it is a Friday – like today – a free afternoon performance of jazz. On either side of the ballroom floor are steps to the exhibition space of the Spirit Level (impossible to balance an egg on an uneven level) and the cloakroom area. The cloakroom – in a way that could only feel natural to the Southbank Centre – has become a practice space for urban dancers. The dancers look into the same mirrors where men once fixed their hats in the 1950s and the bolder women powdered. A group is rehearsing a series of choreographed moves. In a hidden corner, under one of the huge white columns, a pair of young friends are facing each other and reading, rehearsing a script.

Walking through the open spaces of the building it's easy to see why Alan Bartram, in *Bauhaus, Modernism and the Illustrated Book*,

described the Royal Festival Hall as 'still one of the most satisfying buildings in London'.[17] I step back up the stairs into the heart of the building and the sun fires, all gold, across from the Thames and the distant city – through the glass doors and straight into my eyes. I walk across the Level 2 bar, listening to the things that people talk about when they come here: a man is showing a woman a laminated portfolio of door designs. The rising, curling scent of lager intoxicates unexpectedly. As I walk onto the third floor of the building the cacophonic chattering and rising music is punctuated with the trains passing over the viaduct from Charing Cross. A constant metallic squeal and clatter.

Trying to understand the symmetry of the building is the only way to make sense of it. Each room on the east side (blue; Waterloo Bridge: think water) and the west side (green; Jubilee Gardens: think grass) is replicated with its exact opposite on the other side. The structure is as consistent as the doubled hind-wings of an insect. The main hall and ballroom provide the central body. From Level 5 there is a balcony view which looks down on the never-still Thames and the north bank. Laptops clatter: whole businesses seem to be administered from quiet corners of the building. I once saw a man in a suit conducting interviews. Ownership of The People's Palace is often taken quite literally – I once received an email saying: 'Hi

Chris, are you interested in selling the Royal Festival Hall?'

Languages can be heard by the dozen and in parallel time: a polyglottal patter. A woman is talking in French as a man runs a German lesson at a table. Urdu, Spanish, Japanese, Bethnal Green: the cosmopolitan city spills out in the liquids of spoken syllables. When it's late in the afternoon like this, in summer, the light is the main attraction. It streams in crystallised photons through the glass. I've often felt that the building was created to give a feeling that we're momentarily living inside the light from the sun. This is now: you've arrived. That feeling is captured best here, outside on the Level 5 Balcony Terrace. A woman turns a chilled bottle of rosé in a silver decanter facing a man with a fiery red beard. Two men lean in manly friendship against the side of the balcony, looking down at the hundreds of fellow revellers beneath them. It's 18.51, to be exact, early evening, but the May sun is furious up here. Two businessmen, off duty, are necking like herons from two long pints of *Peroni* .

Down below, on the Queen's Walk, those sitting before the Thames cast exaggerated shadows towards the building. The Thames, to paraphrase Gerard Manley Hopkins in another context, glitters like shook foil. Even in the calmness the river moves with purpose, out downstream towards Richmond and then on to Oxford and its source near Kemble. The moment can't be stilled: a woman is talking into her mobile against the water of the river. Life, now: no other.

The current Southbank Centre's artistic vision is to restore the original Festival ethos to the site, to celebrate the buildings and their potential to bring people together to celebrate the arts: arts which can initiate discussion and social change. Led with flair by Artistic Director Jude Kelly the site has changed beyond recognition in the past ten years. Kelly's vision has been to move the centre forward through looking back to its Festival ethos. The programme is curated around a series of festivals that run throughout the year in which ideas and discussion lead towards a broader inclusivity. The festivals are boldly themed to stimulate challenging debate: *Women of the World*, *Being a Man*, *Love* and *Death*, to name a few. Kelly's approach is to tackle the big issues that face society, discussed through the lens of art – and everyone's invited to take part. Kelly says:

> 'For a variety of reasons, we have arrived at societies that place the arts in an area where you achieve once you've moved up through

class, education and entitlement systems. That disadvantages billions of people for whom art is a natural pursuit, but who are made to feel that it isn't.'[18]

Southbank Centre contributes to the long overdue work of removing the social obstructions that hazard people's creative instincts. Deputy Director Shan Mâclennan describes how:

> The restless and ongoing making of Southbank Centre, like the creation of the South Bank Exhibition in 1951, continuously produces new styles of artistic presentation which in themselves make it more possible for more people to think of the arts as useful in their everyday life and relevant to their own concerns.[19]

To call the last fifteen years of the site a transformation would be a gross understatement. When I first travelled down from Liverpool to spend a day at The Poetry Library in 2000 I walked across Hungerford Bridge looking at buildings that rose like the tip of Atlantis from a sea of derelict stone and dust. In the places where hundreds of people are now socialising was a slip-road along which taxis were allowed to circle the building, dropping off the occasional couple who'd set off like explorers into the past, risking the time-freeze. The taxi drivers barely waited to be paid, revving back towards Belvedere Road in plumes of black smoke. The visitors wrapped scarves around their mouths to prevent themselves inhaling debris and coal smoke. Only the Thames glittered with possibility.

I look around now: hundreds of people are meeting, drinking, kissing, cursing, thinking, creating, texting. Social interaction segues seamlessly into participatory art and installations. *The Festival of Love* is just beginning: five months of events and invitations that respond, and question, notions of that great fireship love – in all its incarnations.

Over the years I've heard many stories of those who met and fell in love here. As with all romances, not all of them end well, and artists are particularly good at articulating the bad ones. Perhaps this complicated architectural complex is suited to intense emotional possibilities – labyrinths, bars, music, the river – which attract those forming new relationships towards its landscape of euphoric, always incomplete surfaces and depths? There are those who can't come back to this place of younger delirium: caged emotions are invited to run wild again. In an early draft of his second novel *Albert Angelo* the avant-garde novelist B.S. Johnson based an opening scene around his homoerotic relationship with Michael Bannard. Angelo describes a note that Michael sent him only minutes after catching each other's eye in the work place. They were yet to say a word to each other though the venue for their meeting was decided:

> 'RFH – 7 – Tonight. Coming?' Without asking who had sent it, but sensing, knowing, who it was, he had written 'Yes' on it and directed the messenger to return it.[20]

Many have taken up such a secret calling to these buildings, allowing the emotions to become as much a part of them as these buildings are to the larger map of London. The South Bank suits emotions in crisis and poetry is never far away from that experience. They form an unlikely architectural triumvirate, the Royal Festival Hall, the Queen Elizabeth Hall and the Hayward Gallery. The two smaller buildings look towards the larger building the way two sibling punks might look with awe at their overly formal older brother. The older brother looks away – towards the river and the north – where Portland Stone and post-Bauhaus classicism might be a more expected sight.

The Brutalist buildings of Queen Elizabeth Hall (opened in 1967) and the Hayward Gallery (opened in 1968) contribute to the South Bank's position as being a unique assemblage in London's landscape. The Queen Elizabeth Hall and the Hayward Gallery slide together in misfired shapes, a heliport of angles soliciting shadows to cut skywards along the bric-a-brac of its walls. Between the river and the sky they suggest functionality and seriousness – but there's also something wilfully edgy and challenging about them. They're like exposed engines for which the shell has been lost: the focus repositioned towards their own internal workings. Deconstructed ziggurats that have been cut into fragments and reassembled without instructions. The fact that *Daily Mail* readers voted the Queen Elizabeth Hall as 'Britain's Ugliest Building' in 1967 says everything you need to know about its integrity and challenging aesthetics. And it's on entering the foyers of the Queen Elizabeth Hall that this becomes apparent: when the buildings were first opened the blend of direct light and undecorated angles challenged the prevailing taste. The most radical acts were invited to play the hall: Pink Floyd played their 'Games for May' concert here on 12 May 1967, introducing the audience to surround sound. There's an advertisement for the gig in the Southbank Centre archive which sells the gig as 'Space age relaxation for the climax of spring – electronic composition, colour and image projection, girls, and the Pink Floyd.' Afterwards they were banned from ever playing here again, but not because of the girls: the bubbles produced from a machine stained the new furniture.[21]

The poet John Agard was in residence at Southbank Centre in the early nineties and wrote a whole collection of poems called *A Stone's Throw from Embankment*:

> Gone the days when winding walkways
> formed an up and down maze
> As a new piazza invites a river view
> And ground-level entrances embrace a complex venue.

The twenty-one acres of Southbank Centre, stretching from Waterloo Bridge to the London Eye, will never be anything other than 'a complex venue'.[22]

It's easy to get lost here, particularly inside the Royal Festival Hall. This building has had *Beowulf* performed in its Boiler Room, is connected through underground bunkers and walkways, has a sound proofed-room for the Javanese Gamelan, a ballroom, a Poetry Library and a Spirit Level. I have stood with a sweaty troupe of middle-aged disbelievers watching Morrissey making his 2005 comeback – like a revenant from fifties diner culture – and witnessed a performance artist stage his own death on stage. I've walked past Paul McCartney looking much taller than in 'real life' and stumbled by chance on the French poet Jacques Roubaud giving a reading in the Foyles bookshop. I started work in The Poetry Library when I was 24 and since then my adult life has built up around me: family death, marriage and parenthood have all taken place. Yet I can't honestly say that I am yet to fully understand this complex venue's physicality or its processes. One morning I looked out of the window at work and a rowing boat had been built on the Hayward roof for the *Psychobuildings* exhibition. The Southbank Centre landscape is elemental: earth, water and sky seem to change places each day.

When I came to work here I made a clean break with the working existences that had always felt stalling, stifling that sense of feeling that I was spending the working hours of my life in the right place. Work as the exchange drain: energy for money. Alongside the river, at the centre of the unpredictable – the jewel in the crown – is The Poetry Library. Not that there's much time to write when I'm at work: but stimulation breeds stimuli. On my first day at work Ivor Cutler came up to the desk and asked if I was a poet? I found out later that he asked that question of everyone. It was part of the process of him reaching into his pocket to take out *A Wet Handle*, or another of his micro-books, and read a poem to his newly captive audience. He did reverse the audience for me one time and – asking if I had any new poems – read one of my poems out loud to me that was printed in a new magazine. From then on, until his death in 2006, I saw him in the library and out-and-about on both sides of the river. His moods swung like a pool ball in a stocking but I remember spotting him in the Embankment Gardens next to the station – a few years before he died – dancing in the afternoon as the pigeons landed on him. I still have the sticky label poems he gave me: 'never knowingly understood'. In my copy of his book *A Flat Man* – he always had his publisher make them tiny so he could carry them in his pocket for impromptu readings – he wrote to me: 'For Chris, a man to be respected and enjoyed'. I've been trying to live up to that ever since. He hated noise and crowds but – in a wonderfully gentle paradox – loved nature and attention. A showman loner with a flower in his hat.

The largest public collection of modern poetry in the world has been getting me out of bed for the past fourteen years. The reality of selecting the Selecteds and collecting the Collecteds is far from a life

of books alone, but The Poetry Library has seeped into my poetic consciousness, by metrical osmosis. I've seen poets wilt in its presence as it poses the question: what can you add to all this? The collection grows by up to three hundred items a month, a monster fed by digital printing, letterpress and inkjet. The gifted, the competent and the misguided send their stock: some of it makes it through into the future of poetry that is always already halfway there.

Through reading – in that curiously zigzagging way that collections invite – I've self-educated in Dadaism, Vorticism, Imagism, Surrealism, Objectivism, Black Mountain, concrete, New York (and Cambridge) schools, L=A=N=G=U=A=G=E and conceptual poetics. I have loaned more books than I've bought and stayed late into the evening to read the rarities. I've often given myself the choice of heading to the BFI for a film or staying after work to spend time with Robert Creeley, David Gascoyne or Rosemary Tonks. Dead poets make for such compelling company.

It is surprising that it took thirty-five years of the Poetry Library's life to merge with that of the Royal Festival Hall. The first Poetry International Festival was established by Ted Hughes in 1967 and included an incredible cast of poets brought from around the globe in an attempt to bring voices from across the Cold War divide. Charles Olson, all six-foot-seven of him, sat on the stairs of the hall and refused to take a seat. Every time Poetry International comes around again there seems something so impossible-to-be-true about it: poets who have yet to learn how to use a vending machine somehow wend their way over thousands of miles to arrive. Or not. Charles Osborne described organising the 1970 festival like this:

> The Poets begin to arrive. I sit in my office like some bemused Shakespearian monarch while messengers rush to exclaim 'Thom Gunn has arrived from San Francisco', and 'Soyinka has flown in from Stockholm, but we've lost him' (Stockholm? I was expecting him from Ibadan) and 'I met the plane from Rome but Pasolini wasn't on it'.[23]

And poetry goes on all year and for so many years that it's endemic to the fabric of the place. Edith Sitwell was less worried about fitting in with the crowd and performed her text for William Walton's *Façade* at the Festival Hall in 1962 wearing flowing robes and a hat as if made to make the muse pour words straight into her head. One memorable evening Tom Raworth and Ron Padgett performed together in The Voice Box – a venue that saw thousands of poets perform – before becoming part of The Poetry Library's space.

Looking out of the library window I can see the Hayward Gallery: a beautifully jagged and weather-stained eggbox. Its balconies, balustrades and bridges lead in on itself: stone conduits without a cover. It tricks the eye towards its core, where the reason for its existence – art – takes place. As I look at it now, from the west side, there is a silver slide dangling from a red crane as a workman tries to attach it to the exterior roof of the building: the slide will be the exit from the forthcoming Carsten Höller show, *Decision*. The artist Chuck Close has described exhibiting at the Hayward like this: 'These hard, cold, massive spaces of concrete and stone are surprisingly conducive to the contemplation of images of warm, soft flesh.'[24] The best of the Hayward shows have always made me feel that this space is for artists to make and show work – there are other galleries that exist to spotlight ego. Even the retrospectives have been innovative and unexpected, the most memorable being *Undercover Surrealism*, an exhibition created by turning inside-out Georges Bataille's Surrealist magazine *Documents*. In 2013 I was one of a number of poets who took part in the *Poets After Dark* event, responding to the *Light Show* exhibition. I stood in a room of light – red, blue and green – and read a poem in response to Carlos

Cruz-Diez's *chromosaturation* inside the artwork itself. I made a quick change of clothes after work and emerged for the reading wearing red socks, a green shirt and blue trousers. I even used colour-coded paper to print out the poems. Colleagues never forget these things.

At the 2012 Poetry Parnassus event I was paired with the Serbian poet Ana Ristović as part of the *New World Order* event. As I prepared to soundcheck, taking that deep in-take of air that comes before all achieved lifetime ambitions, I walked up to the microphone to read the start of a poem and heard the words – through the control room above – 'Hello Comrade'. I looked up and saw that the technician was also a fellow union rep, waving through the glass above the stage. When hosting an evening with visual poet Paula Claire I followed as she led the audience out of the library to stroke the fossilised limestone of the walls outside the main hall, asking them to growl as they did so. I joined in – expecting my colleagues to be doing the same – but when I turned to check they were looking at me, arms folded, shaking their heads in dismay. Poetry has taken me to places I'd never thought I'd go to.

Southbank Centre can do that.

'PRISON'D ON WATRY SHORE':
EXPLORING THE BOOKSELLERS AND THE BFI

The booksellers are embedded into the fabric of the Southbank Centre; they even appear on the maps of the site. I've spent hours browsing here – yes, walking from a library to extensive metres of more books – feeling the wind blow in from the river. They are positioned opposite the BFI riverfront, underneath the bridge. From here you can get a view of the juxtaposition of angular line and flowing arches that hold the bridge up. Underneath the bridge light streams through the arches. A series of corrugated beams disappear towards the north side in a perfectly symmetrical formation. Under the first arch, fifty yards out, someone's graffitied the underside of the walls – risking a skirmish with the river to achieve this semi-public tag. They must have swam there with aerosols in their pockets.

I wander around the books: I've bought all kinds here over the years from Ed Dorn to Dave Eggers. The trade editions aren't

particularly cheap, though rarities can be found. If you have time to browse and want something good to read, you'll find it. The prints are worth a look, assembled into themed boxes: fruits, botanical, fashion, dogs, horses. William Blake, Lambeth Everyman, has his own box. I pick out at random: 'Earth's Answer' and read 'Prison'd on watry shore'. Then there are the illustrations that Blake made to accompany Robert Blair's *The Grave*. These were made in 1808, eight years after Blake had left Lambeth: a naked man, ripped to the ribs, hovers upside down blowing a bugle horn towards a skeleton under a sheet. The skeleton, agitated, rises up towards the bugle.

I hear each week in the media that the art of poetry is dead, that nobody cares – but I've never once walked past the poetry box here without someone taking a look. People love to look at old poetry books, especially when they're underneath Waterloo Bridge. I take out Coventry Patmore's *The Angel in the House*, published by John W. Parker on The Strand in 1854. As with The Poetry Bookshop in Bloomsbury 50 years later, here was poetry at the epicentre of London's topography: printed into the public consciousness, deeper than the coal holes. Poetry's changed quite a bit since then but these were hard times that made for the success of less than great poetry. Patmore's book is a tribute to the womanly ideal, She who makes her Husband happy. Despite its popularity at the time the book is now forgotten. Like the cobbled streets of London that steeped back into the muddy shore, this is the fabric that London – and poetry – has modernised and built upon.

The BFI riverfront faces the booksellers pumping out contemporary Muzak through overly-loud speakers. Through the bar, past the plastic glasses and expensive menus, is the library: an oasis. It's one of the few places you can see a finished film script. I've spent a very enjoyable visit looking at how Terry Gilliam laid out *Brazil* before filming. There's also Benugo's bar upstairs: a late-night Lynchian hangout furnished with drapes and soft lighting. I won't say where it is but there's a secret room behind a bookshelf that has a waiter from a previous epoch waiting to serve. Through that room is another room.

I walk along the Queen's Walk, the river chortling beside me, to the four poetry stones placed into the concrete here. They were laid down in the 1980s by the Greater London Council (GLC) to try and cheer the place up, though the GLC chose to embrace London's industrial and foggy past – the South Bank of smoke and ash:

> First, at the dawn of lingering day,
> It rises of an ashy grey;
> Then deepening with a sordid stain
> Of yellow, like a lion's mane.

(Henry Luttrell, 'A London Fog', 1822)

The stone this is laid on is cracked and caving-in at the middle – as if paying homage to the Victorian past that the poem depicts. Although written fifteen years before the Lion Brewery opened in

1837 the 'sordid stain / Of yellow, like a lion's mane' calls forth the South Bank Lion which would sit on top of the factory for over eighty years as the blacking and tanking factories pumped smoke into the air over the river.

The next poem, by Richard Sheridan, provides an unflattering glimpse of 1980s London reality. The poetry selectors at the GLC seem to have been suggesting that, yes, the Lambeth riverside is 'brown and flat', but rather than addressing it they placed instead this meta-stone, Ozymandias-like, to sagely draw attention to the deserted landscape. There is a suggestion in the choice of this text that the South Bank was the depleted cousin of other, more popular parts of London. Although the South Bank had Cuper's Gardens this was closed down in 1753 due to the loose moral vices of its visitors. Ranelagh Gardens, however, was based in Chelsea and not only had fashionable mats on offer, but had also invited the young Mozart to play. Ranelagh Gardens allowed the masque to take off in London and also outdid the nearby Vauxhall Gardens, which is also hinted to in this poem. What the poem in this context suggests is that there has always been a hope that the South Bank would rival other parts of London, a hope so often been misplaced – though the crowds behind me visiting Southbank Centre this evening show that the fortunes of this site have changed.

> Must though in justice,
> Declare that the grass,
> Which worn by our feet,
> Is diminish'd apace,
> In a little time more will
> Be brown and as flat
> As the sand of Vauxhall,
> Or as Ranelagh mat.

(Richard Brinsley Sheridan, 'A Woman of Fashion', 1777)

The next stone, with a poem by Wordsworth, pays homage to the Spenser poem which Eliot later riffed-off in *The Waste Land*. Wordsworth's poem provides a mid-point between both poets, showing how poetic language and legacy is created over centuries, like the current thoroughfares built upon brown flat sand described by Sheridan:

> Glide gently, thus for ever glide,

> O Thames! that other bards may see
> As lovely visions by thy side
> As now, fair river! come to me.
> O glide, fair stream! for ever so
> Thy quiet soul on all bestowing,
> Till all our minds for ever flow
> As thy deep waters now are flowing.

(William Wordsworth, 'Remembrance of Collins')

Eliot seals the quartet, though the stone has been set with a formatting error (which I've reproduced below) that can't be resolved with a thump of the tab button: the long line beginning 'To leeward' begins indented too far to the left:

> The river sweats
> Oil and tar
> The barges drift
> With the turning tide
> Red sails
> Wide
> To leeward, swing on the heavy spar.
> The barges wash
> Drifting logs
> Down Greenwich reach
> Past the Isle of Dogs.

(T.S. Eliot, *The Waste Land*, 1922)

Eliot was a poet of anachronistic contrast: he knew when to position his fag-ends next to his caryatids. In the original text the quote shown here follows on from the lines 'Ionian white and gold' but here we're in the post-Stink of the river: each syllable counts its cost, its value in imagistic weight, amidst the sordid turbulent tides of London commerce. The idea of culture as turning back on itself is captured in 'The river sweats'. The Thames as a porous bottleneck, unable to get out of its own way.

It's the last of the summer on the Queen's Walk. September. In the outdoor sandpit a toddler with blonde hair pushes a toy red bus: a future Boris creating his own playground. A man in a suit and open necked shirt takes the complete top off a ice-cream cornet with a single bite. Even the pigeons' shadows are getting long.

JUBILEE GARDENS:
THE RAIN OF POEMS

Looking at Jubilee Gardens now it's hard to believe that just four years ago this small quadrant of grass was as 'scant as hair in leprosy' (to quote Robert Browning, from another context). For a decade before then picnickers would search for a blooming tuft to park a towel as frisby-throwers practised playful ninjago over their heads. All that could be heard was the busker with a reggae-pedal who put a ragga-edge on everything he played. 'Here Comes the Sun', reggae-style; 'Wonderful Tonight', reggae-style; 'I Wanna Be Adored', reggae-style. Jubilee Gardens was a false peace. Whenever a tourist took a photograph without asking for permission the busker would give a military bark of: 'put some money down'. He later came into competition with the Chilean buskers who could actually *play* their instruments – and played with a smile. Then the mime artists followed, like silver-dipped mannequins. These Oz-like rusties don't do it for the love. They pop out a lollipop whenever a child passes and then put their gloved hand out to parents: gold must pave the palm of silver.

It's hard to remember the old Jubilee Gardens now, the one I took all those lunch breaks on, sitting on the gnarled benches under gnarlier trees – reading poetry. Since 2012 the granite paths have appeared, as well as trees, a play park and a flat green lawn. The spirit of 1951 is back: a Skylon-like column opens lotus-like, flying risk-taking pundits in circles, screaming. They sit in carts with a flag at their back, getting the full view – a view which only goes one way, being blocked on three sides by the Royal Festival Hall, the Shell Building and County Hall. The Thames in front of them like a glistering moat, laid out before this concrete Fantasia.

Then poetry fell from the sky. In 2012 Southbank Centre's *Poetry Parnassus* festival invited two hundred poets to take part, one from each Olympic-competing country. A group of Chileans called Casagrande had 'poetry bombed' a number of cities before, showering poems from a helicopter. They took a poem by each of the poets and turned them into bookmarks with the aim of releasing them in thousands from the sky. At first the wind wasn't right and the poems drifted in flattened wads of snow over the private wall of the Shell Building. Then the chopper was adjusted to make amends for the wind and the poems started to land here, on the grass, where the people were waiting. Children and adults reached up for words in a way that's usually reserved for money. Maybe the answer was in those words, falling by chance into a hand? And chance had everything to do with it: there's divinity in the fall of a sonnet. People climbed trees, declaimed the poems they'd found and gave duplicates to those who'd hit a duck. We found the poems as far as ITV Studios. Later that week a colleague found more on the Royal Festival Hall roof and someone reported a cyclist on the north bank who'd been riding along when one fell into his lap: he read it, realising that the poet who'd written it was a close friend. This is London, where we remain anonymous until a friend's poem falls from the sky.[25]

The Queen's Walk is fizzing with human life today. The fairground carousel – *The Galloping Horses For Your Pleasure* – goes around in cycles, waiting for punters to pay and climb on board. Each of the horses has a different name: Lydia, Ronni, Sue and Stephanie. All ages are welcome. No standing. Then there's the Spiegeltent (burlesque and freaks), advertising spectaculars, ice cream and cocktails. After all that you might need to use the twenty-four hour public toilets which is decorated with dozens of pictures of the Queen through her sixty year reign. Even the attendant, pushing a mop and bucket, wears a Union Jack outfit. Along the rails of the river a man's balancing a wheel on his nose while someone else is doing – something – with fire. The London

Eye looks down on it all, unblinking, a Millenium Eve attraction that has proved so popular it's been allowed to remain. Permanent transience due to public demand. The capsules rotate so slowly it's as if the wheel is a giant hypnotic prop that's been used to put the city to sleep each night. But London never sleeps. The wheel just rests for a bit.

FOUR PUBS AND FISHCOTHEQUE

If you've walked a bit around the central South Bank area you might want a drink or bite to eat. There are dozens of places to eat but finding a proper pub isn't as easy as you might think. My local here is The Hole in the Wall and I'll start by making it clear that you'll either love or hate this pub. Do you usually like pubs that have a picture of a monkey wearing lederhosen on the walls? If you do then read on.

The Hole in the Wall sits halfway down Mepham Street, an oozy kickback to Jacobean London facing the northern entrance to Waterloo Station. This narrow pavement passage intoxicates commuters with the tang of years of urine-relief, the brick saturation of emptied bladders. When Buster Edwards, the Great Train Robber, had served fifteen years in prison following his return to the UK, he decided to go straight and set up a flower stall here, on the intersection of Waterloo Road and Mepham Street. The smell of roses and lavender would have done little to cover-up the overpowering smell of urine.[26]

On the door of the pub, amidst years of accumulated Real Ale awards, is a recent food hygiene award. Of a possible 5 stars the pub has scored 3: GENERALLY SATISFACTORY. The badge is worn with pride. What The Hole in the Wall lacks in bistro is made up for in smells: food is cooked on a small surface alongside the bar, chips lactate in oil, burger fat crackles and spits towards the freshly poured Guinness. I walk up the familiar steps and head straight for the back room, past the front room snug which is crammed with a lads' night out in the early evening. I've been to a few of these kinds of events myself over the years. When a colleague was leaving work to head off to a new career herding lamas, a camera crew from Channel 4 – who were making a film about him – perched their cameras in the doorway as he attempted to make a speech after far too much to drink. He wanted to begin his speech with a quote from a Camus book but was heckled into giving up the idea. On another occasion he walked out of the pub and – forgetting the set of steps – fell face forward and smashed out his front teeth on the pavement. There are more salubrious places to be found.

In the days before the ban the front room snug was a serious smoking emporium. Men sat around the L-shaped sofa arrangement, backs to the trains and buses that should have called them home long before, toking on roll-ups, cigars, pipes and hookahs. Men who for years had told their wives that they finished work at 6.30pm trickled through the door here at 4.30pm, watching the main throng of the commute pass before joining its tail-end after the warm flush of cask ales. After the smoking ban a beer garden was placed in the yard behind the pub and a screen attached to an outside wall to keep the smokers from having to make any split decisions between sport and necessity.

I walk through to the back room: the monkey in the lederhosen is to the right, just after the women's toilets (my wife, Sarah, used to call the pub *The Smoker's Nappy*, based on the combined smell of smoke and urine). The Hole in the Wall is actually bigger than its name suggests. I spot the people I'm here to see, friends and colleagues, standing up against the bar. A few years before I had found myself in a lock-in here, until the early hours of the morning. The short Irish landlord of the time, distinctive for his decayed teeth – which were somewhere between cigarette stumps and Sugar Puffs – had told us to go and wait in the beer garden as he cleared everyone out. We had no choice. We stood in the cold, thinking he'd forgotten us, locked-up and gone home. Then he popped his head out and told us to come back in. We realised that there were a few other chosen stragglers here too and that all attention was focussed around a laptop, precariously placed on the now closed hob. The screen was open on the Light God of *Spotify*, which was open for requests. There was a twist to the merry-making as we realised that the landlord locked people in but didn't take too lightly to people asking to get *out*. At least not before he called Time. The next thing I remember was boarding the night bus which – in my spinning world – was somewhere between a fish tank and a mystery tour.

I drink the Erdinger on tap, a full-bodied cloudy wheatbeer, though if you prefer ales there's always a selection (Doom Bar is a permanent fixture). I look around: faces I've seen coming here for years; locals from the area and off-duty staff from other nearby arts venues. It's the kind of pub where you find that, if someone's getting a round in – and you catch their eye – you're in it. You just might not ever get out of it. Which is what happens now: a man I've drunk with before, who I've talked with a few times in the past – a Cockney comedian – is returning his round for the people he's with and a pint of Erdinger slides along the bar next to me. The last time I saw him was in a pub in Peckham called The Gowlett when he appeared from the gents as if he had an underground tunnel from The Hole in the Wall. I ask him how The Gowlett is: 'I wouldn't know,' he says, 'I'm barred.' He asks me where I drink in East Dulwich and I tell him The Clockhouse (I love the outside beer garden view of Peckham Rye, and often sit drinking London Stout until Blake's angels – one of which he saw on the Rye – start to twinkle in my eyes). 'I'm barred from there as well' he says. He tells me the story as I sip the Erdinger. Fifteen years ago he was in The Clockhouse and noticed some wires sticking out from the wood above the bar – he pulled them and the lights went out in the whole pub. The landlord was furious, and asked if he was responsible? The culprit was furious too, saying he could have been killed. Status determined the outcome: the landlord barred him. He didn't go back for fifteen years and when he did he asked the barman about the old landlord and where he was working now. The barman informed him that he was still here, and was upstairs at that very moment. A few minutes later the barman approached him and said 'I've just had a word with the Governor who remembers what happened fifteen years ago; he doesn't want your kind here – you'll have to leave.'

This is why I drink here: the people, the humour, the stories. The monkey in the lederhosen. After kicking out time I walk slowly along Mepham Street, looking closely at the moss-flecked walls for a fix of authentic London grime. The walls are coated in streams of green ooze, soot-blackened bricks, calcified sewerage pipes. Cigarette stumps mark out the territory as workers from the station's commercial outlets congregate in the warehouse spaces, taking their breaks beneath the opened shutters. The walls are pasted with layers of signage, warnings that run side-by-side with graffiti. Someone has sprayed JFK's face to the wall. Frosted windows have been further barred over with rusted portcullises. Wedged behind one is an eaten packet of chilli prawns.

Walk southwards along Mepham Street, back to the river, and you'll come to Waterloo Road. On your left is a burger bar; the BMW parked alongside it belongs to the owner. If you're hungry there are choices on Waterloo Road: don't be tempted by the burgers. Across the road, on the block nearest to King's College and St John's church – the IMAX cinema marooned on the concrete island like a Ballardian totem of the future – is *Thames Tandoori*. The food is very good though portions are small. Space is also tight and you might find yourself accidentally spooning the lime pickle from a neighbouring table. Next door is *Fishcotheque*, a traditional and proper fish and chips place. When I first met one of America's best poets, Peter Gizzi, we went here, along with his partner Lydia Wilson and artist Rick Myers. Peter told me who to avoid in the States. I went out and bought the beers. He paid for the bill. I owe him one.

A *Subway* recently opened up next door and lives up to its name by being positioned in the arch of the overheard railway bridge. Next to that you'll find The Wellington, a very large pub that is perfectly positioned for the late night commute, with buses heading north and south from the stop outside. Waterloo Station is just across the road. The Wellington is a hotel as well as a pub. I've never seen the rooms but have seen one-night residents slip through slim functional-looking doors, beaming with the alcoholic magnificence that can only come with knowing your bed is a few steps up a staircase from the bar that is sending you to sleep. Between 1994 and 2007, when the Eurostar from Paris to London was resident at Waterloo Station, the first thing the commuter would have seen – as I see now – was a gigantic mural on the ceiling over the bar of Wellington defeating Napoleon's troops on the field of Waterloo. Look downwards: this is a bar that specialises in spirits, the night time lights of outside London coruscates through the bottles that have been assembled from around the world. Nobody ever knows when The Wellington closes; be prepared for a usual last order at 10.45 or a last orders as late as 12.30am. I've sat here with friends on many occasions ordering drinks until midnight, listening to the good quality eighties pop that they often play. There isn't the same quality of character here as The Hole in the Wall though there is the advantage of the flâneurial view from the large windows: the always ticking streets of London – cabs alighting and relighting, buses parking in and then pulling anchor, drunks holding each other up with linked arms – the effect can be somnambulant and narcotic. It's pleasant to drink here until the staff want their glasses back –

though there are always those who want to claim them as their own by taking them out onto the streets to become a part of the blurriness that they've been watching through glass.

WATERLOO STATION

The best way to understand Waterloo Station is through sound. In February 2014 I was asked by academic and sound artist Will Montgomery to contribute to writing a score for musicians that was based upon the sounds of the station at a particular moment. The instructions I received were as follows:

> *stand quietly under the clock on the main concourse at Waterloo Station for a short period of time and listen*
>
> *describe one particular sound that you can hear with as much detail as you can*
>
> *do not include the source of the sound in your description, only how it sounds*
>
> *the source should be ambiguous to the reader*

Here's what I recorded between 9.00 and 9.07 am on 28th February 2014:

Murmurous rumble, sustained but ebbing.
The sound is low, bass-like, moving forward as if on wheels and like wheels squeaks occasionally as if brakes have been applied.

The rumble grows weaker, as if breaking apart, moving further away, and changes in rhythm to contain clap-like sounds.
The rumble continues at a lower volume, now containing the clap-sounds, sometime four, or five, like metal whacking on wood.
The rumble rushes in one direction then becomes distant; the claps are prevalent now, no more than the volume of steady rain and – also like rain – sustained in a steady concentrated pattern.

Rumble is the key word here and, along with the squeaks come claps, whacks and tannoy announcements. The station is named after Wellington's victory at Waterloo (although the station was called York Road in the first years after being built) but there is the water of its name manifested in the architecture: if you look closely at the Portland Stone you can see seaweed enmeshed in it, throughout the station.[27] In each of the twice daily commuter throngs there is a feeling that the station is being flushed of its temporary inhabitants as they pour out under the statue of Britannia, heading towards the Thames.

The migration south for the homeless is part of London's flow – the dispossessed are drawn here like iron filings to a magnet. Waterloo Station and its immediate surroundings is the terminus for those with no clear destination. There's an existing account from someone called Raymond Lunn, in *Londoners*, in which he describes arriving in London from Leeds, determined to make a new start in the capital. After spending the first night on a bench in Cavendish Square he finds himself on the South Bank, spending his nights around the Imperial War Museum: 'Why was I here? Where was I going?' he asks himself. One of the reasons might be the help given at St John's church, particularly through the evening sandwich vans. The current homeless drink on a bench made in tribute to the homeless dead: the forgotten remembered. Things work out okay for Raymond when he's given a studio flat, though he spends his last night drinking strong cider with those yet to find a route out. When he wakes up in the morning after his last night of homelessness he finds that his backpack has gone missing. In an endeavour not to be resentful he blames it on the pigeons.[28]

There is a cyclical history to the capital's attempts to sanitise the station and its environs. In the nineteenth century prostitution was a massive issue and the back of the station was harboured with a road called Granby Street that became synonymous with pimps and prostitutes. When the station was extended in the middle of the century Granby Street was knocked down. Mayhew described the low cabmen pimping women, and John Hollingshead wrote in *Ragged London* in 1861 that: 'unwashed, drunken, fishy-eyed women hang by dozens out of the windows, beckoning to the passers-by'.[29] Hollingshead gives specific mention to the Granby Street area that dominated the back of the current station:

> Each street has got a dingy beer-shop, if not a public-house, and at least one small coalshed, advertising 'an enormous fall in coals'. Such streets run at right angles into the Waterloo Road, cross over that very mangy thoroughfare, and continue into the heart of Lambeth, by the side of the South Western Railway. Granby Street is perhaps the worst sample of a prostitutes' street in this neighbourhood, and the vice it contains overflows in every house and oozes out on to the pavement.[30]

Henry Mayhew describes the conditions of the lodging houses which put so many on the streets in the nineteenth century. Landlords would buy up whole streets, dividing the houses down to the smallest partitions which would then be filled with as many beds as possible. 'There are numbers in Lambeth,' he wrote, 'in the Waterloo Road and contiguous streets.'[31] In the 1990s, when the Bullring was knocked down to make room for the pixelated fishtank of the future IMAX, the homeless moved into the numerous side-streets and alleyways and now make doorways and accidental windbreaks their refuge, outside the plethora of express supermarkets that line up along Waterloo Road.

Standing here, at the centre of the station, the sheer volume and speed of the commute makes the homeless invisible. The clock is the silent God that drives the pulse of human movement. This is the station's distinctive feature and has been a favourite meeting place since the 1920s. The clock has four sides: like the pre-modern belief that the globe was made of edges, it suggests an old world view of time – before Dali made the clock faces melt. Del Boy, in *Only Fools and Horses*, meets Raquel for the first time here, carrying a bouquet of flowers the size of a public shrubbery. In the Kinks' song from 1967, 'Waterloo Sunset', we hear that 'Terry meets Julie, Waterloo Station, every Friday night.' And the station isn't symbolic of the love that runs smoothly. I know someone who's most enduring relationship had ended without closure, leading to years of introspection; one evening, years later, he sat with a drink in a bar at Waterloo Station, looking down on the concourse – looking up by chance at the moment when he saw the woman he was in love with, who'd left him, hand-in-hand with the man she'd left him for. Charles and Diana also set off on their honeymoon from here.

I'm a compulsive hoarder of abandoned notes and ephemera – drawn to the reality of the handwritten. One afternoon walking towards the river through Concert Approach I picked up the following note:

> I THINK THAT I'M OVER YOU I'VE BEEN SAYING I AM FOR YEARS BUT THE TRUTH IS DESPITE THE FACT WE'VE NOT BEEN FRIENDS FOR OVER TWO YEARS NOW NOT A DAY HAS PASSED IN THE PAST 2000 DAYS SINCE WE FIRST MET THAT I HAVEN'T THOUGHT ABOUT YOU I FORGAVE YOU BEFORE YOU EVEN APOLOGISED I NEVER HATED YOU.[32]

Waterloo Station once suggested the modern. It had its own cinema, opposite Station 1, playing current affairs film on loop that commuters could drop into between trains. It was later the site of the Eurostar terminus into Paris, as described in *London from Punk to Blair*: a 'blue skeletal roof welcomes Europeans to London, only to subject them to taxi queues, traffic jams and the still-to-be-redeveloped South Bank.'[33] On my wife's 21st birthday we shuttled through Kent before all went dark; then we arrived under slate-grey skies over Gare du Nord. We had packed a small

toad to leave at Apollinaire's grave, in homage to his fixation with the well-named crapaud.

Over the past year The Balcony has been opened in the station: *Yo! Sushi, Carluccios, Oliver Bonas,* and *Paperchase* reign. Heritage has had an accidental impact: it's now possible to see some of the details of the architecture that has been hidden for decades. The raised surface of the names of places can be read as syllables when you walk at quick-pace: ANTS, WILTS, ON, WALL. Roses and lanyards have been lovingly glazed into coloured glass: London and South Western Railway. The roof looks out of place now: a 1970s geometry of reinforced plastic and angular girder. You see the commuter run for what it is: people dwarfed by the collective. The oppressive dominance of black clothing. The occasional drunk appears like a flute note in the funereal drone.

I'm here at 7am in the morning. The station could be an airport: everything is awake and available for consumption. The sommelier at *Cabin* is like a first aid rep waiting to serve, standing beneath an orange neon in the shape of a wine bottle. Brioche filled with pink flesh leers from silver dishes. *Starbucks* is steaming. I look up: a pug-nosed gargoyle looks loftily out from the wall. A pigeon above it. Alongside the gargoyle a surveillance camera is perched, doing what the masses now do better with their collective handhelds.

The memory of war is a complex monster. You really have to look for the commemorative Waterloo tribute, which is on the balcony facing the concourses. It's a 2015 replica of the medal given to all allied soldiers. There's a quote from Field Marshall Arthur Wellesley: 'My heart is broken by the terrible loss I have sustained

in my old friends and companions and my poor soldiers. Believe me nothing except a battle lost can be half so melancholy as a battle won.' The fact of World War One has been swallowed like jagged granite in the inflexible belly of its history. The World War One memorial requires no quote: its power is in the surnames lost to use or barely heard today. Pittwood, Lovelace, Pegram, Prattington, Holwill, Iremonger. The musical cadences of a lost London.

Next door *Joy* has filled its windows with kitch: a porcelain rabbit in a green birdcage, above a print of a flamingo. A skeleton with glasses looks out from *Kiehl's*: train destinations reflecting back from his lenses. That commuter glaze. *Foyles* is open for the early birds. I ask for the London section and scan through the different takes on offer of the capital city: *Cycle London, Uncommon London, Look Up London, The Art of London, Memories of London, Derelict London, Quiet London, Must Eat London, Meat London, Drink London. Shit London.* I pick this one up, it's by Patrick Dalton. This book is made of real photographs taken in shops, one of which states: 'Shoplifters Will Be Dealt With In A Medieval Fashion'. I walk around the store, looking past the books towards the restored features of the old station: a Victorian bureau with CASH written in caps across the top. The inside is now used for book displays and contains an adult colouring book called *The Secret Garden*. The renaissance around adult colouring books might signify the official end of creativity. Follow the lines. Don't forget to touch. Watch the gap.

On the upper floor a wooden gargoyle greets you on the staircase – you can stare into its closed eyes as you pass. Coming out on the east side of the station is a mountainous rank of bikes. Hundreds of them. An Ai Weiwei dream of bikes. A gargantuan scaffold made of wheels, noodles and chains. If you want to loan one you can get one here, though what was once Barclays blue is now Santander red. The wheels turn the same way. Someone's dropped a pair of glasses and the rushing commuters step over them. I pick them up and leave them on the zebra crossing box – as someone zips ahead on a red bike.

Notes

1. Quoted in the Festival of Britain display in The Royal Festival Hall.

2. Indebted to Charlotte Mullins for much of the information in this chapter. Charlotte Mullins, *A Festival on the River* Op.cit.

3. Simon Winchester *The Surgeon of Crowthorne: A Tale of Murder, Madness and the Oxford English Dictionary* Op.cit.

4. The company who made the lion were specialists in Coade Stone; their fortunes had risen following further restrictions in the centuries after the Great Fire of London that stated that exteriors to buildings couldn't be made of woodwork.

5. Simon Winchester, Op.cit.

6. Inwood, Op.cit.

7. Ibid.

8. Mullins, Op.cit.

9. Quoted in the Festival of Britain display in The Royal Festival Hall.

10. The Skylon was the winner of a competition winner to design something vertical for the site and the name was given by the poet Margaret Sheppard Fidler, who compounded the words 'sky-hook' and 'pylon' to give a strong sense of the futuristic.

11. Dylan Thomas, 'The Festival Exhbition, 1951', *from The Dylan Thomas Omnibus: Under Milk Wood, Poems, Stories, Broadcasts.*

12. Ibid.

13. Dylan Thomas, *Collected Poems 1934-1953* Op.cit.

14. From *Londoners: The Days and Nights of London Now – As Told by Those Who Love It, Hate It, Live It, Left It and Long for It* Op.cit.

15. Mullins, Op.cit.

16. Ibid.

17. Alan Bartram, *Bauhaus, Modernism and the Illustrated Book*, Op.cit.

18. Susanna Rustin, 'Health, Education and the Arts Should be Sacrosanct, Says Kelly', The Guardian, 12 March 2016. http://www.theguardian.com/culture/2016/mar/12/southbank-centre-director-jude-kelly-health-education-and-arts-funding-sacrosanct]

19. Shan MâcLennan, 'Case Study: Southbank Centre London and the Social Utility of the Arts'. Op. cit.

20. B.S. Johnson, Op.cit. For a full account of B.S. Johnson's relationship with Michael Bannard, and his early association with the building, see Jonathan Coe's brilliant biography of the writer *Like a Fiery Elephant: the Story of B.S. Johnson* Op.cit.

21. Grateful for the Southbank Archive which has recently become more accessible through a new Archive studio space on Level 2 of the Royal Festival Hall. It's also worth noting that Pink Floyd guitarist Dave Gilmour has since played live at the Royal Festival Hall – so the staining of the furniture at *Games of May* is now looked back upon as something of a house-warming right of passage. All is forgiven boys.

22. John Agard, *A Stone's Throw From Embankment*, Op.cit. I recently saw John Agard give an extempore reading at the Irish Embassy at the 150 year celebration of Yeats' birth. The Irish Ambassador held a copy of Yeats's poem and Agard asked him to thumb through for 'The Second Coming'. Agard's reading was brooding, uncomfortable, powerful and true to the poem: he slouched into the lectern, drawing the words with an enigmatic timbre of foreboding that Yeats would have approved of.

23. From a document held in the Southbank Centre archive.

24. Mullins, Op.cit.

25. A short film of the Rain of Poems can be found on YouTube and an anthology which includes all of the poems is available to read at The Poetry Library.

26. In the film *Buster* in which Phil Collins plays Edwards, the flower stall was set on Queen's

Walk, in front of the Festival Hall. The film ends with a cheery Buster being gently scolded by his wife – played by Julie Walters – for telling the camera about 'his dream'. He walks away with a wink and a nod to the camera. That was shot in 1988; in 1994 the real Buster Edwards, alcoholic and depressed, committed suicide by hanging from a girder in a garage on Greet Street.

27. Ruth Siddall, *Waterloo & City: Urban Geology Across the Thames*, Op.cit.
28. In Craig Taylor, *Londoners: The Days and Nights of London Now – As Told by Those Who Love It, Hate It, Live It, Left It and Long for It* Op.cit.
29. John Hollingshead, *Ragged London in 1861* Op.cit.
30. Ibid.
31. Henry Mayhew, *London Labour and the London Poor* Op.cit.
32. This note also appears in my poem 'Waterloo' which is included in my collaborative book with Jeremy Reed, *Whitehall Jackals* Op.cit.
33. *London from Punk to Blair*, edited by Joe Kerr and Andrew Gibson, London: Reaktion Books, 2012.

Liquid City cranks the ribs in its masts
          chains them to embankments
     creeks a helix to the sewers
                         jellyfish & hedgefunders
               entanglements of wing & fin
     sails them to Greenwich
          where hulls are burned to superscript
     addendums the date   adds to data
          and plugs an apple in a gasmask
                names it hogroast
pockmarks the walls of stations
     with shrapnel & drill-chaff
                captions for heritage
        pasteurises the details of its residents
          into the commute
     and pours them through centuries
               like missing faces on milk flasks
        Liquid City drinks itself
               spills itself into underground creeks
     brooks   spillways   sewers
     The Fleet   The Neckinger   The Effra
                these are my rivers it says
Go fuck Hades

WEST

THE RESTLESSNESS OF COUNTY HALL

Don't be deceived by the wedding-cake architecture of County Hall: politics is something that happens on both sides of the river. The current offices of the London Mayor are a few miles east along the South Bank at City Hall – a structure that looks like a desktop printer with all of its paper drawers left open. County Hall was the home of the London County Council (LCC) in the 1930s, the strongest political force at the time. Herbert Morrison was the leader of the LCC for six years and kick-started Labour's glossing of their public image through his decision to floodlight the County Hall building: a stage set for modern think-tank engineers.[1]

In the 1980s the Thames was a symbolic divide between the left and right. Ken Livingstone was resident on the South Bank as leader of the Greater London Council (GLC) and was locked in conflict with Thatcher's Tory Government who were based on the other side of the river. In 1981 Ken slung a banner above the inner-curving arches facing the Houses of Parliament: LONDON'S UNEMPLOYED DEC – 1981, 326,238. Lenin had taught Ken at this point how to dress: black gloves, long coat, trimmed blade-like moustache. Thatcher, after undoing the unions, abolished the GLC in 1986. The building is now memorialised in gold lettering : LCC 1889-1965 GLC 1965-1986.

This epicentre of political opposition is now a leisure emporium of Portland Stone labelled Southbank Place. The ribbed arches of power – tunnels of rigorous debate – lead to the gym. The statues of naked men hunched outside the windows are starting to make sense. Ironically, given Thatcher's role in the use of the building, the London Dungeon was based here for a time – it's now Shrek's Adventure with a tagline that would have fitted earlier political wranglings: *laugh, touch and smell the adventure!* On my first trip to London I walked into crippling clocks and lobster phones here: Dali was in residence. Then Saatchi occupied for a while: a room once paced by a combustive Red Ken was filled with a lagoon of black oil. Artist Richard Wilson's piece *20:50* uses oil to create a holographic field, reflecting and refracting the lead-lined window panes and oak panels. 'The oil confounds what it reflects' and – the sign warned – could 'damage clothing if touched'. The piece somehow absorbed – and neutralised – the political quagmire it had been placed in.

There are now hotels built into the building on the west side, overlooking Westminster Bridge. The red badge of Marriott is fixed like a medallion facing St Thomas' Hospital. On the north bank – and so big that it makes you wonder if there could possibly be a river in between – is Big Ben. Time as the big city factor. Don't forget it.

The stone lion that used to sit on top of the Royal Festival Hall now sits staring away, on the bridge, with its back to both the site it was built on and the building it keeps guard on. It looks towards Battersea Power Station, a few miles west – a higher platform and one that might once have been beyond the machinations and endless changes of the city.[2] There are status games in play between London's statues. The Marriott might have historical gravitas as the old County Hall but it can't compete with the Park Plaza on the Lambeth end of Westminster Bridge Road: a gargantuan black UFO which has become its own island. It looks direct at the Houses, like a scientologist's washbowl.

The old County Hall plays to the tourists. Not one, but two, red telephone boxes are locked together on the Westminster Bridge Road side. As I'm about to cross, looking right, a cavalcade of police bikes rip in front of me – one of the drivers blowing a whistle – and the crocodile of school children they're racing towards are halted by a teacher. One bike stops and the driver raises his hands both ways to stop people crossing. Murder? Robbery? Apocalypse? Then comes a stream of silver vehicles with their windows blacked-out: Executive London Commute. A transfer of the prestigious from one meeting to another. Citizens of London stand back and wait for power to pass. The school teacher is clutching a sign post with white knuckles.

As a rule I avoid the riverside walk here, which is always congested with tourists heading to one of the attractions or standing to take photographs of the river. Belvedere Road runs behind and – for want of much else in the way of appeal – does have a *Subway*. If you're hungry, unfussy and on a budget – you're in business. Or as the brilliant Tom Jenks put it on a postcard showing the lascivious poet John Wilmot, 2nd Earl of Rochester: 'want to go footlong for a groat?'[3]

You have to stand under the London Eye to fully sense its scale. An impossible desktop fan that moves at a nano-pace, barely perceptible to human vision. The pods have now been painted the colours of world flags. The reality of being on the Eye is that it's exciting until you hit the halfway point, then the slow descent is tiresome. But London has to be seen at least once from height and this is the best way to do it.

The area around County Hall has become the drifting tourist's *purgatorio*. Facing the river now is The Sea Life London Aquarium. Unlike the work of Damien Hirst, who was part of Saatchi's show, the sharks here are unstuffed. The biggest obstacle is the price of the ticket. Once you're through the tollgate you'll meet an overweight bearded man in lifeguard clothes who asks you to pose for a photo. As he asks you to point aghast at a shark, smiling, you'll next see yourself in an airbrushed image – dressed as a surfer.

Stephen Smith in *Underground London: Travels Beneath the City Streets* describes his epiphany in realising that the attraction he was visiting was much closer to the lost reality of London than he'd previously realised:

> But the mighty River Thames once inundated the very spot where I was now standing, where I was easefully breathing. Today, it's the sunken chamber of an aquarium beneath the former Greater London Council building on the South Bank. Oh sure, it's the South Bank *now*, but the aquarium had been an entirely natural water feature in the days when the river was broader and shallower that it is in the twenty-first century. Schools of eels and salmon had made their piscine living where the tame jellyfish was now moving away from me as lazily as a smoke-ring.[4]

Then waterlife – blue in fin and red in claw – is all around you. Lean silver fish swimming in clouds of bubbles. There is always one fish that goes against the direction of the others, like an accountant brushing against the smudge of the poets. Flatfish appear like plates turning on their sides to reflect discs of light through the glass. Stingrays like pebble-dashed Dysons sweep through the sand. Weird fish – with faces like Picasso paintings – look intelligently into your eye. Parrotfish eat at rock and sand and then spit it out in contempt. All exists in a hierarchical vortex with the dreadnought hulks of sharks circling above. Along the final corridor leading out from the aquarium, a smell rises which reminds me of my schooldays and the hundreds of lost, languorous hours sat next to pond water. The tanks here are murky with roach, perch and tench that stare side-eyed, expending minimal calorific energy. These are Thames water fish. This is Thames water. After the neon and colour of the Atlantic and Pacific we arrive back to the familiar.

And in the spirit of South Bank surveillance, everything watches.

TAKING THE GLITTER OUT AT ST THOMAS' HOSPITAL

I'm sitting in St Thomas' eye casualty waiting to be seen. I have a piece of glitter stuck behind my eye: it flew there, like a burned out star, when I was helping my son to make an improv artwork. There's an aquarium in the waiting room: orange fish slowly twist inside the glass. The hospital is spotless apart from this cubic entity of quail-grey water.

The receptionist sends me for lunch, asking me to come back in an hour, when the doctor's returned. When I worked in a casualty department of a hospital, as a student, I had the same lunch each day: chips and beans. I buy the same now. I sit down in the huge clattering rumbling canteen and then walk along the corridors. Hospitals are becoming increasingly like airports. You can get laid up for the winter but still do your Christmas shopping on the corridors. The last time I came here was because I'd hit my head on a low-growing branch on the Victoria Embankment when I was out running. Seeing stars, the place made more sense to me. Or maybe this corporate arcade has been built since then. Thinking of the hospital's origins – further east down the river, in Southwark – as a medieval place of last resort, as well as burial ground, makes the glitter in the window displays seems all the brighter. Originally located in Southwark, near today's London Bridge, the hospital was named after St Thomas Becket. The moral tone was severe: if you came in with a venereal disease you'd be put in the stocks. Sweat out the clap with shame.

John Stow in his 1598 *A Survey of London* describes St Thomas' as 'a college or hospital for the poor':

> The hospital of St. Thomas, first founded by Richard Prior of Bermondsey, in the Cellarer's ground against the wall of the monastery, in the year 1213, he named it the Almerie, or house of alms for converts and poor children; for the which ground the prior ordained that the almoner should pay ten shillings and fourpence yearly to the Cellarer at Michaelmas.[5]

Stephen Inwood tells us that in 1552 St Thomas' gave shelter to 260 'aged and lame'. This is an early example of social welfare and Stow even uses the word 'workhouse' in association with these hospitals. Of course what began with philanthropic gusto – the strong looking after the weak – later became saturated with the weight of Victorian morality and worthiness. The City Corporation acquired five great properties between 1547 and 1553 (most of them belonging to monastic houses) including St Thomas' and St Mary Bethlehem – or Bedlam as it became known. Both institutions moved to Lambeth in the nineteenth century.[6] St Thomas' moved here in 1862 at the peak of Victorian industry, when the old timber yards had been replaced by the dozens of factories lining the shore. Positioned just behind the hospital was Doulton's pottery factory which made the sewerage pipes that would re-equip the city following The Great Stink.[7] As Jerry White puts it: 'The Lambeth potteries, including Doulton's, behind the Albert Embankment and St Thomas' Hospital, made everything in stoneware: sinks and lavatories, chimneypots and drainpipes, and bottles for beer, ginger beer, blacking and ink'.[8] In terms of sewerage – and the cause of cholera being found to be in the water that ran through the city – the connection between health and the new industries was a very close one.

The best time to come here is on a summer morning and over 150 years after The Great Stink. You can walk through the gardens to the elevated wall along the Thames to gain a viewing platform over the river and the Houses of Parliament. Beyond that is the endless sweep of buses and cabs across Westminster Bridge and the boats passing down the river. There's a temporary hospitality suite with the sound of a piano being tuned, note by sad note.

Facing the riverside entrance – which you can access from the main corridor of the hospital – is one of those curious London architectural intersections in which a number of buildings are fused together from previous eras into one incongruous site: future and past time seems to synch into the present moment. 'The ruins of Time build mansions in Eternity', as Blake put it.[9] Although I'm standing outside it feels like I'm inside: four or five different builds of the city are awkwardly married to this one spot. This is a result of the damage caused by the Blitz in World War Two in which the hospital suffered badly for its proximity to the Houses of Parliament. A metal and glass balcony connects the Victorian section to the geometric sixties' construction. It's like an NHS Millenium Falcon. A bell tower with a weathercock hovers over the sodden prefabs. On the ground – in the middle of this mangled tardis of ruins – is a disco ball which trickles a steady therapeutic stream of water. I look up at a smoke stained glass window and see that I have no reflection.

Warm summer light trellises the walls above with a shadow-patter, falling across the statue of Sir Robert Clayton who was president of the hospital in the seventeenth century. He's

looking away from the river – the river that is always there – towards the hospital. As if he knew the river would soon become a Stygian pool of effluent and the hospital would be cursed by its proximity to the slow-moving treacle of its waters. There's live moss in the stone of his curls. Two cupids are hugging – or holding up – a badge of St George which is on the plinth beneath his feet. Behind him a tesserae of broken tiles forms the wall beneath the arch. Lit pink with the warm lumens of the sun.

I go back inside. There's a lovingly crafted timeline of the hospital which pays tribute to Florence Nightingale. The Florence Nightingale Museum is actually in the grounds of the hospital – there aren't many hospitals than can lay claim to that. Florence Nightingale's name even sounds like a palliative. There's a photograph of men sitting up in beds, during the Blitz, lined up along the embankment wall I've just been walking along.

It's time to go and find the doctor. I look along the corridor through the one eye I can see out of. 'Cakes!' a very well-spoken child shouts looking at a table of home-made consumables that are for sale. There are mosaics on the walls of famous children's stories and nursery rhymes. Puss in Boots blurs before me. I make it back to the Eye Clinic; the young doctor looks at my eye through a series of lenses, staring into the rods and cones I use to look with and never think about. 'Nothing,' he says. 'You're fine.' He sends me off squinting – back towards the endless river I came from.

DOING THE LAMBETH WALK:
WESTMINSTER BRIDGE ROAD AND LAMBETH NORTH

There are tunnels off Westminster Bridge Road that are lined with Blake-inspired mosaics, beginning here on Carlisle Street. Local residents, led by David Tootill, made the mosaics and recorded versions of the poems for the sound boxes which are also here. Tootill talks of why mosaics were the best medium for this tribute: 'Mosaic is such a tough medium that it can go on the street without risk of being damaged, it's 24/7 and it's free; everybody can see it, touch it, and interact with it.'[10] It's a curious experience walking past thirty-six Blake homages in a relatively central London location. The others can be found on Centaur Street and Virgil Street. They exist as visionary depictions that are brushed up against by

occupied, harassed life travelling home on wet Autumn evenings – as Blake would have witnessed in own lifetime. Between two of the works is an arched vacuum that leads towards darkness – inside there is a ledge filled with the remains of crushed beer cans. I step into the road to try to photograph the 'Songs of Innocence' mosaic as a black cab drives towards me, snarling at my heels.

At the end of Carlisle Street the land of paid-for storage hire waits for me. This is the story of the city's Victorian railway tunnels and arches: most remain closed and abandoned, others are put to use by small businesses. And space is becoming big business in contemporary London. In a spirit of industry redolent of the nineteenth century there is money to be made in storage. I walk through to find the extension of Project Blake: 'Visions of the Daughters of Albion' is fixed alongside a graffiti tag from someone called FOULAR. I think of the prolific and ubiquitous poetry activist S.J. Fowler: he might well have organised one of his collaborative poetry events here and invited Blake to take part.

A pipe drips steadily into a moss-lined gutter, past one of the Sons. This is Albion. A cryptic key is left swinging mid-wall. As Blake suggested: all of Albion will come to Lambeth if you look for it. There's an information board for the mosaics which tells us that 'Blake was a paradox: a profoundly spiritual man who detested organised religion'. As I'm looking at the mosaics a man approaches me down the tunnel: it's another poet – and a co-ordinator at The

Poetry School, just down the road – John Canfield. John's also been an actor and a children's clown: he's the best person you could possibly meet down a Blake-themed dark tunnel.

After chatting with John for longer than either of us has time for I'm drawn from the tunnel by the sound of a lamb bleating. At first I think it's John playing a prank but I look back to see his bountiful hair disappearing towards the far end of the tunnel, towards a ringlet of light. I walk towards the bleat and find a sign for Oasis Farm, Waterloo. A picture of a sow suckling five bright piglets entices the eye: OPEN FOR BOOKINGS. The sound of the lamb bleating fuses with the rip of a passing motorbike. 'Lamb' and 'Hithe', I recall, are the roots for place name 'Lambeth': the landing place of the lambs.

THE CROWN AN D CUSHION AND THE NECROPOLIS RAILWAY

Later that evening I'm back on Westminster Bridge Road, at The Crown and Cushion pub, with poet and artist Sophie Herxheimer. If you want a pub around Westminster Bridge Road, along the stretch of Lambeth North station, there are many to choose from. The Walrus, The Horse & Stables, The Steam Engine, The Pineapple. But The Crown and Cushion does it for me. It's an Irish pub with an early-twentieth century feel: a proper Bloomsday boozer. Guinness adverts from every epoch line the walls – the toucan as perennial. Fruit machines splutter in apoplectic seizures: *Cash Monster, Money Pot, Deal or No Deal.* Sophie took part in my 2014 Poetry School course on James Joyce's *Ulysses* and we came here afterwards a few times, with the exiled echo of Dublin's cadences still lisping in our ears. A sip of Guinness was enough to tip us into linguistic meltdown. Above the bar there are a series of sepia photographs of old Ireland. There's a real typewriter attached to the wall.

This book is about real South Bank and here's another real pub. As I remove the top off the Guinness using nothing but my lip and a longer-term plan, I pose the question to Sophie: what, then, is Real South Bank?

'I'm Lambeth born and bred' she says, 'born in Clapham and grew up in Brixton. What do you want to know?' There's lots she could tell me but true to the usual trajectories of our conversations we start with the artist Khadambi Asalache who lived at 575 Wandsworth Road. Sophie shows me the catalogue of his works, which she happens to be carrying in her handbag, which shows how his ornate designs brought together the functional and the aesthetic into one habitable whole. The gap between art and life was non-existent. Over a period of decades Asalache, who was a civil servant working at the Treasury, slowly turned his home – through carving and painting – into a homage to the African home he missed. Even the staircase exists in a *horror vacui*: no surface was left unembellished or unadorned. Sophie points out a picture of Asalache sat in a chair at home with the banisters curving up and away behind him. His black socks are stitched with an argyle weave. He was also a poet. Build block by block was his approach – and let the audience come later. Sophie's hitting her stride now as she talks about how she must have passed him on the street, they lived so nearby. A curl of red lipstick flowers at the edge of her pint of John Smiths.

There's something of the Real South Bank in Asalache's life project – but he lived just outside of the geographical confines of this book. It's my turn for the drinks. A man at the bar, on his own, is asking the barmaids how long they've worked here? One says fourteen years, the other says 'since Jesus was born'. He tells them he's asking because a year ago he came with the Firefighter's Choir to perform at the Park Plaza and they came to this pub for a session

afterwards and got into a singing marathon. The barmaid of fourteen years springs to life: 'I've still got this on my phone,' she says. She walks around to the front of the bar to show him the phone and I huddle in too as she plays it: a group of clearly pissed public service people are singing 'Human' by the Killers, orchestrated by a drunken man in a black suit. I ask him are these all firemen? 'Fire*fighters*', he corrects me, adding: 'Firewomen too'. The he looks back at the film of his shitfaced self with the righteousness of the sober. I take the drinks back to our table. Maybe this is Real South Bank: ethically-driven Firemen orchestrating impromptu sing-a-longs in pubs?

Strange men start to assemble at the bar. An old man who really does look like Jesus leans against the counter. Another man in a purple sweater and a flat cap approaches him, pretending to bowl an imaginary ball. Then more men appear from nowhere, like zombies, returning with black pints and chasers. Last orders. A small bald man in a pink t-shirt dances back to his seat with a pint in each hand – like a torch and a backup candle.

Someone shouts across the room, from a group, 'YOU!' Everyone laughs. I need to use the toilets and follow the sign: 'Roscrea 10'. A town, I later read, known for its pharmaceuticals and meat processing. Inside the toilets a man is urinating with his penis in one hand and a smartphone in the other. I look up: the green glazed tiles are impressive – they could be remnants of the local Doulton's.

As I walk back out someone in the same group is shouting 'ARE YOU IN, ARE YOU OUT?' Everyone laughs. Back at the table Sophie and I try to lose ourselves in poetry: Sophie reads some of her new poems to me. Then I read something I've written, a hybridised prose-poem which tries to capture London in sound: *Sonicopolis* (okay, I confess to Sophie, the title is work in progress). We drain the lasts of the Guinness. As we leave I accidentally capture Jesus on my phone, who's staring into the spinning distance – head on his hands – a thump of dark spirit in his glass.

The world is even darker outside. Westminster Bridge Road was the Victorian termini for the newly dead. As part of the great push to clear corpses from the inner-city Brookwood Necropolis in Woking, Surrey, was opened in 1849. Compared to the Magnificent Seven cemeteries which had developed like a rosary around the city's neck – to paraphrase Lucinda Lampton – the cemetery at Brookwood was gargantuan: 2000 acres of desolate heathland. There was a fantastic twist of Victorian innovation in this development: the dead were taken to this new underworld via train. This location near the river was chosen as the whole of London's dead could be shipped for dispatch via boat along the Thames. The company that ran it was called The London Necropolis and Mausoleum Company and it's here, standing at the remaining offices – feeling slightly drunker now that the oxygen has mixed with the Guinness – that we find ourselves looking up at the former administrative centre of this DLR of death.

The development of the private train station, which stored corpses near Waterloo Station – in a residential area – was not without controversy. As Catherine Arnold makes clear there were 'objections from local residents who were not best pleased at living next to a station for the dead'.[12] In a period of great destitution the corpses would lie with more space – and more prospect of outer London peace – than many of its living. Though the dead weren't outside of the class divide: a First Class ticket was available for corpses, which offered better customer care and a decorated carriage. Bizarrely, the dead were issued with a Coffin Ticket, with the class of travel written on it. The living could travel by the same train too, though they had the option of a return ticket: the dead were one way. Religion was laid down into the structure: there were two lines into the cemetery, North for Dissenters and South for Anglicans. There was even a pub on the south side. There's a story dating from 1867 in which the train driver got so drunk waiting for the return train that the fireman had to drive the train back. From that time on, as it goes, the Company would only provide a free lunch to crew if they hadn't drank more than one pint of beer. Brookwood also pushed the multi-culturalism of the city into its death practices and was one of the first cemeteries to cater for Muslims and Sikhs.[13]

I look up at the arch above and the eight mini classic columns resting above it. The gates are shuttered with steel. When it was opened it had the word NECROPOLIS elevated across the top, the letters standing alone, in sans-serif, like a statement on the city's hatch and dispatch. It now says Westminster Bridge House; the next

door is flagged FOR SALE. It's hard to believe that Necropolis Railway was in use until 1941 until the station – like so much in this area – was destroyed by bomb damage. We cross to the other side of Westminster Bridge Road and, in the roulette of night buses, Sophie's bus arrives first. She runs for it – the Crown and Cushion pushing its shutters up behind us – and makes it.

WILLIAM BLAKE ON HERCULES ROAD

On the corner of Westminster Bridge Road and Kennington Road the London Eye peers over the glass and brick vista of hotels and apartments. Blake would have viewed the Eye as a symbol of Albion – as he wrote in *Jerusalem*:

> cruel Works
> Of many Wheels I view, wheel without wheel, with cogs tyrannic
> Moving by compulsion each other; not as those in Eden: which
> Wheel within wheel, in freedom revolve, in harmony and peace.[14]

There have been countless rebuilds and developments since William Blake lived here, on Hercules Road. The endless clanking and mock-direction of change is moving at an accelerated pace today. Led by luminaries in luminescent jackets – Watch Fiends of the endless shift. Scaffold dismantling, scaffold going up: the hidden structures of the city are remade along the same lines, like sonnets

by half-poets cast in the Shakespearian mould. With these developments around Lambeth North it's the lack of imagination that Blake would have hated most; more apartments for more people with money who wouldn't have considered living here if they could afford to live somewhere else. A plastic hoarding tells us that another Park Plaza is in progress – despite the one that's 300 yards away on Westminster Bridge Road. The Luminescents get to work on it: *G.C.L.: Specialists in Demolition, Groundworks and Concrete Frames.* This is the rational without imagination that Blake warned against.

Blake lived here between 1790 and 1800, writing some of his best work in that period: *America* (1793), *Europe* (1794), *The Book of Ahania* (1795), *The Book of Los* (1795) and *The Song of Los* (1795). He wrote about Lambeth continuously until it became the marshy epicentre of his worldview: the riverside underworld of his personal mythology. Lambeth gave him and his wife Catherine a decade of happiness – it was here that Thomas Hobbs called on them one day and found them naked in the summerhouse, playing out the roles of Adam and Eve from Milton's *Paradise Lost*. Tellingly, it was only after moving from Lambeth to take up a job in Felpham, West Sussex, that the non-alignment of his views with the rest of society began to get him in trouble. Whenever Lambeth appears in his later work it is expressed with affection and reverence:

There is a Grain of Sand in Lambeth that Satan cannot find
Nor can his Watch Fiends find it: tis translucent & has many Angles

(*Jerusalem*)

We have to keep looking obliquely at Blake's work: the tensions in his myths seem to be still playing themselves out as the world continues to change. Using Blake's mythopoeia as a way of seeing the South Bank takes us beyond gamers in a virtual reality to the true core of this part of London.

Why did Blake love Lambeth so much? For a start the house on Hercules Road was huge – especially after the confines of his previous Soho address. He also had a garden that had a fig tree. As a boy Blake had loved nature, walking out as far as Surrey the hills, which at that point rose high over London and could be seen from here. In Lambeth – for the first time in his life – he had his own piece of nature beneath his feet. There was a vine that grew in the garden that he refused to allow anyone to touch – a metaphor that has been equated to the poet's long and visionary lines which he refused to 'prune'.[15] Gilchrist spoke to a woman who, as a girl, had called on Blake here and later recounted:

> Blake would on no account prune this vine, having a theory it was wrong and unnatural to prune vines: and the affranchised tree consequently bore a luxuriant crop of leaves, and plenty of infinitesimal grapes which never ripened.[16]

Subsequent biographers of Blake have failed to come as close as Gilchrist in capturing the atmosphere of what Hercules Road was like back then. Gilchrist had the advantage of speaking to those who'd actually met Blake as well as seeing the streets after just one subsequent development – rather than the many that have happened since. Gilchrist captures the throughways and atmospherics of the South Bank of the 1850s:

> Open garden ground and field, interspersed with a few lines of clean, newly built houses, lay all about and near; for brick and mortar was spreading even then. At back, Blake looked out over gardens towards Lambeth Palace and the Thames ... The city and towers of Westminster closed the prospect beyond the river, on whose surface sailing toys then plying once or twice a day ... The street has since been partly rebuilt, partly renamed; the whole become now sordid and dirty.[17]

I have two favourite anecdotes from Blake's decade on Hercules Road. Gilchrist tells us of how Blake saw a ghost here:

> Standing one evening at his garden door in Lambeth, and chancing to look up, he saw a horrible grim figure, 'scaly, speckled, very awful', stalking down towards him. More frightened than ever before or after, he took to his heels, and ran out of the house.[18]

Blake said that ghosts didn't appear to imaginative men but only to common minds who couldn't see finer spirits – seeing a ghost would have been a terrifyingly normalising experience to him and one that might have been felt to threaten his unique creativity. There is also the anecdote relating to the local circus. Astley's Ampitheatre – London's first circus – had opened on Westminster Bridge Road in 1773. Blake – always walking, always observing – passed the Ampitheatre one day and heard something strange inside. He looked through a gap to see what was happening: a boy was being punished by having a log attached to his foot. Incensed, Blake went into the Ampitheatre to demand that the boy be released. The episode was unresolved but later that day Astley himself knocked at Blake's door to warn him away from interfering with the workings of his circus. A heated argument broke out on Blake's doorstep which, according to artist Frederick Tatham, eventually simmered itself out towards 'mutual forgiveness and mutual respect'.[19]

As always in Blake, joy is quickly offset with the quick chill of experience. If Albion is at war then the light and dark of that war are played out in the poet's mind, wherever he happens to be living: a domestic vine isn't enough to take his gaze from the world. Any happiness in Lambeth was surrounded by the difficulties of living there:

> Remember all thy feigned terrors on the secret couch of
> Lambeths Vale
> When the sun rose in glowing morn

> (*Jerusalem*)

In his long poem *Milton*, Blake describes standing in Lambeth 'with fear & terror'. A decade is a long time in a man's life and Blake – finely attuned with a capricious synaesthesia – also wrote in the same poem:

> from Lambeth
> We began our Foundations: lovely Lambeth!

The urban and industrial were growing all around him and the Victorian churn towards further industrialisation was blackening his doorstep. Gilchrist describes Hercules Road as 'a row of houses which had sprung up since his boyish rambles'.[20] Bentley argues that the place was still largely market gardens and warehouses and although Lambeth had just 1400 houses in 1800 the pace of this change was ripping up the old green marshland. Blake lived here in a hinge period: as the door closed on the marshes the new urban skyline would have appeared as alien and terrifying.

The burnt-out Albion Mill can be seen as a symbol of this.[21] Built by John Rennie this was seen as the newest and most impressive of the new factories, running on steam engines and producing six thousand bushels of flour a week. When it burned down in 1791 its charred carapace was left as burned-out remains for twenty years,

another of the South Bank's circular buildings – or octagonal in this case – that would later reincarnate as the Park Plaza on Westminster Bridge Road.

Approaching the blue plaque on the site of Blake's old house you first pass The Corporation of London badge declaring the William Blake Estate: silvery dragons simplifying the true Albion that Blake saw as split by competing forces. The facing road takes on the mythological grandeur of Blake visions: Centaur Street, which leads back to the tunnels of Blake's mosaics and – alongside that – Virgil Street. Mythology and poetry are everywhere here. I think of Blake's late watercolours *The Wood of the Self-Murderers: The Harpies and the Suicides* which shows Dante and Virgil walking in a shadowy forest. These were painted by Blake when he was in 60s, during a fortnight of illness. All one hundred of them. Virgil Street still has its Georgian houses here, built in 1827, long after Blake had moved but before the house he'd lived in had been demolished.[22] The garden of the corner house leading to the tunnel is overgrown with thriving nettles and light-hungry creepers.

Blake's vines and marigolds – and the fig tree he grew in his garden – appear as a surviving Edenic image before the blacking-out and bricking-up of the area for the factories and warehouses. For the timber yards and breweries, the makers of stone and dyes, the blacking factories and potteries which began to populate the horizon – each of them pumping out their own distinct smoke and scent into the miasmic haze over the river.

Blake absorbed both the grainy textures and spiritual under-wiring of Lambeth. This area that was also home to dwarfs, prostitutes and clowns – and yet was still owned by the Archbishop of Canterbury – was exaggerated and re-imagined in the work he wrote during the prolific decade that he was here. Blake had priests, circus masters, orphans and madmen on his doorstep. The fact that he appeared to his neighbours as strange says a lot for his outsiderness:

> I must Create a System, or be enslav'd by another Mans
> I will not Reason & Compare: my business is to Create

> (*Jerusalem*)

In this poem Blake connects 'Rational Power' with a living form and describes it as:

> a Worm seventy inches long
> That creeps forth in a night & is dried in the morning sun …
> It plows the Earth in its own conceit, it overwhelms the Hills.

The new Park Plaza emerges from the ground facing the spot where Blake lived. The blue plaque faces the exposed apartments which will occupy passers-through from all over the world:

> William Blake
> Poet & Painter
> Lived in a house
> formerly on
> this site.

Despite the non-imaginative trek of false progress Blake would have been fascinated by the people who came here, even as the highest tower of the hotel would have blocked the sun from reaching the garden that inspired his most creative work. And the spirit of Blake can be found here – if you look hard enough – at the end of Hercules Road near Lambeth North station. Wedged into coloured prefabs – in the shadow of the tapering plaza – is Make Space Studios: a collective of sixty-one creative organisations from across the borough. A luminescent workman in orange is standing beneath it, typing furiously into a handheld. Or playing *Candy Crush*.

STINKPITS:
THE PINEAPPLE AND DA VINCI'S

At the end of Hercules Road there's a pub called The Pineapple. There's been a pub of the same name here since Blake's day. It's recently achieved notoriety – not as much as The Dog and Duck Tavern which was situated on St George's Fields and demolished to make way for a different kind Bedlam in 1812 when the Bethlem Hospital was relocated here – but nearly. This version of The Pineapple was opened here in 1870. By chance, a few months back, I met a man who worked for the police force whose job was to take calls for emergency services across London. Given the associations of the south with disrepute and excess there's something quite right about the police having their HQ here. He told me that most of the crimes on the South Bank are committed against 'middle-class skateboarders on a day trip to the area'. Then there are the calls of complaints: ex-partners, domestics, families. The authorities send an officer to move the situation on: no crime committed. Private business. Then there's the sheer ludicrous: those ringing with complaints about being overcharged for photocopies in the local library. Those who report that their Oyster card's not working or that their phone top-up has failed but they've been charged. Occasionally there's a young drunk trapped in a cat flap – lost their keys on a night out and thought they could fit through.

'Most people in London have mental health problems,' he told

me, 'particularly in the south.' They ring up to tell the police that they're being abused and when the officer pays a visit they can't remember lodging the complaint. Then come the silent, mistaken calls – the emergency button on the Blackberry that connects people straight through without them realising they've done it. Unless the person says I want the police / fire brigade / ambulance these are largely ignored. As for Ambulances: 'forget it,' he said. 'Most of them can't make most accidents in time anyway.' He said that you're much better off scooping up the victim yourself and throwing them in the back of a cab for A&E. 'In fact,' he said, 'call the police: might not be best health and safety but at least they'll courier them to the hospital.'

He told me about The Pineapple's notorious public moment in 2009, made famous when *The Sun* ran a story about a number of off-duty officers having sex with a female officer and a civilian in the pub. The rational forces Blake railed against finding the garden of Adam and Eve in a local boozer. O Merrie England.

There's no mistaking the build date of this version of The Pineapple: a gold-foiled meta-stone stamps out its moment of conception: 17th May 1870, glinting with the fact of Henry Finch's hands which pushed it into place – laying the base for the boozy columns to be fitted. This was laid soon after Gilchrist was writing Blake's first biography and walking the streets, describing the changes since Blake had lived here.

The Pineapple is now the regular for the Poetry School students who walk out of the rooms on Lambeth Walk and – glazed by poetry and the night – are led by their worldly tutors for the real educative business of drinking. There's no shortcut to becoming a poet: doing the Lambeth Walk after a golden gallon and still remembering the words of your new poem is one of the steps on the tenfold path.[24] I am one of the few who go elsewhere with my class, to the Steam Engine, which is in Cosser Street, a back road opposite Lambeth North tube. I like the music there, and the late licence. And the Guinness. But I'll never persuade the other tutors – The Pineapple is the regular. Roddy Lumsden writes about it memorably in his poem 'Goodbye John' (which is for the same John Canfield I met in the Blakean underpass a little while back), which describes his group's weekly debauch here, which was often continued in the late night dive of Da Vinci's bar, on Baylis Road at the Waterloo Station end of Lower Marsh. At least until it burned down. Da Vinci's posed as an Italian restaurant by day but after hours transformed into a dark room for those living through various life crises. And poets (which is usually the same thing). Lumsden writes about the group's always renewed commitment to swerving the post-Pineapple Da Vinci's but – in a never-ending sentence which does justice to the liquidated ramble through the old marshes – they always fail:

> We had taken to promising each Wednesday after class not to end up in the stinkpit which served stiffly priced drinks halfway to dawn, but weekly there was a weakening, and we'd strut from The Pineapple, pretending there was an alternative, bleakly denying we were in a soapbox cart and at the bottom of this steepest moral hill was Da Vinci's, where we huddled in the odd light till the eerie became seductive.[25]

Da Vinci's burned down under suspicious circumstances, taking the bargain bookshop next door with it. Within days the developers were in: cranes poking at the smouldering remains. In the South Bank's current property climate there is no burned-out shell – even a 'stinkpit' like Da Vinci's – that has the luxury of a decade of broken dormancy like Albion Mill did in the late eighteenth century. The outstanding question is what will take its place as the area's most notorious late-night hatch in the tradition of The Dog and Duck. Cubana – the Cuban bar on Lower Marsh is very lively of an evening – but it closes surprisingly early. *Join the path* is written on the wall next to a dancing woman. And The Pit Bar across the road – beneath The Old Vic – is far too classy. The poets can't afford the price of the drinks for a start.

WOODLAND FOR THREE PIGS:
LOWER MARSH

Despite being drained in the eighteenth century the marshland that occupied the whole of North Lambeth carries its name in Lower Marsh. The Roman road that had cut through the swamp and brought traffic to Lambeth Palace and the river was extended into new sites of commercial activity. Lower Marsh is shown as a through-road on all of the earliest maps and is also mentioned in the Domesday Book:

> There is a manor of St Mary's which is called Lambeth. Countess Gode, sister of Kind Edward, held it. It was then assessed at ten hides; now at two and a half hides. There is land for two and a half ploughs. In demesne are two ploughs, twelve villeins and 27 bordars with four ploughs. There is a church, and 19 burgesses in London who pay 36/-, and there are three slaves and 16 acres of meadow and woodland for three pigs.[26]

What might have been seen as feral was capable of growth: there was a botanic garden here opened in 1779 by William Curtis but this was replaced by the notorious slum of Granby Street. Granby Street was knocked down in the mid-nineteenth century but it still bears its name here in Granby Place – a cobbled alley adjacent to the Camel & Artichoke pub. Lower Marsh plays low status to The Cut – the cut above – which was once a distinctly working class marketplace. The Cut has the Young and Old Vic, a Michelin starred gastro bar and the underground. Lower Marsh has daily markets, a *Chicken Valley* takeaway, a *Betfred* bookmakers and Waterloo Public Library. The Saturday market offers a brilliantly random selection of specialities – from vintage fabric purses to handmade hats.

I visited a therapist just off Lower Marsh for many months in 2009, walking along here and through the estate at the back to the walk-in centre. The whole turning world of my 33 years spun like a gyre here: as fitting a place as any to work through the tangles. I've

written about this time of my life in my poetry collection *THE RESTRUCTURE*.[27] The illness of a baby. Parental readjustments. Prescribed medication. Burnout. Reflection. As I walk down Frazier Street now it all comes back to me – though the place seems very different in the daytime. They were long days of the night. I walked out after each session into the early evening pitch-black after an hour of pouring out words words words. Back then I hadn't seen before how beautiful the design of these old flats are: Reeves House on Frazier Street is a very English modernist redbrick. These were dark winter evenings. It was around the same time that I started to take a real interest in the stars – as if to try and see myself, and my problems, from as far away as possible.

As if to welcome me back a man on a motorbike revs and raises a clenched fist to a passing truck. Then accelerates towards the red lights next to Christ Church at Lambeth North. I walk back onto Lower Marsh. It's possible to wire money to any continent from almost any shop along here. Greensmiths, a delicatessen selling organic produce, is the foody's dream: 100 per cent pork sausages and fennel salami, artisan bread, chocolate and cheese. Perhaps the higher and lower status games between The Cut and Lower Marsh isn't so clear cut – it's worth travelling from anywhere in London to visit Greensmiths.

LEAKE STREET:
CHROME ADDICTS AND DRONES

Leake Street is sometimes referred to as 'Banksy Tunnel'. Banksy – the gallery-collected graffiti artist – was the first to organise the covering of the walls here with graffiti during the Cans Festival in 2008. This was a massive transition from the performance of E. Nesbitt's *The Railway Children* which had taken place here using a real steam engine a year or so before. Banksy Tunnel actually runs underneath the platforms of Waterloo Station – from York Road to Lower Marsh – and has its own tripadvisor.com page under the title 'Leake Street Tunnel'. Forty-two reviews give an average of 4.5 stars out of 5. You've got to see this. Tom Chivers – whose route for the underground Neckinger is different from Tom Bolton's – includes the Leake Street tunnel, describing the view inside as being like 'the insides of a fossilised dinosaur'.[28] The walls are in a state of constant re-spraying. Each graffito has their moment of ownership in the space while they're there but as soon as they're gone the wall becomes a canvas again. The smell is intoxicating: a heady trip of aerosols and adrenalin. I envy those able to spend entire days fine-tuning a single word – adding depth, perspective and luminescence – in the knowledge that it will be gone tomorrow. This is the spirit of Gustav Metzger's Auto-Destructive Art demonstration on the South Bank in 1961: before the sun expires there'll be more lost art in the world than that which survives the century. Permanence is illusion. And down here there is no sun: enjoy the moment.

Over a period of a year I've seen the following appear and disappear on the walls: FAME; ACK RED WASAS SERA CONCHI; CHROME ADDICT; BEAN DERP; DRONES; SIRE; 1833; RONI. It reads like a script written by a sound poet. This isn't just about typographic free-forming, this is a linguistic art that melds the textual and visual into a form that is at last finding its overground appreciation. Around the dogleg bend of the tunnel – at the Lower Marsh end – a young man and woman have lined up their cans of paint as they study the wall. Halfway down the tunnel there's a ledge where the finished cans are tossed, creating a talismanic shrine.

Inside the three hundred yard tunnel is a venue called The Vaults, which has a gallery, a theatre and a kitchen. Their mission statement reads:

> The Vaults is an arts platform for the bold, the fresh and the fearless. Our mission is to collaborate and conspire, embracing artists from all walks of life to come together and inspire others.[29]

When there are events happening here the audiences spill out into the working zone of the graffiti artists and the whole space fizzes with the high-energy atmosphere of something *happening* – something that the public feels privileged to be inside, something hidden and meaningful – and the artists lap up the attention from their rightful audience.

ALBERT EMBANKMENT AND LONDON'S WATERMEN

Along the Albert Embankment on the South Bank – or 'Surrey side' as it was once known (the north bank is often referred to as the 'London side' – another example of the long history of primacy of north over south) – was once known for its Watermen's Stairs. Before the bridges were built across the river the watermen were the main agents of transportation from one side of the river to the other. These sharp-eyed, river-whetted cabbies were a presence in London life from the thirteenth century onwards, taxiing passengers across the river the way black cabs fly the affluent and late-for-work over the bridges between the north and south of the river. Henry VIII cleaned up the navigation of the river in the sixteenth century and eight years after his death, in 1555, The Watermen's Company was established. Peter Ackroyd, in *Thames: Sacred River*, gives us an insight into the role of the watermen in Elizabethan England:

Many watermen of the fourteenth and fifteenth centuries were prosecuted for taking more than three people in any one vessel. They were forbidden to moor on the south bank of the river, in case 'thieves and malefactors' took possession of their boats. It is a clear indication of the perceived difference between the two shores, with the river acting as a boundary just as it once had between warring British tribes.[30]

Elsewhere, Ackroyd points out something else about the watermen which fits with my view of the lubricious nature of the South Bank – the guttural and liquid essence of their language: 'The violent and blasphemous abuse they used was known as water-language, to which anyone could be subject.'[31] Liquid City has always had its own lived and ever-changing languages and – integral to that – its uses for casting insult and abuse. I don't think a day has passed in my years of commuting in and out of the South Bank when – either on the bus, the tube or the streets – I've not overheard or been subject to the most heinous and guttural insults imaginable. It comes with the harshness and the very real sense of injustice that many people who inhabit the city feel. And the fiery liquids of alcohol don't help.

Looking at John Rocque's map of 1746 there are eleven sets of Watermen's Stairs listed within the South Bank area that this book covers, from Paris Garden down to Vauxhall. There was a set of stairs facing Whitehall, half-way between the current Hungerford and Westminster Bridges, called King's Arms Stairs. Cuper's Stairs were located near the current Waterloo Bridge and ran – in narrow strips of shrubbery and paths – as far back as today's IMAX. Due to the building of the embankments this part of London has struggled to maintain relics of the Watermen's Stairs, though they have often remained as locations of energy and activity – the Festival Pier outside the Royal Festival Hall, for example, near to the site of Cuper's Stairs. There is something very fitting about the Festival Hall being a current site of leisure as this was the role of Cuper's Gardens in the eighteenth century which was also known as a place to go for live music.[32]

Where there's language and the river there's always a poet. John Taylor, the self-declared Water Poet (1578-1653), was a waterman who worked his way up to become the clerk of the Guild of Watermen.[33] Amongst Taylor's works is the brilliantly titled *The True Cause of the Waterman's Suite Concerning Prayers* (1613 or 1614) which took umbrage with the theatre companies who were moving their theatres to the north bank. He is also known for sailing from London to Queenborough in a paper boat using two fish tied to canes for oars. Taylor met the river in less than glamorous circumstances: after challenging another poet, William Fennor, to 'insult each other in verse in public' he was left standing when Fennor didn't show up. Disappointed with the lack of spectacle, the audience threw Taylor in the river and pelted him with offal. Taylor's most famous poem is *Pennyless Pilgrimage*, his account of his walk from London to Scotland with no money, but I prefer this one of nine words: a very early palindrome which – through its wing-mirroring of mono-syllables – reads as fresh today as any 1960s' concrete poem:

Lewd did I live, & evil I did dwel

This also provides a fitting epitaph to many of the lives lived along the South Bank.

At this distance in time it's hard to sense the scale of the waterman industry and thinking of London cab drivers is the closest you'll come to sensing how widespread and prolific this aspect of city life was. As always, the poet-playwrights of the Elizabethan and Jacobean period are a good place to look for registering lost aspects of the culture. In Thomas Middleton's and Thomas Dekker's collaborative play *The Roaring Girl* the character Sir Alexander sets Trapdoor the challenge of finding Moll Cutpurse, otherwise known as The Roaring Girl. Trapdooor responds:

As well as I know 'twill rain upon Simon and Jude's day next: I will sift all the taverns i'th'city, and drink half-pots with all the watermen o'th'Bankside, but if you will, sir, I'll find her out.[34]

Elizabeth Cook's footnote to this quote gives us the strength of Trapdoor's conviction to find Moll here: she quotes Taylor, the Water Poet, who 'asserts that at this time, between Windsor and Gravesend, there were not fewer than forty thousand watermen'.[35] Roughly the same number of authorised cab drivers in London today: black backed beetles morphed from the river's man of war insects.

I'm walking from Westminster Bridge towards Lambeth Palace. Outside the old London Fire Brigade Headquarters a young apprentice fireman is cleaning the doors. I wonder what kind of right of passage a trainee fireman gets on his first day at work? Sent out to get a bucket of stripy water? It starts to rain. He continues to clean the doors.

Moored on the river is a boozy boat, painted yellow. *Tamesis*. The Roman name for the River Thames: *Tam* meaning wide and *Isis* water. There's a sign telling me about Lambeth Floating Marsh: an experiment to try and bring micro-organisms to life. The signs and signifiers of Albert Embankment have to be read with a clear patience for randomness. A rookery of CCTV cameras are perched high on the wall enclosing St Thomas' Hospital. I stop to read a monument to all of the women agents who contributed to the cause of national security. MI6 is half a mile away. The Houses of Parliament are overlooking us. This is a place to watch the watchers, being watched.

LAMBETH PALACE:
AN ELSINORE ON THE MARSHES

Given a choice between sleeping in Lambeth Palace for a night or the Martello Tower on Sandycove Bay in Dublin – where James Joyce spent the six nights that influenced the opening of *Ulysses* – I would go for the disused military defence on the scrotumtightening shore. The building bricks of Lambeth Palace are mongrelised across the centuries: beige towers, brown battlements and pale-grey central atriums struggle to cohabit as one structure. Cobblestone outhouses. It is ugly, as if assembled without clear instruction and with whatever materials were available to hand at the time. Red and grey stumped turrets rise from the old marshland. The mismatched turrets appear like viewing towers whose only purpose is to get a better view of the elegance of the north bank. All of the Palace's very real and riotous historical happenings have taken place in this umber Legoland. When Wat Tyler's rebels arrived in 1381 and chopped off the Archbishop's head – leaving it to putrify like a rancid squash on a hill overlooking the Tower of London – Lambeth Palace was seen as one of the ultimate seats of power. Cromwell's army later invaded the Great Hall on the lookout for building materials. This was the South Bank in which leisure brushed against the choking cloth of politics and insurrection.

The palace houses another great library on the South Bank, one which holds many unique texts of ancient Lambeth: the *Lambeth Bible* (an illuminated book in the model that Blake would later remake in his own image, just half a mile down the road), the *Lambeth Choirbook* and the *Lambeth Homilies*. An ex-colleague at The Poetry Library went to work here for a while. He told me that there was a day when nobody could get any work done in the palace because somebody on the embankment was playing Michael Jackson on loop. Ludic and unpredictable soundtracks play out across this ancient land.

Another ex-colleague, the multi-talented raconteur, director, novelist and filmmaker, James Runcie – who also worked for a while as Head of Literature at Southbank Centre – gives a further insight into real Lambeth Palace. A view worth listening to given that he lived there in the 1970s, as the son of the Archbishop:

> I had secretly hoped that Lambeth Palace would help improve my romantic chances (moonlight over the battlements, the view of the Palace of Westminster from the roof), the funky North London girls that I was keen on (rather than the more suitable Harriets and Amandas) tended to come over all coy at the sight of walls full of seventeenth century paintings, pikes for the Archbishop's private army, and gimlet eyed staff to encounter before they even reached the tower where I lived.[36]

James Runcie's father, Archbishop Runcie, conjured a number of creative projects to engage the wider Anglican community in the UK and beyond. Two of his most effervescent strands were to use Terry Waite to go out to talk to people and to invite six 'religious' poets to a lunch at Lambeth Palace – including David Gascoyne, who in 1936 had tried to free Dali from a stuck diver's helmet at the International Surrealist Exhibition in London. This job was more difficult and ideas around what the poets could do seemed to have run dry before the scones and tea had left their doilies. Asking poets on the South Bank to make a rational contribution to world issues has never part of the agenda.

There is something very stern and unromantic about Lambeth Palace; the ambient lighting is non-existent and the ghosts of the dead, like Hamlet's father on the ramparts of Elsinore, unsettle the twilit walks of the living. Doomed for a certain term to walk the night.

ALEMBIC HOUSE:
A DINNER DATE WITH ARCHER AND STRINGFELLOW

There's a pub I would recommend on the Albert Embankment here called The Rose. It's a warm, old-style boozer that serves good Guinness and food. I launched my second collection *Zeppelins* in the room upstairs. It was the first poetry reading they'd ever hosted. The windows open out onto the Thames at night and the distillations of light from the north bank swell and glister as the alcohol does its work.

Alembic House dominates the skyline but it won't be the exclusive living suite here for long. A new build is taking over the south side of the road, rising splint-by-splint under cranks and cranes. THE CORNICHE is written on the hoardings with uber-cool shadow-dropped text: LIFE AHEAD OF THE CURVE. An 'alembik' is a glass distilling apparatus that consists of two vessels connected by a tube. It looks like the foetus of a Dr Seuss character dunking its head into a basin. Looking at Alembic House – its checker-board of black and white squares – it's not hard to

think what those two vessels might be in relation to this building and its current use. A cistern attached to a cistern.

This is classic penthouse material with little of purification on offer. The main tower is horribly misaligned on a sandwiched layer of concrete that jetties the palatial suites above. Jeffrey Archer's two-floor penthouse at the top looks out with gargantuan eye-like windows – hypnotised by Bentham's prison (now Tate Britain) on the opposite bank – giving the building the look of an accidental offspring of a dalek and an owl. The owl seems to dominate at low tide, as if ready to take cautious steps into the water.

The building's name has recently changed: developers now want us to call it Peninsula Heights. A non sequitur that's hardly worth considering. The building has the Thames before it and the Effra to one side, which means that two halves of this towering peninsula is surrounded by air. Iain Sinclair, in *Lights Out For the Territory*, describes Alembic House and its Archer association like this:

> Alembic House, 93 Albert Embankment, is one of London's worst-kept secrets: anyone who can pick up a newspaper knows that Jeffrey Archer has bagged the top two floors, and spent almost £2 million pounds refurbishing them. A show home for a social balloonist. ... Alembic House was a throwaway secret, the headline kind, part of the package that came with its flamboyant neighbour – Terry Farrell's MI6 palace of the vanities at 85 Vauxhall Cross. An Inca jukebox so blatantly a hybrid of Gotham City and Alhambra fascist chic that you almost suspect someone somewhere, between commissioner and architect, of having a sense of humour.[37]

Previous occupiers of that top floor penthouse have been John Barry, the James Bond composer and Bernie Ecclestone, formula one billionaire. The Hammer House film *Theatre of Blood* ends with Vincent Price jumping out of the window into the Thames: vampiric suicides are at home here.[38] The trailer for the film includes a champagne-drinking dandy exclaiming 'quite insane' before jump-cutting to Vincent Price in black exhorting 'O my god'. Price's body – or at least his stitched-up replica – tumbles like a high-diving Nosferatu into a high level Thames. Everything that Archer hasn't done. Over the image of the drowning man the screen reads *Theatre of Blood* in red dripping letters. A heart with an exposed pulmonary is presented in a black box. 'Can't believe it' another character says: 'his head cut off'. Vincent Price comes back to life – these penthouse figures always do, usually after a dinner party that's got out of hand – ending the trailer at the centre of a burning conflagration.

Out there in the milky depths of popular culture is an episode of *Come Dine With Me* in which Peter Stringfellow hosts a dinner party. He had hired the apartment from a friend for the day. Perhaps it was his inability to do anything with grace – his fingers gnarled from years of touching what he shouldn't – that made the pyrex dishes clatter and sauces refuse to reduce. This makes for claustrophobic viewing: despite the riverside setting the apartment has no windows. Stringfellow has misjudged the temperature, wearing a thick jumper as he meets, greets and dishes-up for his guests. His limpid hair is lacquered with a substance that remains wet for the whole evening. Watching daytime television is like skimming the surface layer of culture as a man of war insect. The goodies are down below: you just have to take a day off work and dip for them.

Today an army of gulls are shrieking and diving into the water. As if the titbits of the vampire are down there in the muddy tapas. Inside the reception a woman is pacing up and down, dressed completely in pink. A statue of Atlas is positioned at the doors – the weight of the world on his back. Albert Embankment does business: men walk with mobiles to their ears or wired mouthpieces held to their lips as the traffic flies and joggers plough. The railway into Vauxhall is constant. I've always loved the Victorian lamp posts along the embankments: a Gothic series of Daliesque black columns

that twist and taper towards the finial of a globe. Cast in iron, into the base of one of the columns, is the frowning face of a man – or the ghost of Christmas Past – placed here in 1870 long before the Alembic House he's looking at gave him something to worry about.

You have to walk past Alembic House to find one of the best pieces of graffiti in the area which simply reads: *Lager*. It's been spray-painted red on top of the green grilles which serve a function for the less salubrious apartments alongside Alembic House. Today it's been placed beside a skip full of white material which is blowing about in the wind like the rags of Miss Havisham – a reminder of the Victorian origins that the playground of the rich rises from.

In the river itself are four white horses, with riders, facing out towards the north bank. A commissioned work by artist Jason deCaires Taylor called *The Rising Tide*. The work is less self-obsessed than Gormley, is genuinely site-specific and has sourced its history well. The stone-grey colour of the horses blends to the white-washed lather of the river. Two horses have their heads dunked beneath the tide as if feeding on the jetsam. The explanatory text tells me that deCaires is an underwater photographer who created the world's first underwater sculpture park, off the west cost of Grenada in the West Indies. Which might explain why two of the horses – the ones with their heads under water – seem to be looking for something more than the sight of Millbank Tower on the north bank. Something more than the former Labour HQ can offer them.

THE RIVER EFFRA:
AN AFTERNOON WITH L'UOMO VOGUE

On the western side of Vaxuhall Bridge is the outfall of the South
Bank's second underground river – quite an impressive number for
a stretch of land of only a few kilometres long. The name *Effra*,
according to Tom Bolton, 'hints at Lambeth's distant past' and
could come from either Anglo Saxon 'efre' – meaning 'bank' – or
the Celtic 'yfrid', meaning 'torrent'. This stretch was once shown on
maps as Lambeth Creek. Given that this area was inglorious
marshland to actually be known as the Creek in its midst suggests
it had long passed its 'torrent' days, even then. The Effra begins in
Crystal Palace and flows – or gargles – through Norwood
Cemetery, Dulwich, Herne Hill, Brixton and Kennington. It ends
by emptying itself into the Thames here, beneath a new-build
empire made from aquamarine glass.

Behind me is St George's Wharf, one of the most peculiar retail
complexes in London. It rises upwards in crenellated fits and starts,
finishing with a series of towers that gather dust like brick-made
moths that can't take flight. In addition to the usual super-brands
this a retail emporium that houses a range of services and smaller
businesses: *Hudson Dry Cleaners, Maxwell Stanley Consulting,
Riverside Dental* (there are lots of examples of lost teeth down on
the foreshore) and – perhaps the worst named eatery on the South
Bank – *Steax and the City American Brasserie*. From the river itself
rise five pillars: the defunct stalks of the old bridge.

In my book *In the Catacombs*, written over the summer of 2013, I traced the Norwood end of the Effra out of West Norwood Cemetery, from where it was diverted in the nineteenth century with the building of the sewerage system. There is a myth that a coffin – with a corpse inside – had disappeared from the cemetery and later been found sailing down the Thames. The river that would later deliver bodies to be shipped out for burial had one returned by underground stream. The myth makes sense: the Victorian industry that turned underground rivers into sewers was also sending bodies by river to take their trains towards burial: an accidental loop was formed.

The Effra has many known midway points too. There are reports of it occasionally bubbling into people's gardens in Brixton and the river can be entered on Effra Road.[40] In *Underground London: Travels Beneath the City Streets* Stephen Smith describes the story of the World War Two bomb that exploded in a street along the Effra's path, exposing the river at the bottom of its chasm. Here, in Vauxhall, it can be heard gurgling back into its source: the Thames. Sometime it's hard to believe that what you can't see is actually there: underground rivers can easily take on a mysterious and spiritual dimension. For me they chime with the imagination – which is also hidden but prone to excitable and often unexpected appearances. Perhaps that explains people's fascination for these rivers: they run just out of sight, like faith, rarely appearing transcendent. We have to keep looking and – to do that – believe enough that we might find them. Before us in the Thames a seven thousand year old wooden structure can be seen on the riverbed

here – near to where the Effra joins the river. This is evidence of the first of London's bridges, built long before the Romans arrived.[41]

MI6 dominates the scene behind me: a hundred small green eyes looking out over the water. The walls rise to a Google-lensed tower made of sand, perfectly symmetrical on each side. The windows are tinged with tinted green – a look that has also been adopted by the St George's complex next door. It serves to make the Thames look browner. At the base, facing the river, is a fountain for penny wishes. Though the water is never switched on: coins lie Queen-up under a sediment of dust. The sandy walls turn slowly more grey. Alongside the river – like a concrete doily left behind at a tea party – is the strange druidical circle which is held up by eight pillars: like an empty monocle to the sky.

On the north bank, in front of the reformed penitentiary of Tate Britain, is the site from which convicts were sent off to Australia. Henry Moore's sculpture – a gnarled, compacted slab of bullion – marks the place with its title: *Locking Piece*.

Further west are the permanently extended cranes of the in-development Battersea Power Station. I can't look at it – never have – without expecting to see the inflatable pig from the cover of Pink Floyd's *Animals*. This morning the tide is high and thrashing with intent at the embankment wall. I walk down to the east side of MI6 where there's a ramp that brings the duck boats in to land. This is where the incident with *L'Uomo Vogue* happened in 2009. After six years I'm ready, at last, to talk about it. The magazine – Italian's version of *Vogue* – wanted to feature some young London artists wearing fashionable clothes, set against the backdrop of the city. They wanted a poet and I was – at the time – still young enough to be worth asking to wear the latest designs. A young woman, a biscotti-thin Italian – who I later suspected of seeing in each night with constellations of cocaine – emailed me, giving me directions to the photographer's house in the suitably named White City. I was to go there on the coming Sunday morning. I was keen and arrived before the photographer was dressed: the emptied-out gin bottles and landfill ashtrays from the night before were still smoking. He made tea, explaining that they'd had an 'artist's symposium' until the early hours.

The photographer had the air of a modernist artist, the kind that had toked-out the remaining space between his existence and artistic work with clinical emotional detachment. He wrapped his green dressing gown around himself as he tried to find a cup to make me tea. Failing, he handed the task over to his 'assistant', a young man in his early twenties who clearly idolised him. Then the Italians came and cornered off a corner of the room to dress me. The whites in their eyes came back to colour – it was clothes they lived for. And they knew how to make a man wear them: distracting the front part of the brain with questions that inflame the creative ego: 'So, they speak of you very highly in London' one of the Italians asserted. The next thing I knew I was wearing what seemed like a ninja-suit with slipper-like sneakers and we were in the back of the car, leaving White City for Albert Embankment. The photographer was arguing with his daughter on his mobile – telling her that he was busy, that she couldn't have money – that they'd have to talk later.

Vauxhall Bridge opened out in front of us and I pointed to the location where I wanted to be photographed. I'd timed the tides so we could get down to the riverbed, between MI6 and Alembic House. The Italians came to life, looking to the photographer for his approval: 'I like this,' he said, looking down at the shore, slowly nodding his head with satisfaction: 'I've not done a shoot down here before.' Then I realised why they call it a *shoot*. I stood still while he thought about where he wanted to put me – a body under command. 'There,' he said, 'crouch down.' I did. 'Now just walk back a bit, yes, into the water – see that stick, pick it up.' A dead branch was sailing past me. 'Lean on it', he said. The ninja suit wasn't as water-resistant as it looked. I could feel Thames water against my knees. I was freezing. Further off towards Westminster a police boat had paused, watching, and then – refusing to save me – went the other way.

The photographer was saving the final denouement until I'd clawed my way back to dry land, shivering and in need of warmth and dry clothes. He pointed at one of the huge stone lions that are built into the embankment wall and told me to go and sit on it. 'Lie down on it and look at the sky, close your eyes as if – I don't know – you've just fallen asleep on the lion.' I caught the faces of the Italians, and the photographer's assistant: no one was laughing. The last thing I remember before I closed my eyes was seeing an aeroplane travelling from south to north, the corner of Alembic House cutting the crystal blue sky in half …

When I opened my eyes the cameras were being packed away. The adrenalin from the group was dispersing, like crabs under rocks. I could feel the cold in my bones and the chill of having to climb out of my body and back into my mind. The photographer, now over the previous night's binge, asked if there was a pub nearby? I suggested The Rose. When we got there I dried-off in the toilets and when I came out the Italians asked what I wanted to drink? I thought of the least continental thing I could think of and asked for a Guinness.

The Guinness turned out to be the only payment I ever got from *L'Uomu Vogue*. They never printed the pictures. They went instead for a guitarist from Shoreditch who'd been planted in a tree in London Fields.

The riverbed can become a scene for anything, even in this spot where there's a tension in being so close to MI6. I came here to find items to be placed inside a limited edition book of a play I wrote called *Shad Thames, Broken Wharf*.[42] The inventory for the found items contains the following:

Vauxhall, MI6, 29/08/10:
Pottery fragment, pink
Ceramic fragments, blue and white
Coconut husk, fragment
Purple alien craft, McDonalds toy gift
Marquis de la Tour champagne cork

Today the ramp is closed with a warning sign that reads 'areas may be wet, muddy, uneven, slippery underfoot and there is a risk of becoming stranded'. All the reasons to come down here. I go down anyway and kick about in the rubble: more champagne corks, a *San Miguel* bottle top, an airline pen, a refined piece of wood.

Strange how the tokens of leisure find their way back to the centre of surveillance.

Notes

1. Stephen Inwood, *A History of London*, Op.cit.
2. At the time of writing Battersea Power Station is being redeveloped 'by an international consortium with a proven track record'. Track record of what, exactly, isn't said. You can read more at: www.batterseapowerstation.co.uk, last visited 04 November 2015. Though, for all I know, you might be booking a table to eat there by the time you read this.
3. This is part of a collaboration I did with Jenks called *Seaside Special*, a series of bawdy literary postcards which can be viewed online here: https://cmtjthethird.wordpress.com/
4. Stephen Smith, *Underground London: Travels Beneath the City Streets*, Op.cit.
5. John Stow, *A Survey of London Written in the Year 1598*, Op.cit.
6. Indebted to Francis Sheppard, *London: A History*, Op.cit.
7. The Great Stink happened in 1858 when the years of effluent that had been discharged into the Thames began to heat up after a hot summer. The smell was said to have been so bad that Disraeli ran from the Houses of Parliament covering his nose with a handkerchief.
8. Jerry White, *London in the Twentieth Century: A City and it's People*, Op.cit.
9. In a letter to William Hayley, May 6 1800, included in Alexander Gilchrist, *The Life of William Blake*, Op.cit.
10. http://www.bbc.co.uk/london/content/articles/2009/03/19/blake_mosaics_video_feature.s html
11. The Magnificent Seven Cemeteries, built between 1832 and 1841, are Kensal Green, West Norwood, Highgate, Abney Park, Nunhead, Brompton and Tower Hamlets. I am writing a series of books about these, which begins with *In the Catacombs* (Penned in the Margins, 2013) and will be followed by *Cenotaph South* in November 2015.
12. Catherine Arnold, *Necropolis*, Op.cit.
13. Ibid, I am indebted to Catherine Arnold for details in this chapter, many of which were checked after the beery evening in The Crown.
14. Quotes from the poems that follow and bibliographical facts are from William Blake, *Selected Poems*, Op.cit.
15. Indebted to the following writers for details on this period of Blake's life: Peter Ackroyd, *Blake*; G.E. Bentley Jr, *The Stranger from Paradise: A Biography of William Blake*; Iain Sinclair *Blake's London: The Topographic Sublime* and particularly Blake's first biographer, Alexander Gilchrist for his seminal *Life of William Blake*.
16. Alexander Gilchrist, *Life of William Blake*, Op.cit.
17. Ibid. Interestingly, given how close Blake was to his wife Catherine – who bound his books for him – Gilchrist contracted scarlet fever from one of his children and died in 1861 and it was his wife Anne who completed his book on Blake and saw it in to print. The book was seminal in bringing Blake to the fore of Victorian culture. Blake's poetry was very much against the hegemony of controlled forms in use at the time; his long lines

and use of the ampersand has a vitality and complexity lacking in so much of the formulaic verse of the Victorians.

18. Ibid.

19. This is account is given in G.E. Bentley Jr, *The Stranger from Paradise: A Biography of William Blake*.

20. Alexander Gilchrist, *Life of William Blake*, Op.cit.

21. Peter Ackroyd, *Blake*, Op.cit.

22. 'Carlisle House and Carlisle Lane', in *Survey of London: Volume 23, Lambeth: South Bank and Vauxhall*, ed. Howard Roberts & Walter H. Godfrey Op.cit. The actual Hercules building that Blake lived in, though by then in altered form, was knocked down in 1917.

23. The Royal Asylum for Female Orphans housed girls between the age of seven to fourteen with the aim of preventing them falling into prostitution. It was located at the end of Hercules Road during the time Blake was here.

24. The Lambeth Walk is a dance derived from the 1937 musical *Me and My Girl*; as Tom Chivers says in his audio guide to the River Neckinger, Lambeth Walk comes from 'Lambeth Wall', the first wall built to keep back the floods of the Thames. He also points out the 1942 piece of propaganda in which marching Nazis were set to the music in a ludic montage is 'an example of one of the world's first video mash-ups, in 1942 the British Ministry of Information produced film which blended the Lambeth Walk song with manipulated footage of Nazi soldiers marching and saluting, a wall of British Surrealist humour against the pomposity of Fascism'.

25. Roddy Lumsden, *Not All Honey*, Op.cit.

26. *Domesday Book: A Complete Translation*, Op.cit.

27. *THE RESTRUCTURE*, Salt Publishing, 2012

28. Tom Chivers, *The Neckinger Pilgrimage*, Op.cit

29. http://www.the-vaults.org/

30. Peter Ackroyd, *Thames: Sacred River*, Op.cit.

31. Peter Ackroyd, *London: The Biography*, Op.cit.

32. John Rocque's map of 1746 is online here www.portcities.org.uk

33. Information on John Taylor from *London in Verse* edited by Christopher Logue, Op.cit.

34. Thomas Middleton & Thomas Dekker, *The Roaring Girl*, Op.cit.

35. Ibid.

36. From James Runcie's website at www.jamesruncie.com

37. Iain Sinclair, *Lights Out for the Territory*, Op.cit

38. Facts about Alembic House from www.skyscrapernews.com

39. Tom Bolton, *London's Lost Rivers*, Op.cit.

40. Peter Ackroyd, *Thames: Sacred River*, Op.cit.

41. Chris Roberts, *Cross River Traffic: A History of London's Bridges*, Op.cit.

42. *Shad Thames, Broken Wharf* was published by Penned in the Margins in 2010 a few months after the play was performed at The London Word Festival. At the time of writing there are a few remaining copies for sale.

Liquid City has seen the back
        of another dry century
    an audience of crows
at St George's Circus
        Mepham Street   The Cut
    this is where it ends   when it hasn't begun
with a mis-synched text
        and a secret fact
    I've seen the news today   & its data
        like black stars in an inkpot
Liquid City fills its cut & paste
            and writes OXO
on a tower of ceramics
    all metropolis needs is a family
and a camera crew
        for another fifteen minutes
    of favouritism
    Breakfast television captures politicians
in the off hours
        blanched at the pancake stand
    The National Watch from Waterloo Bridge
waiting for news from Wellington
        reflected from ITV
    Liquid City speaks truth to power
            but we've all got our truth now
    why buy what we've got?
Power can be borrowed
            in each Styrofoam cup

Liquid City streams our name in it

EAST

CONCRETE REALITY:
THE NATIONAL THEATRE

How has this geometric sand-scraper risen in angular turrets from such wet and unstable ground? Three hundred years ago there was barely a road cutting through these acres of bogland and now this building dominates the South Bank like a futuristic bunker – a beige Minecraft – lit by green neon at night and ribboned with sunlight in the morning and early evening.

The National Theatre is almost its own city: a palace of dust rising over the river. It was built a decade after the Hayward and Queen Elizabeth Hall were opened and has a similar labyrinthine, path-led illogic. When looking up closely at the concrete inside you can see that it makes use of the Brutalist technique of being patterned with wood grain. The inside is the outside. Staircases lead up to balconies which then extend out to further terraces. The towers are imperious end-of industry turrets, as if paying homage to the factories that once lined the river. Crows sit twitching on the edges. The National seems to have landed here ready formed, the architectural equivalent of plug-and-play: connections without wires. From the sky it appears like a well-designed cabinet for London's spare parts. In the rain the stone darkens to the tone of London clay.

Denys Lasdun, the architect of the building, talked about it like this:

I don't want anything to come between people experiencing the theatre and your drama. They have in a way to use the concrete reality of the building, not tarted up in any way. It must be space, walls, light. And the ornaments of the building are people moving around.[1]

Prince Charles has called it 'a nuclear power station' – probably at some point in the Cold War. And there is that austerity to the building, especially on an Autumn morning, before the tourists and commuters pass through – when dead leaves tumble over themselves and the still river starts to wake.

The old bookshop here was a favourite haunt of mine for a long time, browsing the rows of densely-packed scripts in a crammed cube of direct light. Now the bookshop is under concrete, out of the light, straight through the main entrance. You have to walk under the hanging lightsabers from the ceiling and past the stacks of novelty gifts. Earlier this year I came looking for B.S. Johnson's collected plays – which they didn't have. This would have made Johnson apoplectic. Modern theatre, in his view, had already gone wrong. I felt his rage rise for a second, then got distracted by Bob Dylan through the speakers. 'Hurricane': the narrative of a mistreated boxer. BSJ could have done well to listen to it.

While I'm here I flick through *The National Theatre Story* by Daniel Rosenthal: 846 pages even with the endnotes removed and placed online to save printing space. There's a photo of actor Alan Strong, naked, on the back of Nicholas Clay – who's dressed as a horse – taken from a 1973 production of Peter Shaffer's *Equus*. The play is about a psychiatrist who attempts to treat a young man who has a pathological fascination with horses. The caption under the picture reads: *Firth's underpants were only worn for the photocall, not in production.* For the cost of a full ticket underwear was removed.

There is something of the airport to the foyer spaces, which are best enjoyed when you're deliberately getting yourself lost, not knowing – or caring – where you're going. Signs point towards the toilets, which lead to further corridors, towards rows of magisterial doors. Be wary of walking backstage into a live performance of *Hamlet*. The oak-grained pillars are uplit with soft neons. The ceiling is divided into symmetrically-arranged square hatches. Pin-striped benches are arranged under long desks: an English take on the European ideal of shared communal space. The function is to *be* in this space, like Lasdun hoped, to be a person-among-people:

fulfilling the purpose of the building by just existing. The unwritten aspect of this is that this works best if the people are clean and well-mannered. Douglas Murphy in his book *Recent Futures* critiques many of the large-scale architectural buildings of the sixties and seventies because they treated 'ordinary human beings [as] material to be moulded in the service of a grand vision'.[2] I have shirked in the past at the way architects depict people on their maps and drawings: airbrushed Lowrys without faces.

Be careful of the tea here: it's served in teddy bear's picnic cups – the porcelain hoop too small to fit a parched finger in. I've enjoyed having a stronger drink in the bar of an evening, watching the audiences pour out in the intervals and then – after a play, on wet evenings – sliding like bit-drops into the bigger streams of people rushing towards the Thames. On one evening, after a performance of *Jane Eyre*, a consecutive number of women came out from the play hurling insults at their accompanying men: men who'd either left them stranded as they'd gone to the ladies, or had failed to bring an umbrella – or were just guilty of not being Rochester. It was a performance in itself – the kind of humour I needed after paying five pounds at the bar for a small bottle of Hoxton Stout.

The best way to enjoy the building is to bring your own tea, after dark, and look at it from Waterloo Bridge. The fly towers lit with primary neons.

LONDON STUDIOS AND IBM

Here, on the Queen's Walk, crowds press against the riverside railings that surround ITV Studios. Today, teenagers look through the crosshatch trying to catch a glimpse of some superhuman movement in the studio. I ask them who's being interviewed? 'The Saturdays', a teenage boy tells me. In the studio I can see the backs of heads, cut in the same old-new-wave combed-over undercut style. A blackbird flies low, at speed, behind us.

On the Queen's Walk, by Bernie Spain Gardens, a group of Chileans are taking bets from public punters on which silver cup a ball will end up beneath. 'One, two, three', he counts, then says: 'Show me the money'. A woman lays down a twenty pound note. Then she steps forward with her foot, which she places on the cup she's backing. The man reveals the ball inside. He asks if she wants to double? She publically opens her wallet to a streak of crisp twenties. She doubles. 'One, two, three: show me the money.' She chooses correctly again, only this time she pockets the money. I step back and check my pockets, just in case. The spectacle is mesmerising but the profits must be being made somewhere. They walk on further down the South Bank, followed by some new punters who want to play the no-lose game.

Sometimes the cast and crew of *This Morning*, the UK's best-known live daytime show, pile out onto the concrete island that extends from the Queen's Walk to film al-fresco. Last week Eamonn Holmes was placed in a deck chair, wearing a blue suit, his face fixed into a ruddy smile as he waited for a cue. Rylan Clark – fifth-place in the 2012 *The X Factor* and winner of *Celebrity Big Brother* the following year – hovers over him. The journalist, Holmes – who's cut his cloth for the right to be known – and Clark, the whippet-hungry aspirant of a new generation, share near equivalence on this media platform. The parameters of the temporary film set are cordoned off with blue and white emergency tape. People stand with their back to the celebrities, taking selfies against the backdrop.

Earlier this year there was an outbreak of excitement on *This Morning* as Gok Won and Amanda Holden – live on air – spotted David Cameron running past the set with a sweating bodyguard in tow. Lagging behind to make the PM look good. Next day *The Daily Mirror* ran the headline: *This Morning interrupts food segment as sweaty David Cameron jogs past ITV studio.*[3] Amanda, they reported, had shouted: 'OH! David Cameron is jogging on the South Bank!' Afterwards it was reported that: 'Amanda later admitted that she thought Cameron was in great shape.' Then she returned, with Gok, to discussing the best way to make kale chips and the benefits of gobi berries.

The nation comes to those who have access to daytime television – on the South Bank you have to root it out. And you can't plan what you see, this is the white noise of what happens: the mishaps and slips of tongues, the streakers and faux pas, the prime minister kicking back on a jog while most people are at work.

London Studios is an empire, a complicated assemblage fused from whatever was architecturally available at the time of building. All access to these spaces is from Upper Ground, further south of the river. Here, you have to look through the wiry hoardings to get a glimpse of where the action happens. Through the thin shrubs are two black Mercedes and a ramp. Last week there was a group of middle aged women waiting for the new Freddie Mercury: 'Look on YouTube' one of them said to me, 'You'll be converted'.

I walk to the back of IBM, the corrugated layers of its balconies dwarfed by the turrets of the National Theatre. This concrete trinket box has been formed on open land for you to walk through, conceiving your own real and imagined narratives. Leaves are everywhere today: the quick-passing browns and golds of Autumn. Soon there will be more rain, then frost, then snow – the building takes it all, momentarily lightening in shade as the sun dries it out.

Everyone in sight has a phone: photographing, texting, blogging. The powers inside see these narratives reflected back to them through the streams of digital bric-a-brac, organising emergency agendas that try to make sense of what the public *think of them*. In the era of big data we've all got the power to do that now.

BARGEHOUSE STAIRS:
MUDLARKING THE SHORE

I meet Anna Selby, poet and Literature and Spoken Word Programmer at Southbank Centre, early in the morning; she's putting her wellies on in front of the *Giraffe* restaurant at the Royal Festival Hall. We're going mudlarking. We walk towards the Oxo Tower and the site of the Bargehouse Stairs – a landing point for royalty in Tudor times. The gate down to the beach is open and we walk down the rickety steps. This stretch of beach is shown on old maps as Gabriel's Reach.

From down here you can see how built-up the city is and how domineering the embankments have become. It's much easier, when here, to picture how the landscape would have been: mudflats leaking into marshland, the salty ooze spreading to the foundations of factories and warehouses which themselves pumped liquids into the river – waiting for the secretions to return in a different form. I recall some lines from the overlooked British Surrealist poet of old London, David Gascoyne, who wrote in his

1932 collection *Roman Balcony*: 'Mud-flats mirroring / the blue reflecting'.[4] From the view he describes of 'the dome' of St Paul's it's likely that he would have been near to this spot. These oozy shores attract poets.

The embankments made the division between river and land clear: they are statements of man's attempt to further tame and own this landscape that had been a draw for nomadic tribes long before the Romans arrived. Of the thousands who pass through the South Bank each week most of them never come down to the river – it is an exclusion zone for the handheld generations.

The river is still a living one – transport, import, export and the occasional angler on the banks – but far less than at any point in its modern history. In his 2002 book, *London Orbital*, Iain Sinclair makes a strong case that the business energy of the river has moved to the motorway: 'Walking around the fringes of London, I began to think that the true river for contemporary London was not the Thames but the orbital motorway, the M25. It carried the goods and traffic of the world. It hummed and throbbed with a babble of electronic chatter. And it went nowhere.'[5] As the traffic streams above Anna and I – standing at river-level but metres beneath the feet of the walkers – the miasma of London's past can be breathed in. Past lives can be heard again, in the liquid susurration of the tide – which has taken the suicidal and the buried at sea – as well as the trinkets of human living that surround our feet.

The accelerating business of the city on a weekday morning adds to the perpetual gloaming of the shoreline here. To the east, St Paul's appears like a bubble blown from the water; to the west, the Houses of Parliament seems to have been sketched from some idealistic vision of what a major city should look like. Virginia Woolf puts this idea of the city as ongoing assemblage memorably: 'London has lain there time out of mind scarring that stretch of earth deeper and deeper, making it more uneasy, lumped and tumultuous, branding it for ever with an indelible scar.'[6] London is as an extant collage-box devised by those who never spared a thought for what others were doing; an urban model of glued and broken-off bits that have made the city – this clattering work in progress – what it is: a ragbag of enterprises and functions accidentally built around habitual thoroughfares. It's got where it is by being the route that people happened to be passing through. The worn tracks of shoes were the first maps. There's no better place to see that than down here at river-level with the tide tamely licking at your feet.

Or wellies in Anna's case. She's come prepared: for the past few weeks she's been having mudlarking tutorials with an expert who has helped her to date the periods of the most frequently found relics. We're the first ones down here today, walking across the smooth untouched sand. London renews itself each morning through its beaches. Its furrows lift as the sun rises, but only for as long as it can keep the trinkets of its guilt hidden. The handmade curses, the broken lockets, the smoker's last clay pipe. By the end of the day the city is ruined again – an ineffable drunk with its arms around strangers – flying by public transport to the promise of a lock-in. But dawn always comes and the promised new start begins again. This is the only moment to see London in purity.

Anna makes the first find: a tooth – a fang – tapering to a point with a black streak scored through it. It could be from a human – more likely a dog. Then I find a strip of leather pocked with stitch marks. Next we both hit the ceramics. Anna finds a medieval fragment, identifiable by its green glaze which hasn't been burned all the way through. Then the brown ceramics start to appear – as flat and lifeless as calcified cockles. These are mostly broken pieces from Doulton's pipe and kitchenware – Victorian fragments. Something catches my eye: blue and white chips from a Victorian plate – one of them showing the edge of a bluebird.

Anna talks about how sailors travelling down the river could tell where they were with their eyes closed by smelling what came to them from the banks. Meat, beer, fish. Unilever House on the north side is lit radiant with September light, meeting the sun as it curves towards the east. In the commuter churn above us nobody sniffs for fear of missing a text. Then – like a token that indicates where we're all heading – I find a SIM card inside the auburn soup of a tidal pool. SIMs might be the future equivalent of the Victorian clay pipes which are down here in the galley-loads. In the future the remains of electronic cigarettes will score the shoreline – cigalikes, eGos and mods. Dickensian smoking appliances of the now: human vapes. Anna tells me that the Victorian pub served clay pipe carry-outs, break-off pieces of clay that could be taken away and smoked. Holding these stone cigarettes in your hand it's impossible not to think about the mouth that was around it – the speed of that moment – of a mind alive, elsewhere: with the same needs, impulses and addictions as any of the people rushing to work above us.

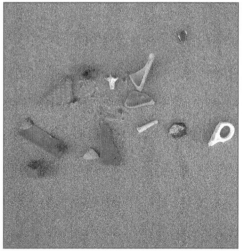

We start to hit at bones, finding something that looks like a love-handle but is long past its ability for loving. I look closely at the inside of the bone which is pitted with tiny bubbles and seems to contain the evidence of its genesis – still readable long after its death. Don't let your mind rove towards potential riches down here – gold, rubies, diamonds – the reality is much more humbling: the dregs of the expired. I stop at the giant sole of a man's shoe, a Reggie Perrin sampler. I look up to the embankment: the many heads of the commuter-pede are moving in the same direction. The person I'll be tomorrow – late for work – or trying to get an advantage on myself as I hurtle headlong into another back-to-back agenda. When the parallax and perspective of today's shore is over. I watch my own shadow as I walk slowly across the sand – as if it's already detached and ahead of me in time.

Work is calling – we both have meetings to get to. Anna walks up the stairs towards Oxo Tower and I follow with two chips of glazed blue porcelain in my pocket. We leave the rest of the finds on the shore, and feel our feet land back at city-level: the flatlands beneath us. We're walking. We've rejoined the fury of the marching shoes.

GABRIEL'S WHARF

In *Thames: Sacred River*, Peter Ackroyd associates the stretch of sand where I mudlarked with Anna with childhood: 'Childhood is often associated with the river ... at low tide, Gabriel's Reach in Southwark still possesses a stretch of sand where children meet.'[7] We're back in the rich mix of Blakean innocence and experience with the warnings – along all of the embankments – that children mustn't play on the steps. I've seen the Thames when it's on the prowl, it uses the embankment walls to its advantage and is quick to close down any remaining dry land with the force of its tides. The Port of London Authority points out the dangers of this on their website: Weil's disease – which comes from the urine of rats left in the water – raw sewage, broken glass and hypodermic needles. For once the authorities aren't being worthy for the sake of it, I've experienced for myself that 'the current is fast and the water is cold'.[9] The Thames rises a mighty seven metres twice a day: enough to dunk a bin wagon or a small cottage.

The artist David Rule wrote a series of texts under the titles ↑, → and ← which indicate the route he walked on the north and south banks, accompanied by a child – his nephew. Rule's gentle, curiously forensic descriptions of the area – history lightened with care for the child's emotions – suggest the enchantment of the area as seen by a child for the first time. Rule describes the dolphin lamp posts that line the embankment here: 'I had a friend who used to be into those angry dolphins on the lampposts. With their broken noses. Remember jumping off that sculpture? I've got a video of it. Remember feeding seagulls chips with Jason? These aren't so big; maybe they get bigger towards the sea.'[10]

I spent one of the most memorable afternoons of my life

mudlarking on the Thames with my son Pavel, on the north bank at Wapping, beneath the Captain Kidd pub. It was an unplanned descent: we got off the train at Shadwell and walked across the dusty A-roads to the cobbled warehouse-lined streets. We found a ladder down to the shore then scraped and hawked the beach for hours, gathering clay pipes, pottery fragments and rusted chains. Pavel pulled an ancient thick rope from the river as if it held the river's plug. The tide began to whoosh towards the high embankment walls behind us, closing down the amount of beach left to walk on. We ran for the ladder that went up a hundred feet so we could get back to the embankment and the view of the river we'd just emerged from. We celebrated our survival at the Captain Kidd, me with a Sam Smiths lager and Pav with a coke.

   Gabriel's Wharf is very different from Wapping. This is a riverside shanty town of eateries and shops, described by southbank-london.com as an 'arty enclave'. Ford Madox Ford talks about how, for the Londoner, emotions attach to parts of the city in abstract and subjective ways (and I'm sure, despite the dated phallocentrism of the male pronoun here, this also applies to women):

> Above all his London, his intimate London, will be the little bits of
> it that witnessed the great moments, the poignant moods of his life;
> it will be what happened to be the backgrounds of his more intense
> emotions.[11]

I can't get myself outside of my past experience of Gabriel's Wharf to see it fresh; it has become tainted by the memory of my dad's illness, before he died, when he came with my mum from Liverpool for a visit and we stopped for a drink. He was planked with meds and suffering from silent fits. And the sadness of the memory is retrospective: more so because it was a hot day and the beer, to me, tasted good. We took a boat down the river to Greenwich.

In the random meld of shops and eateries here there's a samizdat bicycle hire business going head-to-head with the well known bank-sponsored ones: *London Bicycle Tour Company*. Why travel with Barclays or Santander between your legs when you can freewheel on a sponsor-less frame? I've always liked companies that have London in their name: authority through geographical fact. *London Stout. London Bus Rides. London Fish and Chips.* London equals business. London *as* business.

In the centre of this faux-bohemian complex handmade garden furniture is for sale; most if it looks like it has been carved with a spoon: a wooden cat whose neck is thicker than its head. A bench with a back support that's thinner than a toothpick. A rocking horse that doesn't rock. Collectively it looks like a myth in which all of creation has been caricatured then frozen in time. A world of false imitations, waiting for the banks of the Thames to spill over and claim them in its underworld.

Walking through here for the first time in years I realise that nothing's changed. Salads are sold for small fortunes, the smell of burned crêpes floats on the air and overpriced craft goods are still

on the market. Not only overpriced but incomprehensible: suede bags shaped like houses, baby clothes made by hand, knitted scarves and silkscreen prints of local attractions. A yellow London Eye on a hot pink book bag. And in becoming lost in the slipstream of trinkets I've accidentally landed back in the place I had that beer with my dad a decade ago. I close my eyes and taste it. As I walk back out to the riverfront a crowd has gathered over the railings. Down on the beach is an artist who calls himself Martin Artman who's busy sketching a giant Homer Simpson into the sand. People are tossing coins down towards his bucket and his sand-written Twitter handle.

THE NINE MUSES OF THE OXO TOWER

Oxo Tower is another curious construction: a reconstructed bargehouse now containing restaurants, arty-craft shops and a gallery. It is also the home to Redwood Housing. After an event as part of the 2012 Poetry Parnassus festival I went to a late night party here. Simon Armitage, the curator of the festival, had just thrown a bash in Southbank Centre's Festival Village and his mate PJ Harvey had come along. In her presence dozens of poets were relegated to voyeurs of the true legacy of the poetic tradition: the rock star.[12] After the Armitage shindig more booze was called for and the invite rippled out that there was a party in the Oxo Tower. We wound our way back to the south side entrance of the tower, along Upper Ground, through the community-and-business meld

of this part of London, down dead-ends towards towers flying up to the stars. Inside the Tower we took a lift to the top and realised we'd hit the motherlode aftershow: poets from each continent stood on the balcony looking at the river; the Chilean Casagrande group – revelling in their Rain of Poems triumph – stood in worn-out Levis and t-shirts with fags drooping from their mouths, as hidden colleagues emerged from cupboards and bedrooms. There was a rabbit mask hooked on to the coat stand in the hall which I couldn't resist: I put it on, hit the centre of the room, and started dancing. Two years later at formal meetings colleagues – who I thought I'd never met – remind me of the night in the Oxo Tower, when I danced wearing a rabbit mask.

The tower was actually built as a power station at the end of the nineteenth century to provide electricity for the Royal Mail Post Office. Its Oxo name is explained by it being purchased by the Liebig Extract of Meat Company, who made *Oxo Cubes*. It was then used as a cold store. The outside gave a different picture however and was redesigned in an Art Deco look in the 1920s. The use of advertising was ingenious: there was a ban on skyline advertising along the South Bank at the time, so they built the new tower with circular windows and then placed an X between each of them:

O
X
O

After a period of dereliction the building was bought by the GLC and sold back at a loss to the non-profit Coin Street Community Builders who own it now.

The whole length of this part of the embankment has been in development for years: it's under the hegemony of the hardhats. In front of me this morning is an irate builder telling his friend how 'pissed off' he is for being shouted out for doing what he's been told to do. His tightened shoulders are harder than his blue helmet. 'This is what happened in my last job,' he says, 'they got me so fuckin wound-up then I had that accident with the trolley.' I overtake them along the path and stand at the base of the stairs of the complex, looking through to the Bargehouse behind. Virginia Woolf, writing in the 1940s, beautifully captures the history of buildings like this, as they were before the hotels and jewellers came to this part of the South Bank:

The banks of the river are lined with dingy, decrepit-looking warehouses. They huddle on land that has become flat and slimy mud. The same air of decrepitude and of being run up provisionally stamps them all. If a window is broken, broken it remains. A fire that has lately blackened and blistered one of them seems to have left it no more forlorn and joyless than its neighbours. Behind the masts and funnels lies a sinister dwarf city of workmen's houses. In the foreground cranes and workhouses, scaffolding and gasometers line the banks with a skeleton architecture.[13]

Although not technically a warehouse the Oxo Tower presents its outer façade as a narrow shopping complex housing craft industries. Standing on what was once the Prince's Meadow it is home to a series of small glass-fronted shops. The caption runs: DESIGN FOOD SHOPPING ART. There is good hedged bet to be had that most people passing might want to do at least one of those four things.

SOMETHING DIFFERENT ON EVERY FLOOR. A series of points – or unfinished arrows – call me forward. I follow. The day starts late here: it's nearly 10am and the upper levels are closed. I catch my reflection looking into a shop of gifts and crafted ceramics: tiny motorbike sculptures flagged for half price. Hot chocolate. A dinner tray. An emporium of mug coasters. Then come the lamps: desk lamps, Victorian lamps, bulbs that Edison would have killed for. Next is a shop of robots called *Robot Invasion.* I put

my head up for air and the balcony seems to swing out towards eternity. Here lies the quick perspective of the future. Mosaics, fashion, handbags – more ceramics. In the jeweller's window there's a plasma screen showing the jeweller I can see in the store, at work – the screen flies through a montage of his finest triumphs. The arrow points back into the tower: the sign now reads SOMETHING DIFFERENT AROUND EVERY CORNER. I'm starting to feel dizzy. A vinyl points towards AFFORDABLE ART and a framed arrangement of coffee spoons and found bones is tagged for a high three figure sum.

It's a relief to walk around to the back where there's space – and a connection to the origin of the buildings. Yes, we need the lure of life and activity, the pull to see and spend and do – but seeing the old warehouses stand as they did a hundred years ago connects you to a bigger picture. The nearly completed South Bank Tower rises over the warehouses: a red lift crawling up a metal frame. The names of the nine muses of Greek mythology have been spray-painted on the walls of a warehouse: Urania, Polyhymnia, Clio, Erato, Calliope, Thalia, Melpomene, Terpsichore and Euterpe. The tenth muse – The Thames – runs softy just out of view, but within smelling distance of the refined nine.

The bargehouse here would have once belonged to the king and while the play is the thing to catch a king's conscience there is also dance, comedy and poetry. The Greeks gave rightful precedence to poetry with its two Muses for the art, and the South Bank –

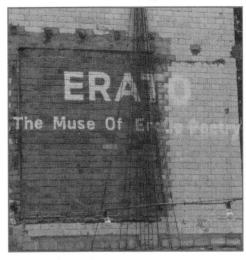

playground and waste land for functionless poets – pays homage to that in the names of Calliope (epic poetry) and Erato (lyric/erotic poetry). Seeing the two poetry muses confirms I'm on the right track in following the winged and grimy tracks of the fallen poets in this book. I sense something behind me. I turn around and look in one of the shops: there's a human-sized figure of an androgynous Minotaur staring from a gold head and the body of a woman. Looking towards the names of the Muses – with its hands on its hips.

BLACKFRIARS ROAD:
GOD SAVE THE SQUAT

When coming from the east, this is where South Bank begins. Beyond, looking east, is Bankside. The division between Lambeth and Southwark – which falls here – has manifested in this split between South Bank and Bankside, though it would have provided a single debauched riverside flow for the Elizabethans and there is no immediate shift in atmospherics between the two areas.

When you stand on the south side of Blackfriars Bridge it's surprising how much hill the bridge has been built upon. It arcs northwards like a rural hump. The new station faces you – a midpoint of static floating in the middle of nowhere – a place to alight in which everything, for a moment, seems possible. If you

have a day with no real plans get a train here and decide which way you'll go – north or south – when you disembark. The station is made in grey glass slats, eclipsing everything from road-level except the bulb of St Paul's. The station seems to be made of crystal, a chrysalis that would break apart at a touch. This station-on-a-bridge might be a new conceit but Blackfriars is an age-old spot of embarkation and alightment. On John Rocque's map of 1746 one of the few details of this area – aside from fields and timber yards – is Falcon Stairs, a stop for the watermen, just a little further on the east side of the bridge. Samuel Pepys often landed here – conveniently close to Paris Garden and the taverns.

Emblazoned against the station bridge is on old shield of arms which declares its ground with INVICTA – Latin for 'undefeated'. In front of me are quadrants of office spaces known as 240 Blackfriars. A geometric Rubick's Cube made of tinted glass. It reflects itself reflected back off passing cars – angled edges hurtling into the void. One day London will just be glass reflecting glass in a matrix of reflections. To the left, along Lower Ground – which runs parallel with the riverside South Bank – the buildings are multiplied in a consistent concrete cream. Brutalist wafers. On the corner of the road, behind me, is a hoarding which shows a designer's mock-up for a new 161 bed boutique hotel. It looks like a suppository with a hatch in the top.

A still-standing red phone box gives perspective to St Paul's in the distance. The creation of the new station has been built around a coat of arms displaying a griffin. Across the river Unilever House is lit white like a remaining segment of a quartered coliseum. Until recently there were two 'William' pubs on Blackfriars Road, one on each side of the road. The Prince William Henry is still here but The Prince Albert, on the western side, is now closed. It was easy to miss, tucked into a side-street next to Christ Church, Southwark. There's barely room to smoke between the closed pub and the church. Slanting oaks are precariously poised over the chapel. Silver shutters over the windows of the pub still give a welcoming 'bienvenue' in mock chalk handwriting – but the ale has long ceased to flow. A man stands in the church gardens wearing a blue suit and woolly beanie, downing from a large *Costa* cup.

Walking up from St George's Circus it's easy to sense how densely populated with housing this area used to be. Stephen Inwood describes how, by 1813, Blackfriars Road was 'a new suburban centre' with 'low-cost humble little terraces'.[14] On first look the imperious rows of perfectly aligned windows – set back into fastidious brown brick – appear to be converted warehouses: but they're not, this is housing that was made for housing and remains as such.

Opposite Southwark tube, at the end of The Cut, is the Palestra Building: a circuit board of glass that looks like it's sliding top-heavy towards the road. A glass biscuit tin left on a plinth which used to house the London Development Agency. The LDA had the dubious responsibility of overseeing economic growth in London. Given the amounts of homeless people between here and the river what did the planners think when they looked out of the window? And the building is all windows: an Argos-eyed hydra hidden by tints. The glass reflects back Southwark station and the speed of the clouds as they go past. Just behind it on Union Street is the Urban Physic Garden, a city space reserved for natural growth. The launch of James Wilkes' *Herbarium* book happened here a few years ago with dozens of poets – who'd written poems about specific herbs – gathering in this hidden enclave for a hidden reading, fuelled by organic cider.

The Surrey Chapel dominated the Blackfriars Road end of the area between 1783 and 1881. This was an independent Methodist and Congregational Church that the architect – Reverend Rowland Hill – 'eloquent, witty, and warm-hearted, and... for many years a power in the religious world' – had built round so that the devil couldn't hide in the corners.[15] According to Walter Thornbury and Edward Walford, who wrote about the chapel when it was still standing, it was 'an ugly octagonal building, with no pretensions to any definite style of architecture'.[16] This was another of the area's distinct circular buildings, formed in the structure of a huge octagon with a quaint bell-like dome at the top. Rowland took advantage of the open fields to preach to over 20,000 people at a time – a following that was only later surpassed by Charles Haddon Spurgeon at the Metropolitan Tabernacle at Elephant & Castle. The chapel attracted religious figures of all kinds and particularly Nonconformists. The spirit of Blake continued long after he left here in 1800 and the glossolalia of the extempore preachers can still be heard on the South Bank on any day of the week. The chapel became known as the Dissenting Chapel until it was refitted for commercial uses in 1881.

From 1910 it became known as The Ring – a famous boxing and wrestling venue. The Ring pub pays homage to this notorious boxing arena which was run by Bella Burge, a music hall performer who later turned to boxing promotion. She had broken the taboo of women attending boxing matches and when she took on the mantle of being the promoter of the venue became known as Bella of Blackfriars. During the Second World War the building was finally destroyed, just as the burnt-out Albion Mill Blake had walked past daily had been over a century before. The building was sliced in half by a bomb, tearing away the walls leaving a piece of the roof in tact. An advert for Guinness was left in place on the remaining wall: THOUSANDS ARE FINDING STRENGTH IN GUINNESS. To get a real sense of the impact of the Blitz here – going beyond the statistics and the dimming of reality across the years – run your fingers over the white tiles on both sides of the underpass beneath Blackfriars Bridge. These cracked white ceramics have been punctured with holes the size of crickets balls, along with the smaller fractures that have spread across the surface. There's a photograph online of the trams crushed by bombs on the 25th October 1940. The drivers were trying to shelter the vehicles under the bridge but the shellfire caught them, flattening the vehicles like cardboard packs.

The Palestra Building – that sliding glass monolith – now stands on the site of the chapel and the boxing ring which continues in the name of the building, 'Palestra' – which is Greek for a public place used for wrestling. There's more to drink at The Ring, a corner pub

on the corner of The Cut and Blackfriars Road. New to London, as a young poet, I was paid £12 in door fees for a reading at St Andrew's on Short Street. I came to The Ring afterwards and palmed it straight across the bar for drinks. Money from poetry has a talismanic magic: for a moment the capitalist order flips on its head with the currency borne of words.

At the end of The Cut is one of the most successful Art on the Underground projects, a text piece which reads *If history could be folded, where would you put the crease?* It then mirrors the same text upside down beneath it. Given the history of this part of London this is a genuinely site-specific work. A huge man with headphones stands underneath the upside down word 'crease'. Beyond is a dated new build which has been graffitied with: GOD SAVE THE SQUAT.

I continue down Blackfriars Road. I'm comfortable here, it reminds me of parts of Liverpool. In the nineteenth century there was a Southwark Mission for the Elevation of the Working Class on this road. I like the *elevation* in use here – which, when I think about it, makes me look up to the top floor of a block of Victorian apartments: quite some drop down to contemporary London. The extant Temperance Hall which still has its name glazed into the glass: SONS OF TEMPERANCE FRIENDLY SOCIETY. This was built in 1875 and used for concerts and lectures – as well as for the all important temperance meetings. Anyone attending these would have had to pass quite a few pubs. I photographed it a few weeks back on the way home after drinking too much in The Hole

in the Wall. The hall still gives an exterior chill of steeliness; white walls glare out through a grille of metal, towards The Crown pub across the road. The Laughing Gravy – another pub – is also nearby on the same side of the road. Then come the super-corporates: *Sainsbury's, Costa, Crush, Pret a Manger.*

The Cycle Super Highway is still being built here. A mechanical digger is trying to claw out a resistant concrete stump. The driver gives up on clawing and then tries to bump it out from the side. His colleague watches. It just won't come out. Seventies' pillars of urban planning stand firm in London clay. Eventually it yields: rusted and calcified, a piece of stone attached to a stump-end comes with it, bigger than its pillar. The audience moves on past the Post Office. Tourists drift back to the Ibis. *Jamboree Foodfest* radiates its buzzword in red neon: SMILE. The yellow digger reflects back from the glass: the driver has removed his hard hat, runs a hand across his brow.

THE PEABODY ESTATE

Peabody Housing Association – one of London's oldest and largest housing associations – has its offices nearby on Westminster Bridge Road. The name comes from its founder, the American philanthropist George Peabody, who made donations totalling half a million pounds towards resolving the slum issue in Victorian London.[22] His obituary in *Illustrated News* in 1869 described him as having 'sought and found his highest enjoyment in putting human affairs right ... and in providing for the comfort, the health, and the sound education of large numbers of mankind.'[23] He was a man in the Dickensian mould of doing Good Works. Peabody has a statue near the Royal Exchange.

By 1897 Peabody Buildings were housing nearly 20,000 people.[24] They were run on a strict tenure and based on a sanitary ideal that meant tenants were part of a greater good and were responsible for helping themselves and thinking of others.[25] The housing that remains on Blackfriars Road – called the Blackfriars Estate – is the best, most beautiful example of this kind. The windows are lit with the quirks of each lodger: the décor of purple blinds and ledges of red magenta – whatever makes the home inside comfortable also adds some furnish to the street. Beneath the central arch and brass finial there is a stone circle which encloses the word *P*. The mark of the philanthropist: Peabody.

I walk through the arch from which a glass ball – once filled with gaslight – hangs, and move into the square behind. This dark narrow passageway opens out into a court overlooked by the windows of hundreds of tenants. On the way in I look at the notice board – an information service for tenants – which gives news on developments relating to the estate. One notice says that landscape gardeners have been appointed to improve play facilities. Another says that people should insure their home. This is real life campus – take your own responsibility. In the background, beyond the estate, is the sound of the crash and tumble of a new hotel under construction.

I look around: a man's sweeping up the Autumn leaves. A silver Mercedes rolls into view behind me. I walk through the back of the first square – yes, there's more – and another square comes into view, deeper than the first, with hundreds more rooms above. Two women are talking about a bad neighbour called Will who's now left the estate. The Peabody spirit is alive and well this morning, the sun is up over Elephant & Castle and vines are growing up the walls. Like the *P* on the exterior I see now that each main door has a letter above its main entrance – an alphabetical system for identifying the blocks. Victorian nomenclature which still works for modern living. A man in a smaller car than the Mercedes starts his engine, then lights a cigarette. All in the right order. The street sweeper has stopped for a text break, leaning on his cart with one hand as he fires into the phone. The wind whispers its lost song of the alphabet through the Victorian court. Despite the works going on behind the estate there is a different set of laws here, another logic. I walk outside of the estate and immediately read a sign that advertises: 'Exciting cutting edge warehouse-style offices: available summer 2016. 3 Valentine Place.' If it wasn't for charities like Peabody there would be nowhere in London for those on low incomes to live. An old building clatters somewhere far off and a crane lifts an unscathed square of new glass up to the clouds. A hoarding reads: *Downwell Demolition: Enabling Solutions.*

ST GEORGE'S CIRCUS

I've been watching this happen for months: the breaking up of the road to make a Cycle Superhighway. I've even been consulted, even though I don't drive or cycle: a letter landed on my desk saying – in longhand – that the shitfest was coming. I brushed it off as a courtesy. Then came the two hour journeys into work, the realisation that any pleasant *ding* made on the bus gave no indication as to how long it would take to reach the next stop. I stood on the bus, waiting, taking videos of the men digging, watching the orange clay fly up around their heels – hoping to at least see something of London's human soup. Centuries of captured history were exposed to the commuters, most of them playing *Subway Surfers* or searching the internet. This earth that's been built over so many times was leaking its

seductive primacy but screens always have more urgency. The frustrated fired on the bell with endless dings. I carried on videoing, hoping to capture clues to the past – shinbones, skulls, Doulton's pipes – anything.

Now the cycle lanes have started to open and the predictable has happened: vehicular status games pervade the daily commute. Buses bump taxis, taxis rail against cars and cars push down on cyclists. And cyclists? They hate pedestrians, treating them like flipper-limbed cro-magnon dawdlers. Non-wheeled descendants of fish. Clones of the Slow Age. The cycle lanes are here and it's all out war. Cyclists turn the corner at St George's Circus, elbows out, flying like one man chariots, eyes peeled sideways to the nearest cyclist to their left or right, teeth bared, all advantage to the next set of lights preserved.

Violence is written into the clay and stone here. St George's Circus was built in 1771 as part of the merging together of the new roads in Southwark.[26] The obelisk in front of me, an anaesthetised Cleopatra's Needle, was built by architect Robert Milne who also built Blackfriars Bridge. The sun is trying to come up behind it, a drifting white disc moving away from the earth that it's denying all knowledge of. There's a constant rattle and chatter of drills as the red crane dangles a rope into a worksite and the luminescent men point upwards towards it. This is the South Bank constant: build, destroy, rebuild. The Shard rises in the backdrop – a silvery hypodermic photobombing every picture. THIS IS BLACKFRIARS CIRCUS a

hoarding reads. Name it before it's here: the hypnotism of branding. I think of Blake's run-in with Astley's Circus over the abuse of the flogged boy. There is always something of the circus to this part of London. The island surrounding the obelisk has now been flattened by concrete. Until last year it was a hybridised urban farm after unknown locals had planted a bizarre range of plants and vegetables on this roundabout, letting it thrive in public view. Cabbages, azaleas, tulips, lavender and a seven foot Christmas tree all appeared. The media named them the 'Guerilla Gardeners'.

I walk away from the Circus and *Chillies Tandoori*, one of a handful of cheap grungy curry houses which I never recommend but very often find convenient. I only found out recently that on the other side of the road, in a red brick building with black tinted windows, is the Feminist Library. The librarians are facing eviction due to the soaring rent prices. I walk past London South Bank University, heading towards Elephant & Castle. Yes, South Bank has a university. My predecessor as Poetry Librarian, Simon Smith, went to teach creative writing here after ten years at The Poetry Library coal face. I always see South Bank University as a poacher of Poetry Librarians.

It won't get me.

Notes

1. Quoted in Patrick Dillon & Jake Tilson, *Concrete Reality: Denys Lasdun and the National Theatre*.

2. Douglas Murphy, *Last Futures: Nature, Technology and the End of Architecture*, Op.cit.

3. http://www.mirror.co.uk/tv/tv-news/morning-interrupts-food-segment-sweaty-6011840

4. The poem is 'Evening on the Thames' published in *Collected Poems 1988*, Op.cit.

5. Iain Sinclair, *Swimming to Heaven: The Lost Rivers of London*, Op.cit.

6. Virginia Woolf, *The London Scene*, Op.cit.

7. Peter Ackroyd, *Thames: Sacred River*, Op.cit.

8. Port of London Authority website at pla.ac.uk/Environment/Metal-Detecting-and-Digging-on-the-Thames-Foreshore The PLA also point out that you need a licence to mudlark on the shore of the Thames.

9. Ibid

10. David Rule, ↑, Op.cit.

11. Ford Madox Ford, *The Soul of London: A Survey of a Modern City*, Op.cit.

12. PJ Harvey was probably writing poetry at the time. She came to The Poetry Library's Poetry Butcher workshop with a poem in 2013 and in 2015 her poetry collection *The Hollow of the Hand* was published by Bloomsbury.

13. Virginia Woolf, *The London Scene*, Op.cit.

14. Stephen Inwood, *A History of London*, Op.cit.

15. Quote from Walter Thornbury and Edward Walford in 'Blackfriars Road: The Surrey Theatre and Surrey Chapel', in *Old and New London: Volume 6* (London, 1878), Op.cit.

16. Ibid.

17. British History Online: http://www.british-history.ac.uk/old-new-london/vol6/pp368-383

18. http://www.nickelinthemachine.com/2009/06/Blackfriars-road-the-ring-and-the-death-of-al-bowlly/

19. Ibid

20. Ibid

21. [http://www.british-history.ac.uk/old-new-london/vol6/pp368-383

22. William Ronald Dalzell, *The History of London*, Op.cit.

23. Quoted in William Ronald Dalzell, *The History of London*, Op.cit.

24. Roy Porter, *London: A Social History*, Op.cit.

25. Ibid.

26. William Ronald Dalzell, *The History of London*, Op.cit.

27. Ibid.

Liquid City writes *You are the custodians*
    The citizens   *The carriers*
      The creators of copy
but first you must learn to breathe
   beneath the rivers
    down where the dead
  are more populous than rats
     you're never more than a whisker away
    from moulds of remains
      of every name walked above
   folded like moth spoor into clay
Liquid City places washbasins
over its streams
    an empire of domes
        a church   a circus
   The IMAX
     and watches the living pray
   to the God of Light cupped in their hands
       heads bowed to it   knitted brows
     the words fly up
  an allowance   a package
   a stream that connects the plague of what was
     to the blue pulse of each of us

SOUTH

A WALK ALONG THE NECKINGER

There are underground river wars afoot. Not in the rivers themselves, but in those who write about them. Is the Neckinger even a real river or – as Tom Chivers suggested to me one evening over beer – 'a bit of made up one'? I am compelled by Chivers's conviction and the maps of different periods back him up. I've walked his route with his Neckinger Pilgrimage audio guide in my ears, being led by Blake an intuition. Can anything more than a gurgling self-drowning stream ever have flowed through marshland? And if it did, where did it flow to? Tom Bolton – whose course in *London's Lost Rivers* I'll be following – pins it down to an exact and convincing geography. Bolton's book covers all of London's underground rivers and is incredibly revealing given its pocket-sized format and the amount of ground it covers. When discussing the Neckinger he tells us that the herbalist John Gerard described the river in the sixteenth century as 'the Devil's Neckerchief on the way to Redriffe'.[1] The Devil's Neckerchief was a slang term for the hangman's noose and it has been argued that the river's outfall in Bermondsey was once the site for executions. It could also be that the curve of the river through some of London's most notorious areas could be the source of its name.

What I'm actually following is unclear: a once natural stream? A

channel for draining off the marshlands? A culverted series of sewerage pipes? I am, however, convinced by Bolton's view that the river (let's call it that, for argument's sake) would have once followed the border between Lambeth and Southwark. I cross-check his route with the map of the Borough that I was sent by Lambeth Council: the eastern edge of this huge, sprawling multicultural jigsaw disappears into the outer realm of Southwark along the route that Bolton lays out for the Neckinger. It makes sense – given man's lazy territoriality – for the landscape to have defined the change in name that would have accompanied different communities. You have that side, I'll have this.

The outfall of the Neckinger isn't beneath the embankment here – I've looked. There are massive pipes rusting under rotting pillars. The building up of the embankment wall here has covered any water outfall and what was left of this river after the drying out of the marshes in the eighteenth century would very likely have become part of the advancements in sewer controls (I'm feeling more confident about that now). I need to remember to keep my head up too, to discover more of the real South Bank. In fact, this is why I'm walking the Neckinger – as a rusted hook to hang the damp fabric of the real South Bank on. It could also be that I have no choice: poets are compelled by underground rivers, poets are dowsers of the imagination – which could explain why Blake and Rimbaud have followed this river's route before.

BERNIE SPAIN GARDENS

This is the name given to this floating area of land between Oxo Tower and Gabriel's Wharf. It's named after Bernadette Spain – one of the Coin Street Action Group campaigners who fought to keep this area for the community. Once a smouldering backwater surrounded with smoke and sodden with damp – 'buffered by dykes and drained by ditches' as Tom Bolton puts it – the grass here has become a crossing land for commuters and tourists.[2] I look back north and guess that the river would have flowed in at the point where I was mudlarking with Anna a few weeks back. A man urgently clings a phone to his head like his mother's inside it. A woman and a child are playing with sticks. I head past them, walking towards Broadwall. Couples are walking in silence. A jogger is clearing his conscience before the evening's inevitable takeaway order. A man in his thirties – iPod in hand – pushes a buggy that has no child in.

Bernie Spain Gardens today is for corporate hire with a company called AIG asking passers-by to do the *Haka Challenge*. On the grass is a large screen of New Zealand rugby players squatting, staring towards the river. A few years ago I stood here dressed as a doctor. Or a Poetry Doctor to be exact. A Poetry Library idea to remedy moods through literary prescription. Want to feel happier? Take a dose of John Cooper Clarke. Working through depression and want to hear another human working through it? Try Hopkins. Suffering bereavement? Have a go at Tennyson. On that day there was a DJ throwing out scratchy remixes for the hours that we were there and – perhaps as a result – uptake for the Poetry Doctor was minimal. It's hard to effectively prescribe with a Rihanna remix between you and your patient.

Along with Jubilee Gardens, this is one of the few grassland areas along the riverfront of the South Bank. In summer you can bring your book and sandwiches and find a hump of hill. There'll be scores of others doing the same but for an hour or two you'll be safe: no one will find you. Though that might be set to change. There are plans afoot to build a Garden Bridge across the Thames which will land by the National Theatre – an idea that has been met by much of the community here with the distaste of force-fed Thames' effluent. The posters in people's windows on Upper Ground – *Say NO to Garden Bridge* – make that clear. The Garden Bridge is another of London's great vanity projects. It was an idea originally conceived by Joanna Lumley, which public-funded dreamers like Boris Johnson and George Osborne engaged with – pledging public money towards it. The design sketches show a bridge that looks like a stretched plant trench pivoted on a viaduct column. Overly green trees extend upwards. Photoshopped pieces of tropical light meld against the backdrop of St Paul's. The website, at the time of writing, says it's still happening: a three hundred and sixty-six long copper nickel structure is coming our way 'to race across, relax in or look back at the rest of the city's sights.'[3] The push is for green: a new floating lush space. The irony of slamming down a massive new concrete structure to achieve this doesn't register in the minds of the power players in this project. Players in the great tradition of those wanting to put their mark on London's topography before they go under it.

The website tells us that there is an area of land along here that has

been earmarked for potential commerce. The grassy area before London Studios is marked on the developers' maps under the cashed-in rubric of 'flexible space'. Flexible: mark on the map now, sell later. This is described as 'Approximately 350 sqm of flexible space allowing for potential exhibition, community, educational, retail or restaurant use.' I don't hold out much hope for the community – even one as resistant and influential as Coin Street – when pitched against the bids for restaurant space along the South Bank. If you listen closely you can already hear the rustle of cloned burger wrappers.

These futuristic designs are airbrushed in a way to make dreamers of us all. A new land that time has yet to allow us to forget. The marketing tries to give us that feeling of walking over water, a feeling which is akin to flying. Freud tells us that dreams of flying are really about sex and the images of bridges created by developers are always smudged with the collective wet dream of themselves and those they aim to build for. The green of the South Bank is Photoshopped on the bridge itself, which flies out over familiar water: a silver rainbow set to trickle gold coins into the local pouch. What's never shown is that the gold is just chocolate money and the real cash – real binary strings of it – are invisibly coded into other bank accounts long before a brick is laid. It's astonishing that the Government has come on board for this. In a fantastic piece of political spin Westminster Council agreed that, yes, views would be obstructed from the other bridges but that the creation of *new views* would outweigh this. We arrive in *Yes Minister* territory: whose views do we accept on whether the outweighing of the old views with the new views is true?

On the leaflet in front of me the consultation with the community is presented as a fait accompli – 'consultation' being a series of tick-boxes that can be marked and returned to the address given: 'this is an opportunity for the local community to provide feedback on the choice of materials ... The location and form of the building has already been approved as part of the planning consent for the Bridge.' There is, however, a chance to input on the toilets: 'There are two potential options for the configuration of toilets – up to seven unisex cubicles or a mix of cubicles and urinals ... We welcome views on the proposed options.' On the diagram fabricated bodies are presented as grey transparencies or featureless black figures stripped of all human urges. We touch the glossy paperwork as soiling creatures, minions of the dream-makers. Even the invisible underground river I'm following would be toll-boothed – if the developers could find it.

UPPER GROUND

Biffa, the side of the van says. A smell of rank banana skins leaks from its rear. A crane swings a container over me, a red elevator rises up the edges of the tapering structure. This is South Bank Tower. Two luminescent men, one in yellow pushing a bin, the other in orange and a hardhat, stand with their backs to each other, texting. The older buildings here – sandstone superblocks – stay where they are: weather-stained and outmoded, like beige décor from a seventies' series of *Parkinson*. A man in a suit walks leisurely

past me, talking out loud to himself – then I spot the earpiece. City of declamatory walkers: even the straitlaced are ranters now.

Upper Ground is taking us through another round of change here. I look for the omphalos, the God, the core of the belief system – there's always one. It comes in a sign: *Luxury Apartments Available Now <<< visit today*. ONE BLACKFRIARS IS COMING. The Jacobean playwrights once debauched themselves on this Bankside-South Bank hinge. Now it's more glazed brioche than bawdy stew.

I walk along Upper Ground, reading the signs as I go. The men who are paid to text have Traffic Marshal on their backs. A brush has been left alongside a *Caution:Wet Paint* sticker. A young man in decorator's dungarees walks with one hand down his trousers and another around a paper coffee cup. Outside the backside of the Mondrian Hotel a Tom Dixon sculpture has been dumped – a bright blue piece of metallic digestive tract. A man in a grey suit is sitting on it, smoking. He looks like he's waiting for a ride to begin, loftily atop this sinking inflatable on the all too rapid rides of the South Bank. In the window of *Lazarides Editions* is a framed Banksy showing three aboriginal warriors aiming spears and axes at shopping trolleys. The tag asks for 32k. These are the anti-corporate corporates who frame the master graffiti-artists and sell them back to the people their work rails against. Tom Dixon's tangled blue tube makes sense appearing here – as it does – like airbrushed faeces.

A blast of warm air rises from the grilles in the road. I cross over Barge House Street and the riverside part of Hatfields before arriving at Stamford Street. A moving lorry shutters past me with its warning audio loop telling everyone to Stand Clear. A man of around twenty stone in weight rides past me, slumped over the bars of a children's bike. The soundtrack to all of this is drilling: the clatter of erected scaffolding, the cacophony of warning bleeps. People only pay attention when everything goes silent.

58 Upper Ground adds to the mishmash of the roads with its fabricated Tudor remains. A CCTV camera is perched across a stained glass window. The entrance side of London Studios – which includes ITV – dominates this deserted futureland. A siren is wailing somewhere far off as a foreman drives a tractor with what looks like a self-rolled spliff lolling from his mouth. A hand down his belt. A massive rugby ball sits in the window of ITV Studios – an unmissable talisman of the never-ending Rugby World Cup. A man in leather lifts a phone to his ear: white noise drifts through the depleted land.

Opposite is The Mulberry Bush, one of the priciest pubs in the area and not one that I'm recommending. At the time of writing a pint of Peroni teeters on the edge of £5. The staff fill the pint to a millimetre beneath the pint-line and then – as you're gearing yourself for the final sweet in-draught at the bottom of the glass – snatch it away for cleaning. In summer the doors of the pub are fully open, facing the built-up grid work of ITV Studios. Production staff, assistants and make-up artists sit facing their place of work, over-using the word 'cunt' in the pauses between cigarettes. Here we go round the life-work imbalance of the exhausted professional. Outside there's a van from a company

called DRAIN DOCTOR – the double doors at the back of the van are wide open so the tools can be reached to clear an executive post-adrenalin private – now public – disaster.

Until the end of the nineteenth century Upper Ground was known as Commercial Road. What that commerce represented – industry, textiles, consumption – has been replaced by a new century's obsessions: media, celebrity, leisure and computing. The transition has been one from a lined avenue of slums overlooking factories, to this current exo-airport on the banks of the Thames. Upper Ground: a platform, a viewing point, a place to stop. Before that this was one of the oldest thoroughfares in this part of London, a descendant of the path which from the Norman period ran along the inside of the embanking river wall. That history still remains in the narrowness and the twists and turns which are characteristic of a country lane.

Looking at the pre-twentieth century maps of the area you can see how Upper Ground – when it was Commercial Road – was very often awash with the effluent from the river. It was common until the 1920s for the river to rise and flood out as far as here – most famously in 1928 – which caused major problems for those living in this area. Gwen Southgate in *Coin Street Chronicles* describes the house her family moved into here when she was a girl:

> Maybe this section should have been called Lower Ground, because it was even lower than Upper Ground! The basement of our 'new' house had been declared unfit for habitation and sealed off, along with the airy and coal cellar, soon after the 1928 flood. The semi-basement kitchen at the back was still usable and not as damp as our living room had been. But it was plagued with black beetles, lovers of dark, damp places. Ugh! ... How they crunched underfoot if you trod on them.[5]

The social housing along here is of high quality now, and these terraces were replaced with buildings like The White House which overlooks the back of the Festival Hall – with its own garden, fountain, and railings which stem from concrete bases that the homeless often bunk-up on for the night. White concrete. Occasional neon. Transience.

I cross into Broadwall, following a Diverted Traffic sign. On the east side is the Southwark-Lambeth divide which continues along

Upper Ground at Paris Garden. Umber leaves swirl in a quick wind. Tom Bolton describes Broadwall as once being a 'raised bank with a causeway along the top'. I'm following the western side of that, past the side entrance to The Thirsty Bear pub. A middle-aged couple with coffees walk past me, plotting out their afternoon: 'well it was free and I thought, well – if there was nothing else to do, why not?' Flagged in every other window are the red and white posters: *Stop £175 Million Garden Bridge.* I come out on Stamford Street, facing the Grecian entrance to the Unitarian Chapel, a Parthenon-like white reconstruction with new apartments obscenely curving behind in black. The chapel was replaced to make a playground for the London Nautical School which later became the smoked-out curvature of modern living you see now.

COIN STREET:
A LONDON COMMUNITY

I have an appointment here, one aimed to bring me closer to one of the South Bank's most well known communities around Coin Street. There's a need to get closer to the people who live here, the communities that have succeeded the lineage from the Victorian slums, the Second World War Blitz and the class friction of the 1980s. A colleague suggested I speak to Joanne Donovan, a member of the Coin Street Action Group who's lived here for decades. She also runs *StorySLAM*, a competition for adults and children to perform stories in front of an audience. Here's someone who not only knows the area but can tell its stories. In fact, when asking her to suggest where we should meet, Joanne recommends *Caffè Mascolo* on Stamford street – between *Pret a Manger* and *Toni & Guy* – because there's a story to it. I later find out that it's a story which demonstrates the essence of community to the area. When *Toni & Guy* had bought the entire block of buildings to open up their salon here – the soaring rates driving many of the small businesses out – the new owners recognised the popularity and character of the café and let it stay. They liked the owner with his broad Italian hospitality and endless jokes.

Joanne's sitting at the back of the cafe, waiting. We say hello and as I pour milk into my tea, realise that our conversation about the reality of the Coin Street community has already started. And that reality is bitter. At the time of writing the Government stay-and-pay proposal for those earning over £40k is threatening to rip through the community. Anyone currently paying rent of £400 per month would see that escalate to the Foxtons' rate of £4,500. The straightforward honouring of the market makes no allowance for those who want to keep their home. Those who've lived here for decades.

Joanne talks about the 'transient people' that come here. A phrase that describes much of what I see every day. This is a transient area, one that – like liquid – is in constant movement. When Joanne first moved here it was a quiet, artsy place, with lights out by ten o'clock in the evening. Many of the struggling artists had been bumped out of their squats following the precedent that had been set from the revisionist Tate Modern. Now millions of people occupy the area for the hours of daylight, returning to hotels and the home counties before dark.

It's the river that Joanne loves most about living here, how it's always changing – often quiet and still in the morning before the boats start to furrow its surface – then restless and tidal in the night. How light changes it too, through the seasons – sometimes even on the same day. She describes that feeling of being closed-in – a feeling that's familiar to me – when being away from water for too long. Living on the South Bank is really about the bond you make with this river that – although now banked – seems to run past the doorsteps. All the people who were here before – and the thousands who now come each day – can't escape its pull, the muddy fact of its existence. All throughways and paths have been laid around its course, creating stages for transience while the ongoing fact of the river runs on. Long past our songs are finished.

I ask Joanne about the divide here, the one between those with and those without. The one that Henry Mayhew and Charles Booth knew in the nineteenth century, that I see every day in the presence of the evicted and homeless. There are the developers and the rich moving into the area of course. Recently there was a video made by the new One Blackfriars hotel development which had to be removed from a screen over Blackfriars Road. This film showed a man who wanted to buy the woman he loved everything. He rolled her in by limousine, bought her a fur coat, showed her the view out across the city by night – its light reduced to red dots – as if powered in standby mode. Then the camera panned out across London, as if handheld by Peter Pan, landing on the apartment that he'd just bought for her. All the way through she doesn't say a word. 'Like Barbie', Joanne says, 'she

just sits there'. At the other extreme are the real homeless, those who look through the bins of those who have just enough. Joanne describes how she started finding ripped bags, often with cigarette butts removed. Then she spotted two homeless men going through her bins, strewing the remains on the floor as they looked for anything worth keeping. She told them they could take what they'd found but they couldn't leave the rubbish on the floor as it attracts the rats. The next day one of the homeless men came back, and asked her: 'did you say it was okay to go through your bags?' On another occasion she heard one of the men whooping with joy: he'd found a t-shirt and some shoes that had been thrown away and would make a good fit for him. While films of fur coats are screened from the top of the tower there are those under its lights who whoop for joy over what they find in people's rubbish.

Living here for decades saturates an individual with all the centuries of human transience that went before. Joanna talks about the Romans and the talismanic curses people flung into the river to place a hex on those who had crossed them. She talks of the Temple of Mithras over in Walbrook, 'Like now,' she says, 'the Romans had brought many different cultures with them.' The tribes of today are the communities and homeless and – way up high, on the other side – the omniscient megabuilders, with their panning films of night time London. South Bank Tower is being extended upwards, the first time ever that's ever been attempted on an already existing tower. The cult of the phallic temple grows each day, mirroring the river it can never be, even as it flows in glass to the clouds. Joanne says her house on the estate at Duchy Street is built on stilts: the supports of the building shift through the marshland and down to the distant clay beneath. When a six feet slab of concrete is fixed on top of the stilts the house is safe to build. She laughs about those who say 'leave the river to be natural' – 'if we all did that', she says, 'then we wouldn't be living here'.

I thank Joanne for her time as she points out her house on Duchy Street. The road name suggests the presence of royalty which was marked in Black Prince's Meadow and the King's Bargehouse. There's birdsong here. Real birdsong. Before we leave Joanne tells me about when her son was away at university, in a rural campus, saying that the thing he missed about not being at home on the South Bank was the sound of the birds.

The concrete obsessives would never believe it.

STAMFORD STREET:
IN SEARCH OF RIMBAUD

Bolton's map of the Neckinger brings me out onto Stamford Street. The poet Arthur Rimbaud lived here for a short period in 1874. At number 178, which – one of Rimbaud's many biographers, Graham Robb tells us – has since disappeared to 'become a bland segment of the A3200'[7]. Rimbaud lived here after the bust-up with poet Paul Verlaine, which began with an insult in Camden – over the amusing way Verlaine walked carrying kippers – and a shotgun incident in a hotel room in Belgium.[8] During his time with Verlaine, Rimbaud had been writing *A Season in Hell*, a title which does justice to the moral-buffeting experience of the reality of living in London with no money. Verlaine, a bullish pug, led their inner-city rambles with Rimbaud in tow, like a whippet in a long coat, refusing to trail behind. Whilst scrimping the gutters as a poet Rimbaud set out to realign the narrowness of society's moral values and – by extension – the limits of the pre-existing poetry to do justice to the modern predicament. Rimbaud wrote a few months later that his new poetry had failed, but he never left poetry behind and he arrived on Stamford Street with his new work-in-progress mutating into fresh possibilities for poetry. It was later named *Illuminations*.

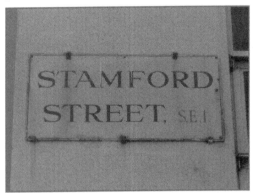

Rimbaud arrived here with a different poet this time: Germaine Nouveau. They would sign up for the reading room at the British Museum adding a false extra name to their real ones: Marie and Joseph. This Biblical symbolism smacks of a Rimbaud rising from the smouldering heaps of his ex, determined to see and doing London in his own way – and enjoying the control. There is scholarly evidence that shows that Germaine Nouveau hand-copied some of Rimbaud's *Illuminations*. It's an intoxicating feeling – even in this rain – to know that modern poetry leaped forward within fifty yards of where I'm now standing.

Nouveau seems to be just what Rimbaud needed after the years with Verlaine. Although Nouveau was older than Rimbaud he would easily have accepted the younger poet as well advanced in poetic achievement. Nouveau stood at less than five foot tall. Rimbaud might also have felt that – if it came to the kind of physical struggle he'd had with Verlaine – he could easily take the upper hand over Nouveau. Yet Nouveau doesn't seem to be a pushover. Graham Robb describes him as 'a short, stocky Provencal with a handsome face and an agreeable habit of gently contradicting everything that was said in the hope of finding a more interesting angle.'[9] Nouveau had lost both parents when young and – no doubt to Rimbaud's delight – had taken a Bohemian flourish to the last of his inheritance. The money seems to have been gone by the time they arrived in London though and Edmund White describes how Nouveau was later to be found back in Paris, begging for money.[10]

There's no better time to come here than on a morning of rain in October. Commuters slide towards bus shelters and offices, darting into unexpected places – like cloned bats – with their opened-out umbrellas. Rimbaud's lodgings would have been at the Waterloo end of Stamford Street. We can get a good sense of the kind of building it was from those that are still standing opposite. Large bay windows – solid functional warehouses for living – with the steps that go down to the basement room collecting all of London's passing detritus. Rimbaud would have walked out from his door facing the current Frank Harris estate agents – which offers prices for three bedroom apartments in the new One Blackfriars from four and a half million pounds. A warehouse that would have been just that – a warehouse – has been renovated and tagged at over two million. 'What is my nothingness to the stupor that awaits you?' Rimbaud wrote in the *Illuminations*.[11]

Nouveau wrote a letter on 27 March 1874 which gives us a flash of what Rimbaud was up to here:

> I left Paris when I least expected and am now, as you see, with Rimbaud ... We have rented a room in Stampfort Street ... in a family where the young gentlemen, knowing a little French, converses with us for an hour every day so that he can improve his

French and I can learn a few words. Rimbaud is also going to work on his English. He knows just enough for our common needs.[12]

'Common needs' was becoming a part of Rimbaud's essential worldview and goes some way to explaining why the *Illuminations* – despite being such a front-on assault to the morals of the sleepwalking masses – has something of the tone of a practical manual. This period saw the transition between the unwashed poet who'd frequented the British Museum with Verlaine and the journeyman who went to Africa to trade in Remingtons. The *Illuminations* offers hands-on advice and critique of the progressive new world – a new world seen through a glass dome, or misted Lambeth window – which reduced this confusing, contradictory city to the poet's own logic. We know Rimbaud took Nouveau to the museums, music hall and the Crystal Palace exhibition which was now based in Sydenham. Nouveau had struggled to keep up with the wiry, restless Rimbaud, writing that 'there's no end to these bridges'.[13] They had a job making boxes in Holborn – an experience that perhaps influenced the text-blocked form of the *Illuminations*. This appearance in the poems between order and control – and the quick interplay of images and ideas – has always appealed to me. Rimbaud, as a citizen holding down a job whilst offering his services as a teacher, knew the difference between surface impression and the wildness of the subconscious. Rimbaud's poems demonstrate how clearly he knew the difference between who a person can appear to be in public and the reality of their personal preoccupations.

The Autumn rains are here: the streets are streaming with sodden leaves and dimly reflected lights. Golds and ambers reflect back from every window. I've decided to find Rimbaud on the wettest morning in months – without anything to cover my head. The rain has flattened my hair to a crocheted matt, is streaming from my forehead and down the back of my neck. The luxuries of warmth and comfort are somewhere else this morning.

Robb cites the references to underground locations and images of the underworld as possible evidence for Rimbaud and Nouveau living in a cellar apartment. This might be true but the interesting thing for me is how at home Rimbaud is in describing a city built upon the dead: he feels more akin with the corpses beneath than with the living that walk above it. The night-lit city becomes a temporary circus for the Living Dead, a mere arcade for the experiences of short-lived sentients. Even when down at this level Rimbaud is resistant to separating the body from the intellect, and suggests how the future London of the clean concrete arts complex would later be built upon a city of filth:

> Now hire for me the tomb, whitewashed with the lines of cement in bold relief – far underground …
>
> At a tremendous distance above my subterranean room, houses grow like plants, and fogs gather. The mud is red or black. Monstrous city! Endless night!

> ('Childhood V')

Rimbaud would also have known about the new building of the embankments and Bazalgette's sewerage systems which made human effluent more visible for its absence – the gunk of the modern metropolis which is out of sight but never out of mind. The brilliance of his new poetry is the ability to jump-cut from the micro to macro:

> Not so high up are the sewers. At my side, nothing but the thickness of the globe.

> ('Childhood V')

As with the modern city, modern literature has risen from the sordid grooves laid down by Rimbaud. The French Surrealist Georges Bataille starts his 1957 novel *Blue of Noon* at the Savoy

Hotel with a character called Dirty overlooking the South Bank where Rimbaud had jolted poetry into the violent and uncomfortable experience it would need to become:

> Dirty dragged herself over to the window. Beneath her she saw the Thames and, in the background, some of the most hideous buildings in London, now magnified in the darkness. She quickly vomited in the open air. In her relief she called for me, and, as I held her forehead, I stared at the foul sewer of a landscape: the river and the warehouses. In the vicinity of the hotel the lights of luxury apartments loomed insolently.[14]

Rimbaud's poem 'Metropolitan' suggests that he would have very likely travelled by tube too (as it would become known two decades later). I look down Stamford Street towards Waterloo Station, looking through the black mist and the vortex of revolving umbrellas: the IMAX looms like a huge basin – the latest in the South Bank's domed architectural offerings. Rimbaud's apartment has been lost to the widened road, somewhere between the new builds of the Coin Street Neighbourhood Centre and King's College Waterloo Campus. The university which has been built up around the old Guy's Hospital and the students still look at outpatients on their way in to a campus which specialises in nursing, midwifery and life sciences. On the Ordnance Survey map of 1896 the word *Infirmary* runs along this side of Stamford Street. Rimbaud would have been very comfortable with 'infirmary' as a description of the unstable layers of the city, and the insecure nature of the human subjects that walk through it.

Rimbaud forged a new poetic order in the *Illuminations*, the kind that's familiar to us now from the speed of the internet and ease of global travel. He was learning the old languages that would facilitate his explorations through Europe and Africa and creating the new language that modern literature would later necessitate. He felt the growing pains of forcing this to happen – before anyone else had realised the necessity for the change. His readers had to catch up. Yet what Rimbaud was surrounded by here couldn't have been more dreary: the architecture of industrialism and the brown brick of worker's lodgings. Graham Robb cites a story reported in *The Daily Telegraph* in 1874 which described Commercial Road as being under seven feet of Thames water which was a staple fact of living here until the embankment was built. The *Illuminations* actually begins with 'After the Flood' which – as with much of the sequence that follows – brings the biblical into the functioning flow of the viral, liquid city:

> – Gush forth, waters of the pond. Foam, pour over the bridge and over the woods. Black shrouds and organs, lightning and thunder, rise up and spread everywhere. Waters and sorrows, rise up and bring back the Floods.
>
> ('After the Flood')

The 'gush', 'black shrouds' and 'sorrows' bring to mind today's masses of commuters. In fact Rimbaud's critique of the crippling condition of mass-packed commuting is so clearly depicted in the *Illuminations* that nearly 150 years later it can't be improved on for the way in captures the city's cramped atmospherics:

> These millions of people who have no need of knowing one another and conduct their education, their trade, and their old age with such similarity that the duration of their lives must be several times shorter than, according to some insane statistics, is the case with the people on the continent. From my window, I see new ghosts rolling through thick, everlasting coal smoke ...
>
> ('City')

I've always found that the South Bank is needed to give perspective on the rest of the city. Rimbaud looks at the new architecture of the city as being built upon an 'acropolis' – a circus that has been made to 'cheat taxi drivers': 'The business quarter is a circus constructed in a uniform style, with arcade galleries.'[15] Although far from the leisure destination it is today, Rimbaud used it as the vantage through which to see London as it's always best to be seen: through parallax. Rimbaud constantly changes his relationship with the objects around him in order to see them fresh. Or at least less *mired* in the filth they exist in. He does this through never standing still, making us try to stay in touch with his heels – like Nouveau over those bridges – fusing his reading, thinking and walking into one complicated, convoluted stream.

By June 1874 Nouveau had moved on and Rimbaud had relocated alone to the playground of his first visit, not far from Howland Street. Rimbaud got ill and called for his mother: the poet like a milk-starved weasel in need of comforting. She travelled with his sister from across the channel. For the next eighteen months

Nouveau would refer to Rimbaud in his diaries as 'Thing'. There may have been something of caution in this, the anonymity of 'thingy' (*that person: you know who I mean*), but still, this is a description that is far from endearing. Yet there's another way of seeing this too: Rimbaud had obsessed so much on the things he'd captured in language so clearly, in Nouveau's mind perhaps he'd become it: a flushed object in the underground sewer, an aspect of the new functioning London. The new poetry was doing away with the false spaces between life and art: all flowers are made to rot. The Thing had left his mark – greasy, unclean, wet with sewerage – on the white sheet of poetry.

It's become so dark in the rain – rain which has saturated each layer of my clothing through to my skin – that the yellow glow from Frank Harris estate agents is almost welcoming. There's a Victorian glow of human movement inside. I take a photo of the Stamford Street sign: in the window next to it is an empty box labelled *Givenchy*. More commuting bats head towards me, joined by a new breed of well-coated puffer people. I wipe my forehead with an already sodden tissue – and keep walking.

AT PARIS GARDEN:
AMONGST THE RABBLE THAT IS THERE

I linger a while longer, on Stamford Street, before following the course of the Neckinger along Hatfields towards The Cut. I'm looking at the Paris Garden, at the opposite end to where Rimbaud would have lived. In the late sixteenth century this was the location for the Elizabethan Beargardens, which John Stow describes as 'the old and new places, wherin be kept bears, bulls, and other beasts, to be baited; as also mastiffs in several kennels, nourished to bait them. These bears and other beasts are there baited in plots of ground, scaffolded about for the beholders to stand safe.'[16] There has been debate over where the Beargdarden was located, and later maps show it further to the east, but Stow – ever meticulous – tells us that 'The Beare-garden [was] commonly called the Paris garden' and the name has remained for this in the strange chicken-bone shaped street which hooks back on itself and into Colombo Street before emerging on to Blackfriars Road.[17]

There were more than just bears on show here and various accounts detail the entertainment which included horses with apes

tied to their backs, a performance which involved apples being showered on the crowd, and a horse being baited to death for the pleasure of the Moroccan Ambassdor. Samuel Pepys visited here in 1666 and then twice more in 1667, writing in his diary:

> After dinner, I went with my wife and Mercer to the BearGarden, where I have not been, I think, of many years, and saw some good sport of the bulls tossing the dogs – one into the very boxes; but it is a very rude and nasty pleasure. We had a great many Hectors in the same box with us (and one very fine went into the pit and played his dog for a wager, which was a strange sport for a gentleman), where they drank wine, and drank Mercer's health first, which I pledge with my hat off.
>
> (14 August 1666)[19]

Not deterred by the Hectors (an early variant of 'hecklers') Pepys returned the following year:

> Abroad, and stopped at Bear-garden Stairs, there to see a prize fought. But the house so full there was no getting in there, so forced to go through an ale-house into the pit, where the bears are baited; and upon a stool did see them fight, which they did very furiously, a butcher and a waterman. The former had the better all along, till by-and-by the latter dropped his sword out of his hand, and the butcher, whether or not seeing his sword dropped I know not, but did give him a cut over the wrist, so as he was disabled to fight any longer. But Lord! to see in a minute how the whole stage was full of

watermen to revenge the foul play, and the butchers to defend their fellow, though most blamed him: and there they all fell to it, knocking and cutting down many on each side. It was pleasant to see; but that I stood in the pit and feared that in the tumult I might get some hurt. At last the battle broke up, and so I away.

(28th May 1667)[20]

Liquid City's watermen take on the butchers and what flows is blood. The Beargarden – with its many spellings (three variants alone in Pepys' diary) – was a place to resolve these disputes. Not so ruffled by the pleasant threat of getting hurt, Pepys was back again a few months later:

To the Bear Garden, where now the yard was full of people, and those most of them seamen, striving by force to get in. I got into the common pit, and there, with my cloak about my face, I stood and saw the prize fought, till one of them, a shoemaker, was so cut in both his wrists, that he could not fight any longer; and then they broke off. His enemy was a butcher. The sport very good; and various humours to be seen among the rabble that is there.

(9th September 1667)[21]

According to Walter Thornbury and Edward Walford – who wrote about this area for *Old and New London,* published in 1878 – Ben Jonson actually performed here and was verbally attacked by Thomas Dekker for doing so. I've heard performance poets from the punk era saying that they existed in a period where they had to entertain or have a glass thrown at them – which proved to be a good education – but I've not heard any of them describe butchers and watermen cutting each other to pieces as part of the evening's entertainment. It's very curious to read Pepys – who is so often refined and sensitive – finding this 'pleasant to see' and 'the sport very good' as for many it proved to be too much. The poet Robert Crowley had written his misgivings about the Paris Garden into verse before his death in 1588:

What folly is this to keep with danger
A great mastiff dog and foul ugly bear,
And to this anent, to see them two fight
With terrible tearings, a full ugly sight:
And methinks these men are most fools of all
Whose store of money is but very small.

And yet every Sunday they will surely spend
One penny or two, the bearward's living to mend.

At Paris Garden, each Sunday, a man shall not fail
To find two or three hundred for the bearward's vale:
One half-penny apiece they use for to give,
When some have not more in their purses, I believe.
Well, at the last day their consciences will declare
That the poor ought to have all that they may spare.
If you, therefore, go to witness a bear-fight,
Be sure God His curse will upon you light.[22]

Thornbury and Walford write that there was an account of a tragedy that took place at the Beargarden in 1582. The account comes from someone called Pennant – who quotes Crowley's poem as a portent of the disaster that happened – when the scaffolding fell and killed and injured over a hundred people. This didn't prevent the entertainments continuing and Queen Elizabeth actually visited in 1599, bringing the French Ambassador with her.[23]

As far as the South Bank goes this seems like a relatively quiet corner of London today – despite the ongoing clatter of dismantling rebuilds. Not so historically. The royal patronage – which continued after Elizabeth's death – was also joined with attention from the rich and famous of the Elizabethan period. The actor Edward Alleyn – famous for playing the lead roles in Marlowe's plays – became the 'keeper of the king's wild beasts, or master of the Royal Bear

Garden'.[24] The profits were huge and in 1619 Alleyn decided to use his money from the Paris Garden (along with significant sums that came from renting out properties and investment in the theatres, including The Rose) to set up a college for 'God's gift' five-and-a-half miles south of here in Dulwich. There have been suggestions that this was brought about through penance from the guilt he felt over funding bear-baiting and stews but this is unlikely as the Southwark vices were so normalised during this period. Alleyn's papers are held at Dulwich College and were salvaged in the 1840s by the biographer J. Payne Collier when he was writing *Memoirs of Edward Alleyn*. These memoirs give a strong sense of the financial machinations, resentments and political – and poetical – infighting that existed along the South Bank in Elizabethan times. This includes a wager between Alleyn and another actor called Peele, over who could excel most in the performance of a particular poetic script. According to Collier, Alleyn not only won but left Peele unable to 'recover from this illness, and we know ... he was dead in 1598'.[25] Poetry as killer: a narrative that has been heard many times since. As American poet Jack Spicer said on his deathbed: 'My vocabulary did this to me.'

When the plague broke out Alleyn took his Lord Strange's Players on tour out of London and in 1593 he wrote a letter to his wife which gives us a view of how the richer houses along here would have been furnished – as well as providing evidence of how strongly attached Elizabethan men were to their tights:

> My good sweete mouse, I commend me hartely to you and to my father, my mother, and my sister bess, hoping in god, though the sickness be round about you, yett by his mercy itt may escape your house ... And, Jug, I pray you, lett my orayng tawny stokins of wolen be dyed a very good blak against I com hom, to wear in the winter.[26]

There is a suggestion that the Beargarden lives on in the name of the pub over the road, The Thirsty Bear. This is an accidental association. The Thirsty Bear describes itself as 'London's first fully fledged self service pub where we aim to marry technology with great food and drinks to ensure you have a memorable experience.'[27] Their website is full of images of people clawing at table-top tablets to pay for cocktails by credit card with the drinks then delivered straight to their seats. The equivalent Beargarden days of scrambling for apples on the ground as fireworks fire

overhead. There isn't even a beer garden here.

The true legacy of the Beargarden is in the coinage that exists in the theatre world's use of the phrase 'Bear-pit'. This is a term which refers to the system for giving opportunities in the theatre to those who wouldn't usually have them. This derivation comes from Alleyn's tenure to establish a school 'for 12 poor children of the Parish of Camberwell'[28] which often led to these children playing many of the female roles in the plays of the time.

Next to Paris Garden is The Mad Hatter, a Fuller's pub. The note on the gold gold-framed door reads 'Behind this typical nineteenth century facade is an up-to-date hotel'. This is the inverse of Rimbaud's poetry which hits us as searingly modern, though absolutely rooted in Victorian issues. Rimbaud wouldn't have been able to afford to dine here: the price of a fish and chip sandwich deranges the rational mind.

The gargoyle overlooking the street – is it Pan or Poseidon? – stares stone-eyed downwards. Forget the fin-de-siecle flavour of these streets – the oversized oil lanterns, the quaint names – there is a CCTV ball hovering above the word *Paris*. As I take a photograph a security man with a cigarette dangling from his mouth asks if I'm okay – 'Just looking at the gargoyles,' I say. 'Ah,' he responds, 'I thought you were lost.' London is a city that refuses to let the wilfully lost remain so; the prevailing logic is to pull those who've fallen off the edges of the map back in to the recognised configuration.

I walk past him, following the underground river into Hatfields.

HATFIELDS

The Neckinger, according to Bolton, goes over Stamford Street then under the defunct chapel and into Hatfields. In the past I've had some success in detecting London's underground rivers by listening for them. The Peck in Peckham Rye gutters out from a rusted grille at the southern edge of the park. The Effra pours into the Thames at Vauxhall. The Fleet, beneath Blackfriars Bridge, unexpectedly whispers from the ground – I heard it one night along the outskirts of Middle Temple. Now it's the turn of the Neckinger: I lie down in the middle of the road and put my ear to the metal covers. Nothing. A milky liquid is trapped in the outside metal patterning. A London cab bolts towards me with its orange light blazing, oblivious to the silent waterway I'm listening for. I stand up, just in time.

Before following Bolton's map of the river down Hatfields I walk past the gargoyles to explore the outside of the massive Dorset House. HM Revenue & Customs. A filthily sellotaped A4 sheet in a plastic wallet says that, as of 30 June 2014, all HMRC Enquiry Centres have been 'replaced by a new service of specialist help over the phone, supported by a mobile team of advisers for customers who need extra help. This service will be accessed through our normal telephone help lines.' The super-verb 'help' refuses to say if this is human help or automated. Then there's the implicit guilt projected through the word 'extra'. The use of the word 'normal'

becomes an emollient for enforced change. Change as fait accompli – language as the cog that puts it into action. Real lived needs lost to the liquid words.

I follow back under the surveillance camera to Hatfields. A trio of Italianesque scooters – one in pink – are elegantly parked in the 'solo motorvehicles bay'. Curtis's Botanical Gardens was set up between here and Cornwall Road in 1779 by botanist William Curtis. Curtis reported that the marshy land was perfect for growing aquatic plants. Hats replaced plants. Hatfields was named after the industries who made linings for hats in the nineteenth century. Bowlers replacing Jacobean stockings. Elegance replacing function. Headpiece replacing codpiece. Here is order, on the edge of the Bear-pit.

The street would have been lined with milliners who dried the skins in their local hat-making workshops. There are tennis courts here now on which an intense game of doubles is taking place. A man hits the ball too far and shouts 'Damn it'. Then the woman he's playing serves with a fierce grunt. Downtime detox.

On a dank rainy October morning the Victorian past feels very contemporary. Hatfields is a curious assemblage these days: the train clatters above what is now a hybridised housing, business and commuter thoroughfare. Cyclists enjoy this quiet slip road that takes them away from the bottleneck of Blackfriars Road, overtaking people walking with a brolly in one hand and a phone in the other. The commercial sense of venture has gone and I can't help wondering if the deli here – pumping out the rising fumes of fresh bread – does much business. This is a throughway for those in the know, beyond the supermarket highway of The Cut.

The aesthetic of Hatfields fails to live up to its functional use. People do their best: potted trees have been arranged to cover silver grilles. This is a different kind of concrete than the Brutalist achievements along the river. Build to sell. Office space equipped with kitchenettes. Pigeons teeter on outside ledges, either dead or asleep. A man wearing what seems to be a Thunderbirds' suit pulls on the levers of an elevator that's yet to be reached by electricity.

I stop at Hatfields Green which marks the old parish boundary between the two boroughs, Lambeth and Southwark. A section of the green is now caged off to conceal the five-a-side pitches. The eight pitches are booked out from morning to dark for competing teams of beer-bellied men between the ages of twenty and fifty who arrive wearing yellow bibs and baggy shorts. A ball flies over the cage – I walk over the muddied green to retrieve it for the watching men, who stand waiting with hands on hips. I throw it back over.

Outside of a closed café kegs are left balancing. Loading bays are piled high with empty boxes, refuting the overlord of the restrictive signage. Max tonnes. Stop. No. Axel load. Marshland replaced with sheer material function. I walk with my phone held high trying to take a photo of the land of clattering nothings – and slip on a wet leaf. That'll teach me to try and write a book about the South Bank while the real people are passing through to their places of work.

There's a clue to the function of the next building: OLO HOSTEL. A British Telecom site on the verge of Rimbaud's London lodgings – it makes sense for the future of communications to land here. When Rimbaud lived nearby there was a particularly notorious group of tenements called the Haunted Houses which may have looked like these Victorian remains opposite the BT site here.[29] A newsagent hatched into the base of the buildings. Two women are walking alongside me: 'Screw it,' she says, 'I'm leaving'.

The river's route goes under and across Roupell Street. The Victorian misery pervades the air here but the housing fetishism of London dominates Roupell Street. As Jerry White writes in *London in the Twentieth Century: A City and its People* this is 'the gentrified nucleus of Roupell Street' where 'the redevelopment of Coin Street produced more of a wealthy middle-class enclave than the revived working class community that GLC purchase of the site for housing in the 1970s had ostensibly promised.'[30] Dozens of raincoated walkers emerge from Waterloo Station, striding with open umbrellas past some of the most elegant Georgian Terraces in London. I once heard that Marc Almond lived here. For me this is the road of the King's Arms pub, one of the loveliest traditional pubs on the South Bank. Midweek suits and feverish poets rub shoulders. I once came here in the afternoon and found the poet Simon Smith at a table with a pint, a Latin dictionary and a notebook – working on his Catullus translations. I pulled up a chair and bought a drink. Then another poet we knew turned up, on his way shopping: I shouted him from the door and he joined us. The afternoon pint turned into a session, the glossololia of the drink flexing the language until late in the evening.

On the left, as you approach The Cut, is Isabella Street, an enclave of hidden restaurants and bars, hidden behind an urban garden of potted plants which fight it out amongst themselves for the little light that filters through the railway arch from the Southwark sky. There's a Greek restaurant here, occupying two of the tunnels, and Jack's Bar. I once sat in the beer garden of Jack's and left a fake fifty pound note on the ground as a social experiment to measure the manners of the leisure-seeking middle classes.

There are none.

DAHN THE CUT

The Cut was built across meadows known as Wild Marsh in the 1820s as part of the urbanisation that drained the area. When The Cut was first built it was known as The New Cut – John Holingshead describes it in *Ragged London* as not differing much from Shoreditch, or Chapel Street, Somers Town, and it may be shortly described as a succession of groves. There are groves of stiff cheap clothing, groves of hardware, groves of flabbylooking meat, groves of boots, and groves of haberdashery; with the stalls of costermongers, filled with fish and vegetables, lining the gutters. There are plenty of gin-shops and a few cheap bakers, and at one corner stands the Victoria Theatre, formerly called the Coburg.[31]

Henry Mayhew wrote about The Cut in *London Labour and the London Poor*. He described the costermongers and street sellers that the market here was known for. Here he describes the scene on a Saturday night, just after the working classes had been paid their wages:

The street sellers are to be seen in the greatest numbers at the London street markets on a Saturday night. Here, and in the shops immediately adjoining, the working-classes generally purchase their Sunday's dinner; and after pay-time on Saturday night, or early on Sunday morning, the crowd in the New-cut, and the Brill in particular, is almost impassable. Indeed, the scene in these parts has more of the character of a fair than a market. There are hundreds of stalls, and every stall has its one or two lights; either it is illuminated by the intense white light of the new self-generating gas-lamp, or else it is brightened up by the red smoky flame of the oldfashioned grease lamp. One man shows off his yellow haddock with a candle stuck in a bundle of firewood; his neighbour makes a candlestick of a huge turnip, and the tallow gutters over its sides; whilst the boy shouting "Eight a penny, stunning pears!" has rolled his dip in a thick coat of brown paper, that flares away with the candle. Some stalls are crimson with the fire shining through the holes beneath the baked chestnut stove; others have handsome octohedral lamps, while a few have a candle shining through a sieve: these, with the sparkling ground-glass globes of the tea-dealers' shops, and the butchers' gaslights streaming and fluttering in the wind, like flags of flame, pour forth such a flood of light, that at a distance the atmosphere immediately above the spot is as lurid as if the street were on fire.[32]

I've been buying fruit from the charming Polish seller on the corner of Blackfriars Road, by Southwark Station, for years – he might be the last of the old street vendors here. On a Friday morning you can get a bowl of fruit for a pound. Next to him is a kiosk selling drinks, granolas and cigarettes. This is a long way from the open air fish vendors of Mayhew's day. Gwen Southgate in *Coin Street Chronicles* describes how The Cut in the 1930s was still animated with its markets over fifty years on from its Victorian height – though significantly the 'New' in The New Cut had by then been lost:

The Cut, a bustling, colourful street market close to Waterloo Station. We did most of our shopping there, not far from the stores that lined both sides of the street – they were too expensive – but far from the 'barrer boys'. Along each curb their hand-pushed barrows were piled high with fruit, vegetables, fish, saucepans, clothing, bolts of fabric and even dead-eyed rabbits and chickens – very dead, but not skinned and plucked. The barrow boys were cheeky Cockneys, yelling come-and-buy messages that proclaimed the superior quality and value-for-money of their goods in a raucous stream-of-consciousness flow that continued even while serving a customer … Unlike today's supermarkets, customers 'dahn The Cut' didn't get to handpick the produce, and woe betide the unwary shopper who didn't keep a sharp watch to make sure no over-ripe plums or damaged potatoes found their way into her shopping bag … My favourites were the fish barrows. I loved the vinegary smell of ready-to-eat winkles, cockles, and mussels and was entranced by the colours and intricately whorled shells of the big whelks. But best of all were the live eels that squirmed, shiny, lithe, and black, in a deep tray just below my eye-level.[33]

At the time of writing there is a war of express supermarkets. Sainsbury's Local were first here and for years the only commercial grocers on The Cut (as well as occupying the only supermarket position facing the station on Waterloo Road). Then Tescos opened one next door to The Ring pub. Then M&S appeared – with deep baize branding – on Waterloo Road, welcoming its shoppers with buckets of fresh flowers. Any sense of the distinct local London life has been removed from The Cut – you have to walk a few hundred yards down to Lower Marsh to find it.

Now The Cut has its Michelin Star standard gastropub in The Anchor and Hope. There is also the Young Vic theatre with its foyer café – which is also good for a drink – and the Old Vic at the Waterloo Road end. The Pit Bar beneath the Old Vic is the best late night place to get a drink in the area. On a cold night ask for a bourbon and ginger wine – then get your chequebook out. My good friend, the poet Simon Barraclough, introduced me to it: one of the many fine introductions I owe him for.

I'm not heading down that far today. I look again at Bolton's map of the Neckinger towards Short Street, crossing in front of the Young Vic. I walk past the Bookshop Theatre here – or Calder's Bookshop as it will always be known to me and thousands of others. In the early 2000s I went to a number of poetry readings here. A decade later I also saw John Calder – Beckett's most important publisher – put on an event here in which he helped to perform readings from some of Beckett's overlooked texts. I look in the bargain books outside: everything from Heidegger to Isherwood. I've often come here of an evening to pick up a Beckett and I always go for the classic Calder editions – no fuss, thick paper, sturdy covers – rather than the Faber reprints. I've often taken the new book – *Watt*, *Murphy* or *Molloy* – on the bus to Dulwich and read it in the garden of the Clockhouse pub overlooking Peckham Rye. With one eye on the book and the other on the lookout for Blake's angels.

On a weekday morning like this, commuters clatter between Blackfriars Bridge and Waterloo Road. A man on a moped drives one-handed whilst taking a call on his mobile. As he drives past – weaving between two motorbikes – a red 'L' plate shines from the box on the back of his bike. London: city of the irreverent underdog. Besuited cyclists ride with silver bikes that fold away small enough to fit into their pockets – each commute is a Sisyphean task of pedalling. A mild headwind becomes a monsoon.

DRINKING WITH PEPYS ON WEBBER STREET

As well as frequenting the Bear-pit here Pepys wrote in his diary that he made use of 'the old house' on Lambeth Marsh to plan a meeting with a Mrs Lane:

> ...and away to Westminster Hall, and there sight of Mrs Lane, and plotted with her to go over to the old house in Lambeth Marsh, and there eat and drank, and had my pleasure with her twice, she being the strangest woman in talk of love to her husband sometimes, and sometimes again she do not care for him, and yet willing enough to allow me a liberty of doing what I would with her. So spending 5s or 6s upon her, I could do what I would, and after an hours stay and more, back again and set her ashore again.
>
> (25th July 1664)[34]

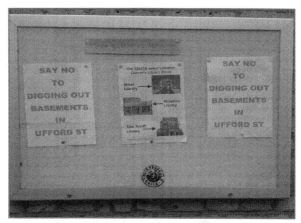

Pepys also drank at a pub on Webber Street, towards which the Neckinger is pulling me now.

I turn on to Short Street, just before the Sainsbury's, and walk past the English Touring Theatre and the pretty latte-coloured terraces that are hidden away here. I walk past Mitre Road and the flats which look tiny but are huge inside – I know a poet who lives in one of them. On the outside wall of some flats here is a notice board that says 'no to digging out basements in Ufford Street'. Red text alert. I look into it online and find a clarifying petition:

> Ufford Street consists of 28 1901 Beautiful Terraced Cottages situated in a Conservation Area. The property concerned is a bedroom Cottage. The buyer needs 3 bedrooms and an Artist Studio. These Cottages were built on what was Marshland and was the original site of the Botanical Gardens. If this was allowed to go ahead it would impact strongly on the adjacent properties and no one knows what the effect would be.[35]

Ufford Street appears as a fairy tale landscape. Arts and Crafts cottages. The estate here was completed in 1902, replacing the slums that were here before. The issue being raised on the notice board is a very local one which seems to be based around the anxiety of living above marshland. Someone is moving in to one of the cottages and they want to dig downward to create a further room; the person behind the petition believes this could have repercussions and send them all sinking further down into the mud. This is credible given that the Neckinger runs along this street, and perhaps it's this echo – this vague worry of not knowing 'what the effect would be' – that drives the petition? Residents go to bed only to be swept downwards by a marshy tide. It's impossible to forget that you live on silt. This isn't the first time that there has been a dispute around the housing on Ufford Street. These properties were sold off in the 1990s despite the locals protesting at Lambeth Palace. The link with the palace is written into the name of the road itself: Ufford was the Archbishop-elect of Canterbury before he died in 1349. Facing the houses here is open space – a children's play area made of wood with a single silver slide in the middle.

I walk to the end of Ufford Street, where it joins Webber Street, and follow the route of the river. You're never far from a pub on the South Bank and Webber Street has a good one in the Stage Door. There's a rooftop garden for warmer weather and a pool table for when it's cold. This is the rebuilt version of the Half-the-Way Inn that Pepys visited with Sir W. Warren on Saturday 5th August 1665 where – like today – he had walked through the rain 'and there I eat a piece of boiled beef and he and I talked over several businesses, among others our design upon the mast docke, which I hope to compass and get 2 or 300l. by.'[36]

A friend once pointed out the disparity between the apartments on both sides of Gray Street which is on the southern side of The Old Vic. They later wrote a piece of prose quoting me as saying 'Why would you live in the good one when you can live in the shit one and get a better view?' It is a testament to the quality of the beer in The Stage Door that I can't remember saying this. I follow the route of the Neckinger over Waterloo Road and into Morley Street. The river, according to Bolton, flows underneath the apartments of

Coopers Close, a tight-packed residential estate where the tenants punch in digits to access the gates, against the backdrop of a stained grey and corrugated mid-century building. This was the site of MI6 from 1966 until 1995.[37] After MI6 moved towards its current site at Vauxhall there was found to be 'a powerful chemical disintegrator' for destroying documents in the building here. This is what happened before shredders. They also found a document which showed that they had access to a private tunnel into Lambeth North tube.[38]

The Neckinger route brings me out at Morley College. St George's Church – like the Houses of Parliament – was built by the architect Augustus Pugin, although this was significantly rebuilt following the Blitz. As was Morley College which was initially set up for the education of working class men and women in the late nineteenth century. I love the gold letters over the door with its classic modernist typeface. Morley College is far from a relic: its current galleries are free and their evening courses ranging from letterpress and book-binding to zoology, massage and millinery are open to all. The college's education centre is further along the road here, on King Edward Walk. I look closely at the brick walls of the building: it is bomb-pocked with black holes. A wooden door carries faded letters which read: KEEP LOCKED WHEN NOT IN USE. A *Costa* cup has been left in a metal hatch in the wall. The evidence of the war that led to the freedoms of the next century's luxuries. There's a runic stone in the ground here and five wooden pillars. At the end, before Lambeth Road, is the Wellington Mills estate. This was once the site of a blacking factory and before that, the Lambeth Asylum for Girls. The river has brought me out where the mad were brought for remedial attention: like a giant aquamarine crocus, Bedlam dominates the landscape.

BACK TO BEDLAM:
THE IMPERIAL WAR MUSEUM

The underground river has brought us here: to the ghosts of the incarcerated insane. The Imperial War Museum now occupies what was the third site of the infamous Bethlehem (or Bethlam – from which the word Bedlam derives) Hospital. The current museum is the actual asylum building. The hospital moved to St George's Fields in 1815 and was – at the time – the modern incarnation of the now outmoded asylum (just as the Moorfields building had

been before when it moved from Bishopsgate in 1673).[39] The hospital had already achieved notoriety through its Moorfields era due to the public being allowed to pay to witness the patients: 'as if to point out that lunacy is undignified and absurd, the inmates were on display like so many wild beasts in a zoo; they were ravening creatures that had to be manacled or tied.'[40] The price of admission was a penny. In the fifteenth century some inmates were allowed to pay the 'madman's pound' and leave Bedlam – which was located with symbolic fittingness in Bishopsgate just outside the walls of the City of London – but had to wear a tin badge on their left arm to signify their association with the institution. It was also seen as symbolic by many Jacobean playwrights that London was home to the only mental institute on in the country: it has been harder to stay sane – but more easy to hide it – in London.[41]

During Bedlam's period on the South Bank staff were employed as 'Bethlem Watchers' and were paid to watch the patients during the night, ensuring that they didn't commit suicide.[42] Moving Bethlem here didn't put an end to the leering crowds and prison-like treatments and the case was reported of one patient being held in chains here for fourteen years.[43]

If you walk through any crowded part of London today and look around you'll be witnessing scores of mentally ill people. The population of London in 2013 was 8,400,200 which – given the accepted rate that one in four suffer mental illness in their lives – indicates that a quarter of these people, 2,100,050, will experience mental ill health.[44] London needs its mental institutions the way a desert needs its oases. It's good news for everyone that these places of refuge are no longer open for public baiting although the Elizabethan bear-baiting approach to the mentally ill could well be seen as continuing into the modern era through the media. To be a celebrity and vulnerable is to be the bear that is whipped and cajoled.

The grounds of the old hospital are in what is now known as Geraldine Mary Harmsworth Park. The land was bought by Lord Rothermere who gave it to the London County Council on the basis that it would be used as a park – in return he asked for it to be named after his mother.[45] These open grounds of old Bedlam now include a Tibetan Peace Garden, a World Garden, a Soviet Memorial, an outdoor gym, a sports court, a café and a children's playroom. There's also an Ice Age Tree Trail which includes dozens of tress which are native to Britain. Those that the Ice Age killed off now thrive, including a Strawberry Tree and a Wych Elm. Hooded figures pace with their dogs, walking the stress off.

Looking at the pale green dome of the museum you have to remind yourself that this massive structure is standing upon drained marshland. A gargantuan asparagus tip in a waterlogged soup. For centuries this land was seen as unusable for anything and although everything might now seem solid here – cobbled walkways and crisp fallen leaves – I remind myself that I'm also following the underground river which flows around the outskirts of this imperious structure. The wind is strong today and the children's play park is empty: the swings, like pendulums, move by themselves.

A tree sculpture emerges from the open field. A gold-brown twist of carved wood with a ball at the top. 'The artist Morganico has been commissioned to sculpt the dead London plane tree' the explanatory text tells me. In front of the museum are two massive grey naval guns – with upstanding yellow shells – pointing towards St George's Road. A section of the Berlin Wall says CHANGE YOUR LIFE.

Standing at the North Entrance is the best place to sense what it would have been like to have been incarcerated here as a patient. The huge rectangular windows suggest the distant rational world which was closed off to the patients. Beneath that is the imperious oak door of no return. Higher up are smaller windows – those of minimal light – where I imagine that the work of assessing the patients was done. The building itself seems to work with the same hidden complexities as the human mind.

The Greek majesty of the columns and Doric arch give a classical gravitas to the enterprise although – as with a lot of London architecture – there are mixed influences here. The crocus-leaf dome has a hint of Babylonia about it. What would the nineteenth century patients have made of that dome? It casts a panopticonic eye across the grounds. I stand here feeling watched by the ghosts of the mad – the watched who were prevented from having such a clear view out. There's a balcony across the top which would have been well out of access for the suffering. I walk through the grounds, past a dog agility course that has been carefully constructed with ramps and hoops – designed to push canine prowess to the maximum. Humpty Dumpty is painted on the wall in the children's area. A climbing frame is webbed and ready for action.

I walk towards the West Entrance, past the Imperial Café. Through the wet mist is the outline of a Parisian-style street kiosk shifting cups of PG Tips to shadowy figures. Even the design of the kiosk is domed. The walkways of the garden flow in a circuitous route as if the reality of lost minds has been reproduced through the landscape. Walking as process – in circles – around and around. I turn back to the building. What would have been blocked to light in the days of the asylum is now made to look inviting: tall glass windows show the café inside with cakes piled on towering plates and a fridge of chilled *Sanpellegrinos*. Above the café some of the windows have been filled-in with bricks.

The galleries are open from 10am every day. It's a relief to find that you can access the building without having to walk through the epic opening arch. I'm first here: a jovial woman checks my bag, which just happens to be a khaki satchel that I bought from the army store on The Cut. I walk down a lengthy amber corridor looking for the main foyer. Another throwback to the purgatory of lost minds. And what the corridor opens out into is, indeed, a reminder of a different kind of madness: a life-sized Spitfire is wired to the roof. A Mark V tank with a wooden battering ram strapped to its side is perched on the fringes. Were these things really invented? A huge rocket aims towards the roof, its internal wires exposed. A kayak with what looks like a gun underneath. An undeclared missile. If there's a way to kill, it's been invented and is on display here.

It's worth visiting just to see Walter Bayes' artwork *The Underworld*: a huge panel canvas which shows civilians in World War One sheltering in the Elephant & Castle tube. That caption tells me that 300,000 Londoners went down into the underground to escape bombs in the war – twice the number who descended to the tube during the Blitz. This might have been the only occasions in history that Elephant & Castle has been sought as a place of sanctuary.

It is to Elephant & Castle that the Neckinger will be taking me next – both Bolton and Chivers agree on the route of the river from here: it's written into the name of Brook Drive. The infamous seventeenth century Dog and Duck was based here, which offered restoratives from its spas. The 'laxative springs' it boasted were – after it was closed at the end of the eighteenth century – declared unsafe: marshland fluids are not a way to restore the human body. I follow the gentle curve of the Georgian terraces along Brook Drive. Even the offshoot roads here carry echoes of the once visible river: Castlebrook Close. *New apartments.* We're said to be getting

bigger as a species – leaving Tudor hatches and Stuart cottages behind – but the houses being built here for ordinary habitation don't indicate that. It's perfectly conceivable to work an entire lifetime to clear the mortgage on an urban pad that is no bigger than a Wendy House.

A bin wagon pulls alongside me smelling – curiously – of fresh pastries. The road pulls me forward with its hypnotically cloned bay terraces windows – each finding relief in floral stucco. All that Pugin was against: a layer of decor without the substance. It seems plausible to live a quiet life here – birds singing above – which is impossible to believe given that I'm on the edge of one of London's most notorious and dangerous roundabouts at Elephant & Castle.

The ever-present building cranes have switched from red to green here. I think of Rimbaud again and his poem 'Voyelles' in which he says that the letter 'I' is red, and 'U' is green: these mechanical structures spell out the opposite. Numerous cranes carrying the ever-present luminescent men are writing 'I's in the sky as if with gargantuan crayons.

The birdsong ends. The road ahead is rammed with trucks and lorries heading to the pinched knot of the Elephant. The crush to leave the city comes to a bottleneck here: desperation, anxiety, purgatory. I walk past Dante Road to where the semi-circle of the London Eye is visible again.

I come out at St Mary's Churchyard, the parish church which was demolished for road widening in 1877. This was one of the old city churchyards, now revamped as a leisure emporium for the

nouveau-commuter. Thomas Middleton, the Jacobean playwright described by T.S. Eliot as 'one of the more voluminous, and one of the best, dramatic writers of his time' was buried in St Mary's on July 4 1627.[46] He lived in Newington Butts – as Elephant & Castle was then known – and St Mary's was his local church. It seems right, looking at the architectural confusion of today's Elephant, that Middleton was one of the few playwrights to achieve equal success in both tragedy and comedy.

Middleton collaborated wildly, including with Rowley on *The Changeling* and with Dekker on *The Roaring Girl*. If Eliot is right that Middleton's greatness 'is not that of a peculiar personality ... He remains merely a name, a voice, the author of certain plays, which are all of them great plays'[47] then it's also true that the Elephant sweeps across the living and dead here regardless of the strength of personality: the mercurial Middleton is wiped from the face of the area as easily as the bombastic and filibustering Charles Spurgeon. Middleton might well have approved of a book like this: from 1620, until his death seven years later, he was an official Chronologer of the City of London.[48] Ben Jonson, who Middleton had opposed in the War of the Theatres, succeeded him in this role. Today we have Iain Sinclair – a voice all the more necessary for not being authorised.

London silenced Middleton. It has been mooted that he was banned for writing for the theatre again after the Spanish Embassy took umbrage against his satirical play *A Game of Chess*. The fact that he could be banned from writing for the theatre and still become an official Chronologer of the City shows how powerful a medium the theatre was at this time. Most of the people who saw plays couldn't read them.

I walk out onto the grass that remains above the churchyard and see a sign for Elephant Park: 'an inspiring place to call home'. I find myself at the base of the red crane that's appeared at the back of every photo I've taken for months. This will soon be *Elephant 1*. These developments are increasingly being given names of numerical grandeur redolent of space missions. Blast off into déjà vu.

Am I imagining the tang of pondwater just before the Metropolitan Tabernacle? We've reached the tangled knot of the Devil's Neckcloth, where the Neckinger prepares to swing back on itself towards the Thames: as if catching sight of the Elephant – and the new developments – the river's instinct is to rush back towards the rutty bank of the Thames. Southwark Council's investments are generated towards *allowing* for investment. If you sat out the wilderness years here and made a home of it then it's time to hold up your hands – the wind of change is coming. Take refuge in knowing that any séance spirit will come down on your side. Council workers use a Ghostbusters-style machine to blow dry leaves from the path of the park. I notice a text written on the outside wall of the leisure centre – a huge Modernist 'A' standing alone in a window. Acceleration? Addiction? Aftertaste? The new properties are coming to cleanse the sourced waters of this ancient thoroughfare. Property and leisure: the new gods.

ELEPHANT & CASTLE

The roundabout is a carousel that enforces dizziness without you needing to move. At last they're filling-in the hobbits' network of subways – the ones my wife was scared to walk through at night when she worked in the student bar at London College of Communication at the start of the century. Urban trenches glossed with mosaics. I know someone who – at some point in the nineties – took acid with a friend and got trapped in the subway network. They spent the night looking for a way out, following a leading light back to the north before arriving at the same corner for the hundredth time. The Elephant exists in a perpetual catatonic Groundhog Day.

Like the Bethlem Hospital the system could be a manifestation of the lost mind. Today the island in the middle of the roundabout shimmers like the coral that shipwrecked swimmers head for: the sharks of taxis and buses clamping for their heels. At the centre of the island is a square diamond – the Faraday Memorial – that strobes at night with the vampyric reflections of vehicular headlights.

Elephant & Castle isn't ashamed to state the obvious: its name is written in the red ceramic elephant with a tiny grey castle on its back which hovers before the shopping centre. At the same time the place is completely unknowable. The parts of the shopping complex that haven't been lacquered with lick of paint for decades have turned the colour of nicotine: the whole complex is like an experimental pub ashtray. I think of the scene in *Jurassic Park* where the T-rex looks into a locked car. Which way out from the past we've humanly engineered? Drivers must sense this in the accusing wing-mirrors they glance at before speeding into one of the chicanes that shoot like electrical charges from Faraday's Cage.

This isn't a place for meandering. Charlie Chaplin – born nearby in 1889 – had to move to America to develop the walking stick stroll he became known for. His name lives on in Charlie Chaplin's pub which is always open for late night drinks. The pool table couldn't double as a bed: the balls are never off its back. The doorman is a dog – an Alsatian – playing bouncer as the real doorman snogs a woman in a corner.

When I saw The Fall play at The Coronet – a venue which exists as the cracked plastic egg at the centre of the Elephant lucky bag – lead singer Mark E. Smith walked on stage saying: 'Say goodbye to architecture'. You can see what he means. Smaller businesses have been pushed to the outskirts of the Tescos which dominates the area like the lodestone at the centre of the toad's forehead. Parallax is pushed towards expressionism: your eye drifts from an outdoor stall selling rugs, out across the road to the Metropolitan Tabernacle – built in the Greek style – where 'The Boy Preacher' Charles Haddon Spurgeon held audiences in their tens of thousands captive for hours.[49]

I walk past an abandoned bike, with no wheels, which has been locked to a rail. Yellow crosses have been painted onto a brick wall. An electricity box at foot level has had its cover removed. Neon flashing above closed shops. Tags from squatter graffiti-artists: BETTER SQUAT THAN LET HOMES ROT. London's sprawling language banquet is reduced to a stock here: noodle bars and buffet restaurants. The always present builders – the luminescent men – walk the artificial bombsite they've constructed: transient overlords. At least until the contract is delivered on.

London developments are endless. Projects are underfunded, forgotten, then re-imagined in a different form by graduate planners. In front of me now I can see that the three lane roundabout has been downscaled to just two – cones signal the fact in red and yellow swirls. For once, the late night commuters and the drivers agree: they all want to kill each other. Stress becomes a universal language.

The Heygate Estate – once home to 3,000 people – is no more; demolished, it remains under wraps: detritus to the wind. The bin bags above the remains are held down by car tyres which appear like rubber rings in a pool of tarmac. Alongside the tube a new build towers between two off-gold columns. The old Elephant & Castle pub has long closed down too, its faux-Rococo lettering is peeling away, serif-by-serif. The single syllable PHANT remains, as if longing for a lost OM to complete it.

The Metropolitan Tabernacle is now a baptist church. Along the hidden course of the Neckinger water is offered as the source of renewal. Dunk, start again. Alongside it, a man in a forklift sweeps grey clay over some ornate tubes, newly laid, and the vinyl in the window behind reads: *The Future Generations of the Creative Industries*. We can't forget the source that we're above – the river that's brought us here. And rivers, like roundabouts, can bring you back to where you started. With the tunnels now gone the walker is diverted through the dug-up earth towards the only remaining memory of the last five decades: The Michael Faraday Memorial. The diamond in the toolbox. A stainless steel hard drive, facing all four directions at once. A compacted skyscraper. Inside is an electrical substation for the Northern and Bakerloo lines. It was built by artist Rodney Gordon and has been here since 1961, invacuating all white noise into its cubic force field. At night it flicks to neon: a disco theme with a spectrum of colours twisting behind its hologrammatic windshields. Each square incarcerates a

headlight. This is a true memorial: Faraday as the young local apprentice who came from nowhere to put his name on the map. Like Chaplin before him. The memorial seems to invite its own erasure but is so rooted in the psyche of London as to be immovable. Just like Elephant & Castle itself.

Notes

1. Redriffe was an historical name for Rotherhithe. I am indebted to William Rendle & Philip Norman, *The Inns of Old Southwark And Their Associations*, Op.cit.
2. Tom Bolton, *London's Lost Rivers*, Op.cit.
3. www.gardenbridge.london
4. Edward Walford, *Old and New London: Volume 6*, Op.cit.
5. Gwen Southgate gives a colourful account of what it was like to live in this area in the interwar years in her book *Coin Street Chronicles*, Op.cit.
6. Tom Bolton, *London's Lost Rivers*, Op.cit.
7. Graham Robb, *Rimbaud*, Op.cit.
8. Verlaine had left his wife and child to elope with Rimbaud to London in September 1872 where they had lived with no money, renting in Bloomsbury and Camden Town. After a return to Paris for Christmas, they had returned to London with a flourish but after Rimbaud had laughed at the way he walked down the street towards their Camden Town apartment carrying a bag of kippers, an incident involving a knife had taken place. In Brussels in June 1873, Verlaine shot Rimbaud in the wrist and was arrested. They met for the last time in 1875 after Verlaine had been released from prison and had converted to Catholicism.
9. Graham Robb, *Rimbaud*, Op.cit.
10. Edmund White, *Rimbaud: The Double Life of a Rebel*, Op.cit.
11. Arthur Rimbaud, *Complete Works, Selected Letters*, translated by Wallace Fowlie Op.cit.
12. The mis-spelling of Stamford is true to Nouveau's original letter. Quoted in Charles Chadwick, *Rimbaud*, Op.cit.
13. The six bridges that I've covered in this book would have been just four at that time – thought the two men would have went well beyond the parameters of today's South Bank.
14. George Bataille, *Blue of Noon*, Op.cit.
15. 'Cities II' in Arthur Rimbaud, *Complete Works, Selected Letters*, Op.cit.
16. John Stow, *A Survey of London Written in the Year 1598* Op.cit.
17. Ibid
18. Henry Benjamin Wheatley. *London, Past and Present: Its History, Associations, and Traditions*. 3 Volumes, Op.cit.
19. Samuel Pepys, *Diary of Samuel Pepys – Complete Edition*, Op.cit.
20. Ibid
21. Ibid
22. Poem quoted at http://www.british-history.ac.uk/survey-london/vol22/pp66-77
23. Walter Thornbury and Edward Walford, *Old and New London: Volume 6*, Op.cit.
24. J. Payne Collier *Memoirs of Edward Alleyn, Founder of Dulwich College: including some new particulars respecting Shakespeare, Ben Jonson, Massinger, Marston, Dekker & c*, Op.cit.
25. Ibid

26. Ibid

27. See The Thirsty Bear website at www.thethirstybear.com

28. J. Payne Collier *Memoirs of Edward Alleyn, Founder of Dulwich College: including some new particulars respecting Shakespeare, Ben Jonson, Massinger, Marston, Dekker & c*, Op.cit.

29. Graham Robb, *Rimbaud*, Op.cit.

30. Jerry White, *London in the Twentieth Century: A City and its People* Op.cit.

31. John Hollingshead, *Ragged London in 1861*, Op.cit.

32. Henry Mayhew, *London Labour and the London Poor*, Op.cit.

33. Gwen Southgate, *Coin Street Chronicles*, Op.cit.

34. Samuel Pepys, *Diary of Samuel Pepys – Complete Edition* Op.cit.

35. https://www.change.org/p/lambeth-council-say-no-to-digging-out-basements-in-ufford-street?source_location=petition_footer&algorithm=promoted&grid_position=4

36. Samuel Pepys, *Diary of Samuel Pepys – Complete Edition*, Op.cit.

37. 'Walk This Way South Bank: London Eye to the Imperial War Museum' http://www.southbanklondon.com/walkthisway/TheGuides.html and http://www.british-history.ac.uk/survey-london/vol23/pp77-78

38. Tom Bolton, *London's Lost Rivers*, Op.cit.

39. Indebted to Peter *Ackroyd's London: The Biography*, Op.cit.

40. Ibid.

41. Ibid.

42. Simon Winchester, *The Surgeon of Crowthorne: A Tale of Murder, Madness and the Oxford English Dictionary*, Op.cit.

43. Peter Ackroyd, *London: The Biography*, Op.cit.

44. *London Mental Health: The Invisible Costs of Mental Ill Health*. Available online as a PDF, with an introduction by Boris Johnson, here: https://www.london.gov.uk/sites/default/files/Mental%20health%20report.pdf]

45. Tom Bolton, *London's Lost Rivers*, Op.cit.

46. 'Thomas Middleton' in *For Lancelot Andrews: Essays on Style and Order*, Op.cit.

47. Ibid.

48. Elizabeth Cook's introduction to *The Roaring Girl*, Op.cit.

49. Tom Bolton, *London's Lost Rivers*, Op.cit.

Liquid City is not Paris
       the suburbs
     are not for flâneurs
its lights flicker fin de siècle
          when least expected
   then clasp to blackness
like collapsing hindwings
      lit red by sulphur
Liquid City mudlarks the remains of middle managers
  in the Thames
detects them by SIM cards
   then checks them in at airports
     they raise their arms
   in flight simulacrum
the city that made them discharges them
       memories stick like fog
to the hoardings of conferences centres
   air lifts them above the river
      like bonfire men in prayers
  raises them   raises them
    until all that is left is the soles of their shoes
 and a lost tie   a strung vowel
     noosed at low tide
  to a boat's gallows

NORTH

VIEWPOINT:
BLACKFRIARS BRIDGE

The pavement across Blackfriars Bridge is wide and expansive: there is none of the Hungerford Bridge bottlenecking here. Along the bridge there are a number of stone enclaves with concrete benches inside them, sentry positions from which you can switch from the stream of moving bodies into the position of silent voyeur. The railings are Lilliputian in size, a trip hazard for anyone over six foot who's just left one of the pubs on the South Bank or Fleet Street. They are carved beautifully on both sides in a red and white Baroque design: in appearance at least, Blackfriars Bridge – first built in 1760 is the most regal of all of the South Bank's bridges.

There's only one view left from here now, which is to the west. The narrowing Thames pulls the eye to the stone-skimming arches of Waterloo Bridge. The new Blackfriars Bridge station has blocked the view east – but does at least give us another view back, as a developer – or government official – would argue, when disembarking or boarding a train on that bridge. Over the top of the razor blade slats of the station the Tate, the Shard, The Walkie-Talkie (20 Fenchurch Street) and – further east – the brick cone pustule of St Paul's can be seen. Standing on the east side of the bridge gives you the best chance of seeing the outfall of the Fleet under the station bridge – though the tide has to be low and the light favourable. Tom Bolton details how to find the best platforms for this in *London's Lost Rivers*. For me, the Fleet is a river to be listened to. You can hear it in a hole cover at Ludgate Circus which leads down into the fourteen foot relief tunnels that now contain the flows of the Fleet inside Bazalgette's complex sewerage system. I've heard it further west, on the outskirt of Middle Temple. The sound rises up in a charged susurration which invites you to lower your body towards this centuries-old flow.

When I'm here I can't help thinking of my wife's trips to work at Tate Modern – pregnant, with my son, Pavel, growing inside her – listening to Rammstein while crossing from north to south. Pav has yet to develop a taste for German Neue Deutsche Härte music. She spoke to him on the bridge as she walked, her voice and the distinct rhythms of the music contributing to his early formations – and the person he's become.

The new Blackfriars Station runs adjacent to the bridge. This is the only bridge in London that you can disembark a train on. At night it is a Gamer's paradise: as if you're inside the working processors of the city, the fly-green flex of the matrix. On an early evening in winter when the whole of the north side is flanked with chequered office lights it's tempting to think of those miles of office spaces as filled with secretaries, admin assistants, managers. But the majority leave, vacating office space and repopulate the city, joining into joggers' groups or merging into the huddle under the heater-grilles of beer gardens. And then there are those clattering into the stations at speed, heading towards suburban homes. Remaining night workers ghost office space.

These people and the ones streaming past me now are – in the context of London's history – motes on the windscreen of the city's history. On the north bank here the remains of a Roman barge has been found containing ragstone from quarries in Kent – the same stone that has been found in the walls at Tower Hill.[1] The Romans didn't claim this land through flowery offerings and – despite the refined railings of this bridge – Blackfriars has been associated with violence throughout its history. During the Gordon Riots of 1780 around 40,000 people gathered at St George's Circus to protest the Catholic Relief Act and attempted to destroy the tollbooth at Blackfriars – before going on to attack any Catholic property that stood before them.[2] In 1982 Italian banker Roberto Calvi was discovered swinging from a scaffold under Blackfriars Bridge with

$15,000 in three different currencies in his pockets. He had shaved off his moustache. The events are murky: the Vatican, it was discovered, had paid $224 million to 120 creditors in 'recognition of moral involvement'.[3] Leopold Bloom, the main character in James Joyce's *Ulysses*, associates this area with violence – even from as far away as Dublin:

> Desperadoes who had next to nothing to live on to be abroad waylaying and generally terrorising peaceable pedestrians by placing a pistol at their head in some secluded spot outside the city proper, famished loiterers of the Thames embankment category they might be hanging about there or simply marauders ready to decamp with whatever boodle they could in one feel swoop at a moment's notice, your money or your life, leaving you there to point a moral, gagged and garrotted.[4]

Samuel Pepys writes about the bridge during another of his diversions from his official duties, which always led him southwards to the liberties of this area. Monday 15 June 1665 was a day of mixed domestic and professional events, in which Peyps drinks too much, takes the frustration out on his son and rues the absence of his wife:

> Thence by barge with my Lord to Blackfriars, where we landed and I thence walked home, where vexed to find my boy (whom I boxed at his coming for it) and Will abroad, though he was but upon Tower Hill a very little while. My head akeing with the healths I was forced to drink to-day I sent for the barber, and he having done, I up to my wife's closett, and there played on my viallin a good while, and without supper anon to bed, sad for want of my wife, whom I love with all my heart, though of late she has given me some troubled thoughts.[5]

The first Blackfriars Bridge was opened in 1769 and served as a popular route into Paris Garden and the emerging cheaper properties along Blackfriars Road. The marshy fields joined up the other major centres north of the river. Ackroyd talks of the building of Blackfriars Bridge as marking 'the real development of south London'.[6]

Blackfriars Bridge is a distinctive landmark; the draining of the Fleet here marks a feature in the city's natural – and culverted landscape – that has long been written into poetry and lore. John Stow described the Fleet as 'goeth by London walls, betwixt Friars

prechers Church and Ludgate.'[7] The King's Fleet Prison was built on the banks of The Fleet in 1155 next to the The Blackfriars – a monastery for Dominicans.[8] By the time the Fleet was being built over in the 1760s it had become a sewer. In fact, as Stephen Inwood points out, complaints about the smell had begun as early as 1290 when 'local residents were beginning to complain about the stench of sewerage, rubbish and butcher's waste in the Fleet, which overpowered the smell of the Whitefriars incense'.[9] This use of London's waterways as sluice precedes The Great Stink of the Thames by 650 years. At this point it was known as the Fleet Ditch: a floating sewer. Yet it remains as part of London mythology through the fascination people have had with the city's underground rivers. The Fleet is the best known and most celebrated of all these hidden rivers, running from the eastern boundary of Roman London along its five mile route from Hampstead – under King's Cross – and down through Farringdon and Holborn to empty into the river here, beneath Blackfriars Bridge.

Shakespeare lived for a while at Blackfriars before moving to Southwark: a movement that is traced by thousands of commuters each day. He bought a gatehouse just a few yards from the Blackfriars Theatre and his King's Men acted there from the winter of 1608.[11] Although Shakespeare glossed over much of the factual presence of London in his plays it is fascinating to think about how much that presence – the always changing light, the noise, the rush of the Thames – might have influenced the storm in *The Tempest* or the sea change in *Hamlet*. The Thames can't be ignored by any writer, and Shakespeare was no exception: it alters mood and impacts on all attempts at creative invention.

In more contemporary times, the poet Jeremy Reed – who I collaborated with on a collection of poems called *Whitehall Jackals* – has written a poem about the Fleet. Throughout the collaboration Jeremy was very much focused on his milieu of Soho, Charing Cross Road and Seven Dials, while I covered the neglected banks on both sides of the river including Wapping, Bermondsey and Rotherhithe. However, it was the Fleet that inspired Jeremy to write his poem of the same title in which he associates the underground flow of the river beneath him with the pubs in which he'd meet friends for drinks:

> to feel its drive into the underground,
> but it's not clear where water starts,
> unlike a road, it's shoplifting impulse
> traffics into a dark gritty corridor.
> We stand above it as we talk,
>
> a disturbed system of tunnels and tubes,
> aquifers, islanded from the rain,
> and I can feel the drop under my feet
> into the Fleet pit, as I buy a round
> and feel the fourth or fifth light up my brain.

Underground rivers might threaten to pull us down but they also light up the imagination: poets are the semaphorists of its presence.

Walking northwards the bridge rises – slowly – to the central apex of its hump, before it descends again on the north bank towards

Ludgate. The north side claims its rightful people as they gather speed before arriving at Unilever House. While walking on the bridge you can feel most yourself, historical – in flight – but the north bank levels that feeling out as the bridge is reduced to land and coliseums of corporate banks.

Today I walk along the north bank heading east towards Waterloo Bridge, looking at the South Bank from distance. From here the buildings on the South Bank can be seen for the anachronistic hotchpotch that they make – Sea Container's House, the Mondrian Hotel – appear as out-dated ideas of the future rehashed for maximum corporate potential. The Oxo Tower stands like a modernist one word poem. Then comes the quiet absence of the beach and Bernie Spain Gardens before the cultural monoliths – London Studios, IBM, the National Theatre – dominate the view. Browngrey fly towers and stone balconies stretch as far south as the eye can see, concealing the old view of the Surrey Hills.

VIEWPOINT:
WATERLOO BRIDGE

Waterloo Bridge was the bridge used to cross the river by William Blake, from his house on Hercules Road towards the lure of his birthplace in Soho and the further city. Whenever he walked too far north, he said, he always ended up feeling ill for days.[12] Fountain Court on The Strand was the place of his last home before he died in 1827. From there he had a view of the Thames from the end of the street and – beyond that – Lambeth, where he'd spent the happiest decade of his life.

The bridge was designed by Giles Gilbert Scott, an architect that connects my current cities of occupation – London and Liverpool – through two of my favourite buildings: Liverpool's Anglican Cathedral and Battersea Power Station. Both make epic claims on the skyline.

Due to Waterloo Bridge being positioned on a bend in the river it is from here that you get some of the best views of London in both directions. This is the throughway for buses heading south, the 59 to Brixton, 171 to Catford, the 176 to Penge (one of the few London places to have its name rooted in the Celtic – hence its peculiar, slightly vulgar look and sound). Looking eastwards, St Paul's is an off-white yellow bulb set against the spluttering red

neons of the City and the Isle of Dogs. Historically, all pulls northwards. Waterloo Bridge was actually called Strand Bridge until the victory at the battle of Waterloo when it was given its current name. Along with the Millennium Bridge it is the only bridge on the South Bank not to be named after its location.

In 1832 the physicist Michael Faraday conducted an experiment using Waterloo Bridge.[13] He used a wire that traversed the river to observe the electricity generated by the river's motion through the Earth's magnetic field. I know this from working with the artist Rick Myers on his exhibition for The Poetry Library called *Faraday's Synaptic Gap*.[14] The exhibition was in two halves: one part in The Poetry Library and the other in the foyer of the art library at the Courtauld Institute. Myers's audio piece – to be listened to whilst walking across Waterloo Bridge – connected the two locations. Working with the US-based Myers on this exhibition gave me one of those moments of satisfaction as Poetry Librarian – one of those moments when I knew I was in the right job. Rick asked me to send him some Thames water at the same point in time at which he had sent me a white noise machine from the States: both passed each other as they crossed the Atlantic. It takes four and a half minutes to walk across the bridge at a leisurely pace. I timed it for Rick's audio piece: a fractured, beautifully layered and anachronistic assemblage of facts and perspectives of Faraday's experiment and the bridge itself:

Waterloo Bridge was situated about 60 feet west of Somerset House on the north bank, and about 90 feet west of the Waterman's stairs at Cuper's Bridge on the South Bank ... On January the 12th, 1832, Faraday conducted an experiment where he suspended a 960 foot length of copper wire from the toll house on The Strand side, over six arches, to the sixth pier ... Faraday hoped to observe the electricity generated, as the river flowed, between east and west, across the Earth's magnetic field ... Despite rigorous checks for other causes for the unpredictable deflections his results were still inconclusive. He asked the watermen about sewage contaminants near the shores but they assured him otherwise. Faraday noted the turbidity of the river and the bad weather during the days of the experiment.[15]

All of human life is here. It's like being inside the hydra-head of London with all personality threads vocalising their presence at once. Business colleagues talk about recent audits as an accelerating jogger flies past; a 100 year old woman ploughs into a headwind on a silver zimmer. Somerset House, which can be accessed via Waterloo Bridge, once held the records for all of the births, deaths and marriages in the UK. We pace the river in our personal mythologies of historicalness – stressed, in conversation or dreaming – forgetting that we're also a tick on the vast swathes of data captured for census.

The bridge's physical appearance of *lightness* – which comes from the elegance of the nine arches which appear in the form of a perfectly skimmed stone – conceals the bridge's history of murder and suicide. As Chris Roberts points out in *Cross River Traffic: A History of London's Bridges*, looking at the bridge from distance gives the impression that the passing people and cars are floating.[16] But in the nineteenth century bodies descended to their end here without the hope of flight: Waterloo Bridge was known as a site for suicides. By 1840 one fifth of London's suicides were from here – an average of 40 a year.[17] As the bridge with the most open views in both directions I'm intrigued by the tension between very personal defeat and public spectacle: the last workings of exhausted consciousnesses spurning themselves to enter the statistical body. Dickens wrote in 1860:

The river had an awful look, the buildings on the banks were muffled in black shrouds, and the reflected limbos seemed to originate deep in the water, as if the spectres of suicides were

holding them to show where they went down. The wild moon and
clouds were as restless as an evil conscience in a tumbled bed, and
the very shadow of the immensity of London seemed to lie
oppressively upon the river.[18]

'Black shrouds': the exact same image that Rimbaud used in his
poem 'After the Flood' (quoted earlier). Around the same time that
Dickens wrote this a heap of human remains was found in a carpet
bag. A witness described a 'person in female attire' lowering the bag
from the bridge. Thomas Hood wrote his poem 'The Bridge of
Sighs' about a woman hurling herself from the bridge; the short four,
five, six and seven syllable lines – and alternating end-rhymes –
suggest the unfeeling drag and pull of the tide:

> The bleak wind of March
> Made her tremble and shiver;
> But not the dark arch,
> Or the black flowing river:
> Mad from life's history,
> Glad to death's mystery,
>   Swift to be hurl'd –
> Anywhere, anywhere
>   Out of the world!
>
> In she plunged boldly –
> No matter how coldly
>   The rough river ran –
> Over the brink of it,
> Picture it – think of it,
>   Dissolute Man!
> Lave in it, drink of it,
>   Then, if you can!
>
> Take her up tenderly,
>   Lift her with care;
> Fashion'd so slenderly,
>   Young, and so fair![19]

More recent deaths have occurred here. For years the BBC ran
its World Service from Bush House on the Aldwych, on the north
side of the bridge. In 1978 Georgi Markov, a worker for the service
– who was also a Bulgarian dissident – was crossing the bridge to

the south and felt a sharp stab in his calf. He turned to see a man with an umbrella and bowler hat walking away from him. After Markov died a few days later it was found that his calf had been punctured with a platinum pellet of ricin. The KGB had sent their assassin dressed as a businessman – parodying the properness of the English to get to Markov.

As this suggests, this isn't a bridge without politics. There's a famous photograph of Herbert Morrison, leader of the London County Council between 1934 and 1940, pulling a slab of granite from John Rennie's old Waterloo Bridge – surrounded by the press – to make way for the new bridge. If the bridge that followed is synonymous with modern London this could largely be attributed to Morrison, who – according to Stephen Inwood – 'was an urban administrator of exceptional energy and ability'.[20] At the same time this Government introduced a Green Belt policy though which the London County Council encouraged – and subsidised – the other London boroughs to create open spaces.

Alberto de Lacerda in his poem 'Waterloo' suggests that the bridge offers 'enchantment'. Waterloo Bridge is not a structure built to get you somewhere but is the experience in itself. The north side of the bridge is built-in to the riverside court of Somerset House and its forecourts and cafés. If you continue walking straight ahead you arrive directly onto The Strand and the once notorious – now gentrified – Covent Garden. If you stand on the bridge on the north side and look west, the sudden bend in the river before Westminster gives the illusion that the Houses of Parliament could easily be on the South Bank. Trains draw slowly into Charing Cross. The London Eye, from side on, leads like a ladder to nowhere.

Enchantment is here – at least for those walking to the South Bank. Then you get that feeling of pushing against the northern walkers, knowing you're heading the right way, to the right place: walking away from the city's secularisation and bureaucracy. The enchantment of experience and excess. As you get closer to the South Bank, the angles and edges of the Queen Elizabeth Hall and Hayward Gallery dominate the view. Light and shadow defines how you see it – that angle, in this light, just once: for you. As you walk down the steps alongside the National Theatre a tiny mosaic is set into the bridge: a swallow on a tiled blue background. On a day of clean sharp light there is a feeling of having arrived on the concrete set of a spaghetti western. People stand taking photographs of what looks like nothing – walls, space, light.

A collective documentation of simply being here.

VIEWPOINT:
HUNGERFORD BRIDGE

The current Hungerford Bridge makes no sense. In fact, there are *three* bridges here, albeit closely aligned. There is the railway line into Charing Cross – crosshatched with steel girders – and, on either side of that, two footbridges. The one furthest west is called the Jubilee Bridge and was built in 2005. From the two footbridges there are tremendous views in both directions – you just can't see them both from either bridge. If you're on a train, on the middle bridge, you experience the world in a series of quick shutter-like flashes through the blurred grilles of steel girders.

When walking around the base of the Hungerford Bridges on the South Bank side you experience an anachronistic London time-freeze: the new steel has been built upwards from Brunel's original stone base. The modern rises from unshakeable Victoriana. Apparently Brunel – late in his life – was upset when he heard that the version of the bridge he had built was going to be torn down.[21] Now his ghost is encased in the statue of him, on Albert Embankment, near to the Walkabout pub. Sitting duck for traffic cone hats and communal ankle urination. In reality Brunel's spirit is more likely to be here on the south side. Two miles eastwards, at Rotherhithe, you can visit the Brunel Museum and the entrance to the pedestrian tunnel under the river.

Looking over the rail of the bridge down to the tide-stained and

moss-flanked embankment wall you can sense the old industrial South Bank. You can smell it in the calcified tide – awash with Victorian claypipes and banked ephemera. Ooze and grunge. What else can we expect from the bridge which brought the poète maudits Verlaine and Rimbaud from Paris in 1872? For a moment I'm back with the rambling poets, thinking of how they would have landed at Charing Cross, straight into the markets and bric-a-brac stalls which can still be found here, on the entry to the backend of the station from the bridge. Scarves and handmade jewellery can be bought – if you can linger long enough around the tang of urination to browse the stalls.

Charing Cross station is becoming a cloned parody of all London stations, the same stalls replicate themselves: *Boots*, *M&S*, *WH Smith*, *Costa Coffee*, *Caffe Nero*. There are pubs here, but only use them if you haven't got time to explore the Coal Hole and the Lyceum on The Strand – both Victorian pubs with a range of beers.[22] There's also Gordon's Wine Bar on Villiers Terrace, at the bottom of the narrow, slowly rising hill that meets Embankment Station. You walk down a narrow staircase to a candle-lit pit smelling of candles and tannins. It's a favourite haunt for leaving dos in the area, though if you're in a group of more than four it can be a squeeze. In summer, chairs are lined along Embankment Gardens for al fresco drinking under the stars. Opposite Gordons is the *Holland & Barrett* where I tried to wrestle a rising depression with St John's Wort. It was like fire-fighting lava with a water pistol.

I walk back along Hungerford Bridge, to the South Bank. A

troupe of around forty teenage Germans are walking towards me –
it's good news that this bridge is twice the width of the old one, the
one that was here when I was getting to know the area in 2002. When
rushing to work from the tube there was no space to pass the human
traffic. That bridge was a temporary structure, a bailey bridge (built
by the military) which had passed its use until a new one was needed
to allow the visiting hordes to cross the river to the south.

There have been other things I've found out too, about this
bridge. In 1999 two young men were beaten-up by a gang and
thrown into the river. One of them, Timothy Baxter, died. His
mother, Linda Baxter, has published a collection of poetry called
Losing Timo which tells the story of that evening and candidly
simmers in the rage that she felt over losing her son.[23] Poetry as
catharsis. In 2004 there was a homophobic attack on the South
Bank side, a man beaten by another man, just after midnight. The
darker associations that the Victorians had with Waterloo Bridge
have – in recent times – leapt across to Hungerford Bridge. It's my
least favourite of the South Bank's six bridges. Dark forces may well
have entered during its years of disrepair, following the 1951
Festival site's abandonment. The bridge was ill-kempt, untreated
and puddle-soaked. It is also possible that, as this part of the South
Bank has become positively re-energised, that the problematic era
for Hungerford Bridge has come to a close. I can believe that when
looking out across the Thames towards St Paul's and seeing the
Southbank Centre's colours and vibrancy across the acres of

riverside here. If this is the case – and the hex of bridges works logically – then Westminster Bridge is in for darker years.

VIEWPOINT:
WESTMINSTER BRIDGE

'Earth' – Wordsworth wrote – 'has not any thing to shew more fair'.[24] Most of the original watermen's stairs might be gone along the Albert Embankment here but Westminster Bridge was built with the wherrymen in mind: twin flights of stairs meet each other at the base of the bridge, on the south side. A slim pipe emerges from the mossy wall. These stairs are closed off from the public now: when the powerful authorise a practice it's already dead. A graffiti artist has made it to impossible heights to spray the word BAGS across the bricks.

There's a steady current heading east along the river this morning, towards Oxford. Cigarette cartons, crisp packets and broken branches from the recent winds all float along it. A Wat Tyler of detritus ready to land at Gloucester Head. A steady trickle of people and joggers are moving over the bridge in both directions. Unlike the wide Blackfriars Bridge – with its emporiums of stone platforms – there is nowhere here to sit and take a view. During a peak midweek morning like this you're forced to move at the same pace as everyone else.

Big Ben looms over the bridge, a parody if its own celebrity status. How can you truly see fresh – as if the first time – what you've seen so many times? Architecturally it doesn't disappoint. The huge clock face of Big Ben – or Elizabeth Tower as it's properly called (Big Ben is the name for the bell) – symbolises the bridge's commuting function. London won't wait. 'You want to say you did something in your life, right?' it seems to ask. A cyclist flies past with a camera attached to his helmet, tracking his journey straight to digital. I photograph the tourist photographers who are memorialising the memories before they've happened. Big Ben starts to ding: *Do, do, do*.

I walk around the Houses of Parliament towards Lambeth Bridge. The Paris attacks were a week ago, November 2015. Two machine-gun-ready officers, wearing all black, stroll through the grounds here. Numerous pairs of Bobbies have been paired along the main gates like rotten pineapples bobbing in sticky waters. A young woman – text-firing into a pink phone – apologises for walking into me. I overhear one of the policemen telling another what his wife does for a living. Can't stop. A singular policeman sits alone in a black box, arms folded, facing Westminster Abbey and the sleeping poets. But this is no time for the poets to sleep. The policemen hold back the crowds until the last of the black cavalcade of cars have passed through. Under the arch of the Horse Guards is the crosshatched silk of old spider webs: they've been building through decades of debate and can only be seen in certain light. I ran past here the day that Batman climbed onto the roof of the

houses as a 'Fathers 4 Justice' stunt. A bloated crow on a turreted gingerbread. For ten years the political activist Brian Haw was camped on Parliament Square in protest against US and UK foreign policy. His army sunhat was so wildly laminated with badges that it began to take on the look of an army helmet: KEEP MY MUSLIM NEIGHBOURS SAFE, one of them read. He sat, often hand-on-bearded-chin, staring into space. A knot of confused outrage at the bridge of his nose, staring at the statue of Cromwell: another unlikely outsider to take up residence here. The initial suggestion to have a Cromwell statue was debated in Parliament in the mid-nineteenth century and has had opponents in the house as recently as 2004, when a group of Members of Parliament (including Labour MP, Tony Banks) suggested that it should be reduced by fire to its component parts. The converse has happened and the statue was refurbished for the 350th anniversary of Cromwell's death, in 2008. He stands left leg forward in the classic boxer's position – with a bible in one hand and a sword in another. A black lion positioned on the plinth beneath his feet.

VIEWPOINT:
LAMBETH BRIDGE

At the base of Lambeth Bridge, down beneath the embankment wall, is a shingle-strewn beach. A short stretch of sand disappears under the fast ripples of tide. A juvenile seagull cocks the ground

like a Teddy Boy at the plaza. Pigeons rove in pecking packs. An ancient landing stage for boats sits firm in the mud. Under the bridge there is a black heap of sludge and broken stones, at the base of an old pier. A siren can be heard ringing from somewhere on the South Bank. When viewing from here there is no wonder that the powerful and influential have so easily transformed the south side of the river to *other* throughout its history.

Visually Lambeth Bridge is the punk's bridge: it is pitted along its flanks with pink and black anti-vandal spikes. It has the feel of a DIY bridge. At either end there are pillars decorated with pineapples, ostensibly symbols of welcome though with an echo of the fruits gained through imperialism. Forget any sense of a people's bridge: this was built by the powerful, providing essential connection from north to south and allowing the rich to further expand through the new routes and possibilities of the South Bank's previously castigated land. It is functional and incredibly simple: five skimmed arches. Like Blackfriars Bridge and Westminster Bridge the rails are made of wood, though these are slightly higher here – perhaps to give some protection to ambling politicians, flushed with post debating-chamber intoxicants. The gothic lights along here are still in place along the edges, the electrics caged in wind-protecting glass. Black spikes have been placed at the bottom of the lampposts which gives the view a clear sense of precaution – as if medieval punishments await those who err. As I walk across a man stands looking out east: his whole life in his bag. He walks north across the bridge as a National Express coach runs alongside him. City of exits and entrances, endless departures.

VIEWPOINT:
VAUXHALL BRIDGE

Vauxhall Bridge marks the site of London's most ancient crossing. In 1998 a series of 3500-year old oak posts were found here – the remains of a bridge – not far from where the Effra empties into the river. The Thames was much wider then and, as Chris Roberts suggests, the bridge might have led to an island in the middle of the river.[25] The feeling of being watched doesn't pass here and knowing how far back in time people have lived here adds to that feeling. Across the river from here is the former Millbank Penitentiary, now Tate Britain. It was originally planned to be constructed around Jeremy Bentham's Panopticon principle but was eventually structured in the shape of an asterisk: six fronds extending from a central chapel. Black rose of the Thames. It's not just the South Bank that has been built upon marshland: the early attempts at building the prison were met with the problem of subsidence, until a concrete raft was devised to give a secure foundation. These are the mulchy foundations that modern British art rests upon.

Millbank Prison faced across to Vauxhall Gardens where hot air balloons were to be seen floating up from the marshy land and the Turkish Tent was a draw. In 1844 Mister Barry – a clown from Astley's Ampitheatre hated by Blake – sailed from Vauxhall to Westminster Bridge in a washtub towed by geese. A huge crowd gathered to watch. This is what people did in the days before Netflix.

On both sides of the bridge are a series of bronze statues of women representing both the trades and educational industries. I associate Vauxhall with one of London's most lively gay scenes which centres around the Royal Vauxhall Tavern: London's oldest surviving gay venue and also a listed building. This was originally a Victorian music hall, built on the old pleasure gardens, which has since become a place of gossip, legend and avant-garde performance. I've been here to see my younger brother perform his music on many occasions, most often as part of a Duckie evening. I can remember sobering up enough one night to see the next act emerge: a group of men – or women – wearing gasmasks and leather boots, wading out onto a smoke-filled stage. Morrissey wrote one of his best albums – *Vauxhall and I* – inspired by the area and the comedian Cleo Rocos recently claimed that she visited here in the late 1980s with Freddie Mercury, Kenny Everett and Princess Diana who was dressed a man: 'When we walked in ... we felt she was obviously Princess Diana and would be discovered at any minute. But people just seemed to blank her. She sort of disappeared. But she loved it.'[26]

Chris Roberts writes that 'Vauxhall carries on its tradition of hedonism into the twenty-first century, with more nightclubs in the area than just about anywhere else in London.'[27] In Craig Taylor's book *Londoners* there is a first person account from a dominatrix whose office is not far from Vauxhall Station: 'everybody has a sub and a dom side', she says, then tells us that London is 'one of the kinkier cities in the world. I don't know why. It has more fetish clubs, more mistresses, the biggest fetish clubs ... I can go to the Oxo Tower in rubber for lunch, as I did on my thirtieth birthday – a rubber blouse, a rubber corset and high boots ... There's a complete mix of people here so if you see something weird and outrageous, well ... it's just London.'[28] It is right that when I went to such lengths of depravity for *L'Umo Vogue* that it was here, between the old prison and pleasure gardens, at the site of an ancient civilisation.

If you want a quieter drink then look across the river to the Morpeth Arms on the north bank, just next to Chelsea College. This is a Young's pub which has a quaint Victorian parlour room, originally built for the prison warders from the penitentiary next door. It has a large round bar at the centre – which makes it hard not to be sociable. I spoke to a barmaid here once who told me this was the only pub between MI5 and MI6. There'll be no trouble here then, I said.

Notes

1. W.R. Dalzell, *The History of London*, Op.cit.
2. Lindsey German & John Rees, *A People's History of London*, Op.cit.
3. https://en.wikipedia.org/wiki/Roberto_Calvi
4. James Joyce, *Ulysses*, Op.cit.
5. Samuel Pepys, *Diary of Samuel Pepys – Complete Edition*, Op.cit.
6. Peter Ackroyd, *London: The Biography*, Op.cit.
7. John Stow, *A Survey of London Written in the Year 1598*, Op.cit.
8. Ibid.
9. Stephen Inwood, *A History of London*, Op.cit.
10. Tom Bolton, *London's Lost Rivers*, Op.cit.
11. Stephen Porter, *Shakespeare's London: Everyday Life in London 1580-1616*, Op.cit.
12. Iain Sinclair, *Blake's London: The Topographic Sublime*, Op.cit.
13. This was the previous bridge by John Rennie, which was built in 1817.
14. The correct title for the audio piece is *Fa ra day's sy nap tic gap – for headphones and Waterloo Bridge*. At the time of writing there is a book relating to the exhibition in development which I am planning to write something for – that will be called *Fa ra day's sy nap tic gap*.
15. Rick Myers, *Fa ra day's Sy nap tic Gap – for headphones and Waterloo Bridge*, Op.cit.
16. Chris Roberts, *Cross River Traffic: A History of London's Bridges*, Op.cit.
17. Ibid.
18. Charles Dickens, *The Uncommercial Traveller*, Op.cit.
19. Thomas Hood, *Selected Poems*, Op.cit.
20. Stephen Inwood, *A History of London*, Op.cit.
21. Chris Roberts, *Cross River Traffic: A History of London's Bridges*, Op.cit.

22. The Lyceum has the advantage of being a Sam Smiths pub, but the Coal Hole has real pies on its side.

23. Linda Baxter, *Losing Timo,* Aberystwyth, Honno, 2004

24. William Wordsworth, 'Composed upon Westminster Bridge, September 3, 1802' in *The Collected Poems of William Wordsworth*, Op.cit.

25. Chris Roberts, *Cross River Traffic: A History of London's Bridges*, Op.cit.

26. http://www.telegraph.co.uk/news/newstopics/diana/9963557/Freddie-Mercury-smuggled-Princess-Diana-into-gay-bar-disguised-as-a-man.html

27. Chris Roberts, *Cross River Traffic: A History of London's Bridges*, Op.cit.

28. Craig Taylor, *Londoners: The Days and Nights of London Now – As Told by Those Who Love It, Hate It, Live It, Left It and Long for It*, Op.cit.

Build it round to keep the devil out
    Liquid City says
        smooth those corners
  Diablo likes keyholes   cellars   converted lofts
 especially those pocked with Blitz spittle
        the acne of history
    pocket the cheque and fold it in the top pocket
  like a watermarked tissue
        the coins that keep the dawnlight out
  toss them to the footmen
    like nickel that bungs the sand of time
and drips in sheets of rain
        in this   thy cistern   my citizens
    the devil will be flushed
    then the day is back with its arsenal of tickboxes
  an aubade of quick questionnaires
      who would write graffiti   Liquid City asks
  when you can put it on Twitter?
 This day that began in orange
       ends in black
nothing in between but the blocks you walk
   the eternal mudflats
      and those eyes you love
that stop you from sinking

BEYOND

APOLLINAIRE'S STOCKWELL

I'm standing outside the house of Apollinaire's first love, Annie Playden, on the road he later immortalised in his poem 'The Emigrant of Landor Road'. It's a half hour walk from Vauxhall Bridge, along South Lambeth Road. Whilst trekking my way through this contested area of south London I've been thinking about Apollinaire's origins: his mother was Polish and unknown father apocryphally Swiss-Italian. This area has historically become home to many immigrants. I walk past the tube station where the Brazilian Jean Charles de Menezes was mistakenly shot dead by police two weeks after the London bombings of July 2005. One bullet in his shoulder, seven in the head.

The eateries along South Lambeth Road and Stockwell Road bare their flags: Portugese, Spanish, African, Italian and English: *Three Lions Cafe, Full English Breakfast, £4.95*. Apollinaire visited Annie Playden here twice.[1] Playden was a Victorian middle-class South London girl who he'd met in Germany two years before and proposed to on a clifftop. Sensing Apollinaire's passion and waywardness she no doubt considered the drop before giving a direct answer. On his London visits Apollinaire stayed with his Albanian friend Faik beg Konica; first visit in Islington and then, when he returned, in Chingford. The distance between south London and the north would have been an awkward one to travel. I went to college in Highbury & Islington and experienced how the tube plunders northwards through excavated earth decreasingly punctuated by stations. There is a note in Apollinaire's notebook of the time, detailing the directions across London and the cost of the underground fare:

Retour a' Angel
Tube en face passé
Demander Clapham Road
4d^2

Modern developments were kind to Apollinaire the commuter – the one available branch of the City & South London Railway (now the Northern Line, Bank branch) connected him to where he needed to be: to the woman he was adamant to woo. When Apollinaire was in love there was no sense that he would ever fail in his quest. One of the few things he said about Annie – that isn't in the two poems he wrote of the experience ('Song of the Poorly Loved', as well as 'The Emigrant of Landor Road') – was that she had 'great tits & a behind'.[3] In 1962 an Apollinaire obsessive tracked down the still-living Annie to interview her[4]; he had met her once before in 1951 – the year Lambeth was celebrating The Festival of Britain and the Royal Festival Hall was being built anew by immigrants. When told about it, Playden was astonished to hear that that she'd been captured in some of the century's most enduring poems, confessing that, at the time of knowing Apollinaire, her family lived in fear of him: 'One night he rang our bell late: I didn't want to open the door, but my mother said if we didn't he might break it down. We lived in constant fear of his fits of rage.'[5] The poet was desperate – the poet who once described himself as a 'creature of whim' – and had written a letter from Paris not long before in a state of agitation: 'I'm afraid of being cuckolded and am miserable. Console me!'

I walk past The First World War cenotaph – a modernist slab spattered with huge painted poppies – and read the lines from Laurence Binyon's 'For the Fallen': 'At the going down of the sun and in the morning / We will remember them.' Violette Szabo – a French-born English Special Operations Executive agent during the Second World War – has her own shrine. She was also in the Stockwell line of immigrants: her French mother had met her father, a London cab-driver, during the The Great War. She was influential as a code-breaker before being tortured and killed by the Nazis.

An old woman in front of me tumbles on a raised stone flag and hits the floor outside the tube stop, her silver stick rolling towards the road. In seconds there are six or seven of us are helping her up. 'I should get my daughter to help with these bags' she says. I walk past the tube stop and a stall selling flat caps.

I arrive on Landor Road. Annie's family lived at 75 which has

now become 75b due to a flat conversion. The door is a brazen
bright red. Annie said of Apollinaire, fifty-seven years later, 'He was
extraordinary in London, too, on both times he came.' One day he
bought her a hat; on another he brought a feather boa. A buddleia
bush reaches over the wall of number 75 and settles on a wheelie
bin. Along the pavements – decomposing in the June heat – are bin
bags oozing with the sweetly-sick treacle of emptied super-strength
lager cans. Opposite is a pub called The Landor. This could be the
ghost-structure of the pub where Apollinaire wrote about seeing a
'hoodlum' whom he mistook for Annie:

> One night in London mist and flame
> A corner boy who looked like my
> Lover came up and asked my name
> But what I saw in that one's eye
> Made me lower mine in shame

('Song of the Poorly Loved')[6]

This is the strength of a desire that has forgotten its fixation with a
specific source. There is the nagging regret – and shame – of one
who has stood for far too long in the same place, chasing shadows.
Blushes in the dark are wasted on everyone.

Across from number 75 is the Italia Conti, an Academy of
Theatre Arts which was founded in 1911. Here is a link to
Apollinaire's Swiss-Italian father and the internationalism of the
area. Between his two visits to London, in Paris, Apollinaire had

been visiting *La Descent* soirees at St Michel and had mocked the Symbolist heritage of the venue's forebears. I walk past the Post Office Bakery (*London's first organic bakery*) and find a sewing shop called SEW OVER IT. I look again at the poems in front of me. Part of Apollinaire's making new – and strange and modern – in 'The Emigrant of Landor Road' is his lurid picture of a tailor's shop. In the poem the tailor has taken the heads off the mannequins and left them half-naked.[7] A symbol of the shunted lover. The rage felt by one who stands for hours outside a red door that remains locked.

I stand a little longer, sensing the hopelessness of a man whose hands have been described as tiger's paws and whose jaw – in photographs – juts with pride and forthrightness. His limbs, in photographs, are heavy in a tight-fitting suit. He would have walked up the eight stairs to the door of the woman he came from Paris to win. His knuckles rapped, repeatedly, on the door. Accepting defeat would not have come easily.

Playden, in 1961, remembers seeing him off on the occasion of his first visit: 'I remember Kostro waving goodbye to me at the station ... Was it Waterloo? Victoria? He was half inside, half outside the window.'[8] Apollinaire was known for being half inside and half outside many things: as a painter amongst the poets, the coiner of the term Surrealism and the inventor of the Calligramme – there would be many more passions that would occupy him fully. When excitable his mind could easily see danger as erotic – as he would when writing a poem that describes a flare, seen from a First World War trench, as a 'pretty redhead'. He was always between 'order and adventure'. Shortly after his visit to London he would meet Picasso and influence the artist to take a new approach to his work, capturing the fleeting modernity of the city through paint. He would alter poetry forever with the writing of *Alcools* and *Calligrammes*. But despite all this, Apollinaire always maintained that he was badly loved in London.

NIGHTWALKING WITH DICKENS

'Some years ago, a temporary inability to sleep, referable to a distressing impression, caused me to walk about the streets all night, for a series of several nights.' So begins Charles Dickens essay 'Night Walks', an essay written for his column as 'The Uncommercial Traveller' in the early 1860s.[9] I start my walk –

following his route – in the converse state to his description of
sleeplessness, at the end of a long day and evening's work, in the last
hour or so before sleep. The day's work done, the evening passed:
I've been waiting for the pubs to close to start my walk. Only then
does London change, when most of the people with homes have
vacated. The city is taken over with the homeless and the diaspora
of transient inhabitants. When the real cold comes in – on a
November night like this – and something close to silence begins.
As close to silence as London ever gets.

At this time of night the streets are beyond surreal. I see what
Matthew Beaumont means now when he says 'The nighttime is
another city'.[10] Not enough has been said about Dickens the
Surrealist: the creator of ghostly palimpsest Paul Dombey,
puppeteer of the ultra-industrial backdrop of the city, the man who
made one of his characters spontaneously combust.[11] Dickens made
his nightwalk in March, I'm here nine months – and over 150 years
– later. The hands of the clock are the same: half-past twelve.
Dickens invented a word for those still out at this time: 'houseless'.
This is a kind of temporary homelessness of a body outside the
confines – and safety – of four walls. Despite the end-of-the-day
tiredness, all my senses – the rods and cones at the back of my eyes
– are fox-sharp. My nerves hooked to the movement of each shadow.
    I remind myself what a new phenomenon this is: to be able to
walk at night without suspicion of arrest. 'Who walks alone in the
streets at night? The sad, the mad, the bad. The lost, the lonely. The

hypomanic, the catatonic. The sleepless, the homeless. All the city's internal exiles.'[12] This is Matthew Beaumont again. His book tells us that in the late Middle Ages nightwalkers were knows as 'noctavigators'. Wanderers without purpose: stragglers. In Elizabethan England there was a curfew on being outside the confines of the City after 9pm in summer and at dusk during winter. But this is historical. These days one in eight of people in the UK work nights – we've become used to the flux of human traffic after dark.[13] Though it always feels different to be out in it yourself, alone. The old social unconscious is hard to shake off.

Dickens made the distinction between walking 'straight on end to a definite goal at a round pace' and that which is 'objectless, loitering, and purely vagabond'.[14] I realise that – if stopped for questioning – I would form the latter. To say 'I'm writing a book' is a very different – and less plausible – reason, than saying: 'I'm heading to my shift at St Thomas' hospital'. Though I wouldn't be the first writer for whom the act of writing has landed them in casualty.

In his essay 'Poor Mercantile Jack' Dickens takes us on a journey through the docklands of Liverpool – also at night – and despite being accompanied by police officers it's not the city's poor inhabitants that receives his satire, but the law. The four officers he walks with are lampooned as 'Mr Superintendent', 'Trampfoot', 'Quickest' and 'Sharpeye'. Despite the police officers attempts to look down on the black residents, Dickens sees things his own way and writes about them with affection. Trampfoot is keen to show Dickens 'Dark Jack':

> But we had not yet looked, Mr Superintendent – said Trampfoot, receiving us in the street with military salute – for Dark Jack. True, Trampfoot. Ring the wonderful stick, rub the wonderful lantern, and cause the spirits of the stick and lantern to convey us to darkness.[15]

There's a scathing spittle of satire against Trampfoot's attempt to conjure a genie here. And what Dickens concludes – after being taken to a dance and drinking several lemonades there – is that 'If I were Light Jack, I should be very slow to interfere oppressively with Dark Jack, for, whenever I have had to do with him I have found him a simple and a gentle fellow.'[16]

These are the 'midnight streets' where Blake heard 'the youthful harlots curse.'[17] I see what Dickens means about London – and he referenced Borough and Old Kent Road on the south side as specific examples of this – when he said that it 'has expiring fits and starts of restlessness'.[18] The intoxicated magnetize, he suggested: 'when one drunk staggers into the shutters of a shop another will soon be along to fight with it'.[19]

I have arrived, like Dickens, at Waterloo Bridge. He describes looking at the bridge's tollkeeper, wrapped in shawls against the cold , resistant to the dawn. The only contented person to be seen. 'The bridge was dreary' Dickens says: it still is. He wrote of the water dripping from all around him: 'Drip, drip, drip, from ledge and coping, splash from pipes and water-spouts.'[20] When Dickens looked out across the river he saw murkiness.[21] Tonight there's neon as far as the eye can see: the deep blues of the *Pizza Express* logo on Belvedere Road, the seventies' orange of *Brasserie Blanc.* There's no *drip drip* tonight but there is a fierce hurtling wind coming in off the river. Waterloo Bridge has been rebuilt since Dickens walked here and there are now numerous ways to access it from the South Bank – each of them impossible to find at night. A red staircase spirals up between the BFI and the Queen Elizabeth Hall. Beyond the BFI – which is advertising a season of 'films to fall in love with or break your heart' – I look for the solid base, a staircase worthy of the tollkeeper Dickens described. People are parting around a revving cab, a young woman among them shouts: 'I love you all!'. A man is walking more slowly than I am – hooded against the wind, wearing shorts. Earphones beneath his hood. There is a new kind of nightwalker, one that isn't homeless – and not even houseless – but simply *here.* Transient. Passing between rented beds.

Since the attacks in Paris the only thing to cut the silence is tension. The occasional person I pass would have ignored me a few weeks ago – now we are quickly glancing, checking. Creating a narrative as to why the other person is out at night. I walk up the imperious steps to the bridge. When my eight year old son heard the news about the attacks in Paris he asked 'when will the war be over, is it finished?' The London I'm writing about now – as for any London writer – is mostly unknown. Things change before text goes to print. Could Dickens have imagined the future zeppelins over the foggy streets he loved? The blitz of shrapnel? Bombings at Russell Square? The words go down as mere impressions – trapped in time – waiting for the city to flex, or fracture or morph – into a new incarnation. To see Dickens as really here you have to think of the modernity of the Victorians, the man who could write that: 'each century [is] more amazed by the century following it than by all the centuries going before.'[22] A man passes in a black beanie – listening to his headphones – heading north towards the Strand. To the ghosts Dickens said that he saw in the windows of the closed theatres.

What has not changed is the aloneness of the transient houseless. This has exacerbated. Dickens described an incident at St Martin's Church in which a beetle-like, ghostly man in his twenties seemed to disappear before his eyes: leaving the rags he was wearing in his hands. Occasionally, in the day, people walk across the South Bank and stop to ask for directions. This rarely happens after midnight. People walk because there is safety in walking. If someone was to make contact unexpectedly we'd all turn to rags and disappear. Last night I was on the night bus and the driver – stopping the bus – came up the stairs to ask a child aged about nine who they were with? Faces in phones, sleeping, drunk: no one had noticed the child. Then a young man – getting some downtime with his iPod at the back of the bus – appeared to claim back responsibility for his younger brother.

Dickens walked northwards to the theatres, watching ghostly shadows appear in the upper windows. He then went on to Newgate Prison – along the north bank to Billingsgate Wharf – before crossing back on London Bridge to the 'Surrey shore'. Then to King's Bench prison, and with good reason: Dickens – agitated in mind and unable to sleep – was haunted by his childhood experience of visiting his father in the debtor's prison at Marshalsea. The experience changed the way he looked at the poor throughout his life. He then walked to Bethlehem Hospital – the current

Imperial War Museum – and into the parameters of this book: 'partly, because it lay on my road round to Westminster'. He also had an idea that had occurred to his overactive, sleepless mind: 'Are not the sane and insane equal at night as the sane lie a dreaming?'[23]

On Blackfriars Bridge Road a new bus stop has been planted in the freshly laid concrete. The mulch of root and bone has been replaced. A man stands next to the pillar, as some do, bobbing on his toes with a *Metro* in his hands. A cyclist goes past with an orange Sainsbury's bag swinging from the handlebars. Two men walk together, laughing at the behaviour of someone else they've just been in a bar with. It's nearly one o'clock in the morning now and still the people continue to surface: Orpheus figures led by the underworld of their phones. Apologies sent to sleeping lovers. No one stands still – even while standing.

A bus passes: the number 4, making its way to Waterloo. A blast of hot air streams from its reignited exhaust. Two men pass me, talking in Spanish, smiling. In the dark, after midnight, the passing shadows of others can be whatever we want them to be. Dickens saw no cyclists at night. There were no candles for the nightcyclist. And the cars, now, never end – on the bridge there is a constant stream of full-beams heading towards me. The next language floating on the wind is German as a young man – like a thin Rainer Werner Fassbinder – walks past, expounding emphatically. Then the white noise of the never-silence comes again. It is these torrents of people and movement that define our night London from that of

Dickens. South Bank speed. The city sleeps – like fish – with its eyes open. On the other side of the glass are those who bother to watch. The 188 bus stops and opens its doors, though there's no one to embark or alight. Commuter ghosts.

I walk back to Waterloo Road. A man in a suit – his tails like cut flippers – marches against the backdrop of another Sainsbury's window, with an umbrella and a batch of newspapers. Three students stumble into the shop. There's no need for an end goal – another drink or a home – it's perfectly possible to just *be* in today's night London. This new breed of the transient know that it's possible to simply be here, out under the stars – night is the same as day, working and dreaming are the same thing – being away from something is as good as being present elsewhere. These are not the houseless but the consenting revenants. I jump the bus. It follows a cyclist without a light towards the Elephant & Castle. A tree branch thumps the window as we approach St George's Circus. This is the night bus: the known route cloned for after hours. The night bus is a kind of living hearse for the drunk – the aggressive and the lost – but tonight the experience offers some level of serenity. It is emptier than usual – as if the recent bombings took place in this city – and I watch the reflections from the front mirror reflecting those behind me: a woman, with a ribbon in her hair, reading the *Metro*. The rest are texting. Quiet last words: it feels like we're all writing them now. Leaving a data trace of where we are.

Touching text.

Responding.

Meaning it.

SHAKESPEARE'S REAL GLOBE

We've walked down through Bridewell from the stairs of St Paul's where – just after the audio started rolling – I slipped on the steps. Poet and literature producer Tom Chivers tried not to laugh but Sarah Dustagheer – Lecturer in Early Modern Literature at the University of Kent and co-author of *Shakespeare in London* – couldn't help it. The moment says a lot about my approach to London's past: start high up, where the tourists are, and end with my head in a disused pipe. At least there's Sarah to keep us on course. We're supposed to be talking up my new poetry collection *Speculatrix* which has a series of poems spoken by characters from

Jacobean drama. *Speculatrix*: a female spy. The watched who watches. An essential coinage, lost to Latin. There's also an echo of 'speculation' here too: the watchword of modern London.

In reality the last few hours have become what we always knew they'd be: an excuse to recreate an old London which is always happening now. A London which never really disappeared but has also never truly become what it will one day be. The still living voices of the poetic lexicon pitch their coinages like darts into the Bear-pit of the daily commute – you just need to carry a Jacobean play with you to hear it.

Fortunately audio can be edited, wiped from the surface. London doesn't work like that. With St Paul's behind us, we pass through the Stationer's Hall – where all Jacobean plays where registered – then down Ludgate Hill towards Farringdon Street, stopping at the point where the River Fleet once ran. And still does, beneath the traffic flying towards the South Bank or veering towards east London and the two financial organs: the heart in the City, and the distended liver of the Isle of Dogs. Tom is the curator of the expedition but as an underground-river obsessive he's already off ahead of us, recording the sounds of his own shoes as he races towards a steel cover on the pavement. Then his ear's to the ground. He stands back up, rocking on his heels, his nostrils flexing: 'Smell that,' he says, 'that's the Fleet'. He's right: a rich mossy tang curls up to the senses. Joseph Bazalgette no doubt diverted some of The Great Stink to this hidden river: more hybrid water-current than organic Styx.

We walk back east – our route creating a runic letter C-shape on the face of London – stopping at the Cockpit pub in Blackfriars. The Cockpit has nothing to do with the old playhouse of the same

name though this was, Tom tells us, the scene of his stag night drinks. It's one of those tiny, corner-building London pubs: there's barely room inside to shake a tied-up bachelor wearing a Viking helmet.Heading towards Upper Thames Street we duck in to the church of St Andrew by the Wardrobe, where the choir are conducting a pre-Christmas evening matins – adding another sonic layer to our journey. All rectors since 1693 are written on the wall: a roll call of lost, disciplined faith. Sarah maps out the nearest remains – or at least known sites – of the Jacobean playhouses: The Curtain and The Theatre in Shoreditch and – in the direction we're heading – The Rose in Southwark. There's one particular site we want to find though: Shakespeare's real Globe. Not the reconstruction on Bankside further east but the real one – slightly further south from the muddy shore.

As we're walking we talk about the Jacobean playwrights as a huge band of competing and collaborative talents. Dekker, Marston, Jonson, Middleton, and – the greatest of them all, in my view – John Webster:

> If the buttery-hatch at court stood continually open, there would be nothing so passionate crowding, nor hot suit after the beverage.[24]

Stultifying wants, impossible desires, claustrophobia – there are few laughs in Webster – and when it came to audience response and further commissions, he paid for it. The most gifted are rarely rewarded in poetry: they sit picking their warts as the merry songsters are served hot cakes from the buttery-hatch.

Money continues to surface as we walk. My past lack of it; the frustration of trying to get out of the way of the problem via payday loans: that modern form of usury. A frustration which frothed with the spittle of Jacobean language in *Speculatrix*. We stand at the crossroads of Ludgate Hill for a while, outside the berry-red hoardings of the Santander bank. It's possible to spend an afternoon watching the adverts that appear on ATMs now. Flash animations of archetypal life predicaments. Middle-aged men enjoying a pint, relaxed in the knowledge that their accounts are in order. An old couple smiling on a cliff-top (death, the ever-closening force, represented in the white cliffs). A baby, pleased to be alive: our familial happiness is the bank's big concern. Everything promised – grab it quick, happiness doesn't come knocking twice.

I tell Sarah about the fix I get from Jacobean drama: the tension between those with and those without is always ready to switch. The same tension that also ran through the 1980s – everything's yours to have: aspire, speculate, invent, patent. The old lie based on the reality of a minority – which is why so many Jacobeans went to the playhouses to see the fortunes of lowly characters played out before them: characters whose fortunes convert them from guttersnipes to booty-holders. And why, centuries later, people protested the Poll Tax while those with time on their hands bought a mixing desk or invested in stocks. Sarah puts this well: in the Jacobean plays we see the clash of old money meeting new. The great buy-in to class and status. George in *The Knight of the Burning Pestle* is a kind of Del Boy: this time next year Rodders we'll have a sack of a thousand guineas.

As usual I've said too much: money signed away like an elastic candy string of zeros and ones pinging back interest before anything is tasted. There's a power to walking through the city – especially towards the South Bank – and raging against these forces. This is what underground rivers are for: a lilting backing track to the sound of your own improvised glossolalia. Later, when I listen to the audio of our talk, that sense of hitting the purple patch – the city rising to meet our efforts to find its truth – is justified in the dialogue at the Santander bank on Ludgate Hill. It reads like the script of a Jacobean play: this drive to capture the old truth now, to pin it in language now that we've aired it:

Sarah Dustagheer: They were seeing the beginnings of the capitalist system of credit and debt. So instead of trading in gold, silver, tangible materials, it's being replaced with intangible ideas. You can't touch the money, you can't see the money. It's being taken out of the hands of ordinary people. It becomes global, it becomes commercial. In 2008 we saw the repercussions of a system that began in the Jacobean period.

Chris McCabe: The idea of a bank run, when everyone comes for the money at once. In the Jacobean period that would have been everyone running for the signed bits of paper, the tally sticks and IOUs. The beginnings of the zeros and ones we know are flying around us all the time.

We move towards Bridewell, originally the palace belonging to Henry VIII. By the Jacobean period it was known as the site where sexual crimes were punished. Next door was the Blackfriars precinct, where plays exploring outlandish sexual possibilities were often performed: the id runs wild while the superego sleeps. The correctional forces need to let the people have their moment, fearful of the powder keg – as Sarah puts it – that comes with thousands of young men and outsiders hearing radical ideas. Forty years later the city was cleansed by fire, the old lines incinerated. Yet the shape of the Blackfriars precinct remains. We walk down Carter Lane into Playhouse Yard. Sarah talks of how the neighbours complained of the noise here: easy to see with these small, narrow streets. A single coach would jam the whole thing; today it would only take a cab or a badly parked Audi. And this was the theatre for the rich: six pennies was the minimal fee for access. The Globe could get you a standing space for a penny.

As we walk towards Millennium Bridge I suggest to Sarah that anyone renting property in London should read *The Alchemist*. Sarah takes the provocation forward: all this change in Jacobean London was being lampooned by Ben Jonson who realised that the idea of turning base metals into gold could be an image for changing identity and escalating social status. In my poem 'The Alchemist' I used the notion of alchemy to suggest the contemporary commute: people leave home with the idea of themselves intact but after bottlenecking with thousands of besuited clones they emerge into their public and professional moulds. In Jonson's play the baser characters have something that the privileged will never have: a language that *lives*. There is a quality of insult in *The Alchemist* that can be smelt as keenly as today's Fleet. The opening few lines has a character asking another to 'lick figs' – figs being anal piles. The fact that Jonson was classically educated suggests everything about the class tensions resident in the literature of this period.

The three of us walk up on to Millennium Bridge, a tin-thin twist of cotton silk that sways in the wind as we look at it. A hammock for sleepwalking commuters. The twin rails open out towards the ever-functioning Tate Modern. Blue lights pulsate along both sides. The Jacobean audiences, and Shakespeare, would have walked across the river using London Bridge, heading towards the Liberty of the Clink and the playhouses. Adding in a visit to a stew or Paris Garden – if they were making a night of it. The watermen would have been perched for punters. When heading in this direction the river invites forgetfulness: a Lethe filled with horseshoes and leather appendages, SIM cards and *Coke* cans. The blue lights pull us forward.

Walking on Millennium Bridge never feels right – it doesn't even *sound* right. A hollow reverb meets each footstep. Pilchard flesh mulched by a coiled lid. Which partly explains my resistance towards the tidal pull of the Tate and its art-as-product shop. We stop halfway across the bridge.

The north bank is well behind us now, the evening matins left for those walking the fringes of the ancient City. We look towards where we're heading: the reconstructed Globe seems to be expecting us, as it might justly expect anyone within range with an interest in Shakespeare. Shakespeare lived on the south side of the river, at one point near Paris Garden and then – in Spring 1599 – in a house near the Globe that is now lost. He would have heard the rivets being hammered down as he wrote the words of the plays to be performed in it: *Julius Caesar* or *Henry V.* Given the politics around the building of the theatres and the performance of plays – and the likelihood of Shakespeare being a catholic – there is no surprise that his mind was on political intrigue at this time.[25]

The south side of the Thames was the site of four playhouses: The Globe, The Swan, The Hope and The Rose. Today's Globe is painted a gleaming Dulux white and its Tudor décor is in a pristinely touched-up black. But we're looking for the site of the real Globe, the one that I described in my poems as being 'like a shitbasin of rivets, a cistern of balconies'. Sarah thinks that the 1997 rebuild is about right in its detail, maybe a bit too big, but 'if Shakespeare rose from the dead and found himself outside of it, I think he would squint and say you've got it just about it right'. I like the image of a squinting Shakespeare: he would no doubt return like Lear, a revenant confused and intrigued by contemporary London's accelerating appetites.

As we walk we talk riots. The Jacobean authorities allowed Shrove Tuesday as a regulated kick-back time, Sarah says. I recall how I was sitting in a restaurant with two other poets, just down the river – on the South Bank – when the last riots happened in London in 2011. Which were closely followed by riots in Liverpool. The South Bank was deserted that night: the leisure-seekers ran for cover, leaving the homeless and the poets behind. I look towards the Tate Modern: business as usual this evening. There's a dripping human trickle of black-wearing ticket payers entering the old power station at the front and then – like hospital entrants just fitted with colostomy bags – emerging from the side doors, loaded with new appendages in white *Tate* plastic bags.

The correctional threat benefitted the playwrights, we agree. They couldn't say – directly – what they meant. London dressed itself as the continent. Names became embellished and exotic. Shakespeare hid his Catholicism in the loft. Elizabeth, flattered by the prologue, took her eye from the analogous king whose lands were under threat. The writers were sycophantic *and* deftly skilled in the cut of contemporary satire. More discerning audiences knew what they meant, but who could ever prove it? Looking back at the dome of St

Paul's for a second I'm reminded why I'm less excited by metaphysical poetry which, in my view, is the source of the origins of the workshop poem. The prize-winning John Donne imitation piece. The poem as a snow globe: give it a shake and watch the poet's orchestrated scene settle in your mind. An easy trick to turn and one that leaves the poem unreadable a second time. I like explosions in every line: the poem that remains mysterious. As a child the first shake of a snow globe was magical but the magic waned when I realised how the thing worked. But getting lost in brambles made the gap between play and life disappear: and the scars were there to prove it. The real poetry of Jacobean London is in the plays not the poems: the stew of forms, the unwieldy language, the collapsing lines that tangle themselves in images of death and desire. The plays house the growing pains of the historical canon. I remember now, as the wind blows over the river, that Webster didn't write an introduction to John Marston's *The Malcontent*, he wrote an *induction*: let the waters break. The coruscation of light across the river moves in silver Vs, like lexical swans.

We walk across to Bankside, the firm landing of the embankment which not so long ago would have been true to the early modern experience of muddy sludge. We walk past the new Globe, heading to the unlit backstreets. In 1989 the remains of The Rose were found and now there's a programme of mini-plays that take place in a small theatre there. Marlowe's final play, *The Massacre of Paris*, is advertised on a flyer that's attached to the back door. Not just the remains of the playhouse were found, Sarah says, but 'items such as swords, pins, shoes, the debris of early modern playing and performance.' We cross Park Street, straight across the road,

checking both ways for a horse and cart – we've gone outside of the reality of contemporary London – and arrive at a Georgian building which reclaims the ground of Shakesperare's original playhouse. Underneath the newly listed buildings here will be further remains of the early modern audiences, including objects which might have belonged to Shakespeare himself. But the Georgian building is listed and the city's heritage interests are – as a rising investor in the city might put it – *Jenga'd.*

Outside of the rush of the already hurtling twenty-first century, lost in the cracks between the early modern and the future, there's only one thing left to do, Tom suggests: read one of my poems on the street.

And that's what I do.

Notes

1. Facts about Apollinaire's visits to London and affair with Annie Playden are from Francis Steegmuller, *Apollinaire: Poet Among the Painters*, Op.cit.
2. Quoted in James Campbell, 'To London, for love' published in *The Guardian*, Op.cit.
3. Francis Steegmuller, *Apollinaire: Poet Among the Painters*, Op.cit.
4. This interview is included as an appendix in the Steegmuller book but annoyingly the person conducting the interview isn't named
5. Ibid.
6. From Apollinaire, *Selected Poems* (translated by Oliver Bernard) Op.cit..
7. Ibid.
8. Francis Steegmuller, *Apollinaire: Poet Among the Painters,* Op.cit.
9. Charles Dickens, *The Uncommercial Traveller*, Op.cit.
10. Matthew Beaumont, *Nightwalking: A Nocturnal History of London, Chaucer to Dickens*, Op.cit.
11. The character is called Krook and this takes place in *Bleak House*
12. Matthew Beaumont, *Nightwalking: A Nocturnal History of London, Chaucer to Dickens*, Op.cit.
13. http://www.independent.co.uk/life-style/health-and-families/health-news/three-million-britons-working-night-shifts-and-endangering-their-health-10438592.html
14. Charles Dickens, *The Uncommercial Traveller*, Op.cit.
15. Ibid.
16. Ibid.
17. William Blake, 'London', in *Selected Poems*, Op.cit.
18. Charles Dickens, *The Uncommercial Traveller*, Op.cit.
19. Ibid.
20. Ibid.
21. Ibid.
22. Ibid.
23. Ibid.
24. John Webster, *The White Devil*, Op.cit.
25. Indebted to Michael Wood http.bbc.co.uk/history/tudors/Shakespeare_later_01.shtml for facts on Shakespeare's houses and *The Norton Book of Shakespeare* for the dates of the plays.

Liquid City is not Paris   I said that   it is not
        it is moving because Paris has stopped
        the dust still flying in mica chips
  lost notes   the unsung   abandoned drinks
            the sound of the Seine in sibilants
      syriasyriasyria
            this is not that   not on the Old Kent Road
        the Poundland or the Chicken Cottage
              the Cash Converters closed
      where Chaucer's pilgrims crossed the Neckinger
          the devil's neckloth
      Cities do that sometimes
            they hang themselves between stream & build
      like a creature of fire & water
                  cancelling elixirs with sterile lime
poets strap the beast of time to a florist's back
        like Apollinaire who sang his lyre in fog
      his back to the Seine
          The day's go by   he wrote   I still remain
      Under the Pont Mirabeau there goes the Seine

        The days go by I still remain

WORKS CONSULTED

Peter Ackroyd, *Blake*, London: Vintage, 1999

Peter Ackroyd, *London: the Biography*, London: Random House, 2001

Peter Ackroyd, *Thames: Sacred River*, London: Chatto & Windus, 2007

Apollinaire, *Selected Poems* (translated by Oliver Bernard), London: Anvil Press Poetry, 1994

John Agard, *A Stone's Throw from Embankment*, London: Royal Festival Hall, 1993

Catharine Arnold, *Necropolis: London and its Dead*, London: Pocket Books, 2007

Alan Bartram, *Bauhaus, Modernism and the Illustrated Book*, London: British Library Publishing Division, 2004

Georges Bataille, *Blue of Noon*, London: Penguin Books, 2012

Matthew Beaumont, *Nightwalking: A Nocturnal History of London, Chaucer to Dickens*, London: Verso, 2015

G.E. Bentley Jr, *The Stranger from Paradise: A Biography of William Blake*, Yale University: Yale University Press, 2003

William Blake, *Selected Poems*, London: Penguin Classics, 2006

Tom Bolton, *London's Lost Rivers: A Walker's Guide*, London: Strange Attractor Press, 2011

Charles Booth, *Life and Labour of the People in London*, Bibliolife, 2009

Gilly Cameron-Cooper, *Walking London's Waterways*, London: New Holland Publishers, 2011

Geoffrey Chaucer, *The Canterbury Tales*, London: Penguin, 2005

Charles Chadwick, *Rimbaud*, University of London: The Athlone Press, 1979

Tom Chivers, *The Neckinger Pilgrimage* (audio tour), 2013, heard by permission from the author

J. Payne Collier *Memoirs of Edward Alleyn, Founder of Dulwich College: including some new particulars respecting Shakespeare, Ben Jonson, Massinger, Marston, Dekker & c*, London: Printed for the Shakespeare Society, 1841

Jonathan Coe, *Like a Fiery Elephant: the Story of B.S. Johnson*, London: Picador, 2004

Elizabeth Cook, introduction to *The Roaring Girl* by Thomas Dekker and Thomas Middleton, London: A & C Black, 2000

Joseph Conrad, *Heart of Darkness and Other Tales*, Oxford: OUP, 2008

William Ronald Dalzell, *The History of London*, London: Michael Joseph, 1981

Guy Debord, 'Theory of the Derive', 1956 in *Situationist International Anthology*, Berkeley, CA: Bureau of Public Secrets, 2007

Charles Dickens, *The Uncommercial Traveller*, London: Mandarin, 1991

Patrick Dillon & Jake Tilson, *Concrete Reality: Denys Lasdun and the National Theatre*, London: National Theatre Publishing, 2015

Domesday Book: A Complete Translation (with an introduction by Geoffrey Martin) London: Penguin Classics, 2003

T.S. Eliot, *Collected Poems 1909-1962*, London: Faber and Faber, 1974

T.S. Eliot, *For Lancelot Andrews: Essays on Style and Order*, London: Faber, 1970

Ford Madox Ford, *The Soul of London: A Survey of a Modern City*, ed. by Alan G. Hill, London: Everyman, 1995

David Gascoyne, *Collected Poems 1988*, Oxford: Oxford University Press, 1988

Lindsey German & John Rees, *A People's History of London*, London: Verso, 2012

Alexander Gilchrist, *Life of William Blake*, Kindle Edition, 2013

Jonathan Glancey, *London: Bread and Circuses*, London: Verso, 2001

Stephen Greenblatt (editor), *The Norton Book of Shakespeare*, London: W.W. Norton & Co, 2008

John Hollingshead, *Ragged London in 1861*, London: Smith, Elder & Co, 1861 [available online at http://www.victorianlondon.org/]

Thomas Hood, *Selected Poems*, Manchester: Carcanet Press, 1992

Stephen Inwood, *A History of London*, London: Macmillan, 1998

B.S. Johnson, *Albert Angelo* in *Omnibus*, London: Picador, 2004

James Joyce, *Ulysses*, Oxford: Oxford university Press, 1993

Joe Kerr & Andrew Gibson (editors), *London from Punk to Blair* (second edition); London: Reaktion Books, 2012

Christopher Logue (editor), *London in Verse, edited, with notes and with illustrations chosen by Chrisopher Logue*, London: Penguin Books, 1984

Roddy Lumsden, *Not All Honey*, Tarset, Northumberland: Bloodaxe Books, 2014

Chris McCabe, *In the Catacombs: A Summer Among the Dead Poets of West Norwood Cemetery*, London: Penned in the Margins, 2014

Chris McCabe & Jeremy Reed, *Whitehall Jackals*, Rugby: Nine Arches Press, 2013

Shan Mâclennan, 'Case Study: Southbank Centre London and the Social Utility of the Arts', 2015, in Stephen Clift and Paul M. Camic (editors) *Oxford Textbook of Creative Arts, Health and Wellbeing: International Perspectives on Practice, Policy and Research*, Oxford: Oxford University Press, 2016

Henry Mayhew, *London Labour and the London Poor*, available online at http://www.victorianlondon.org/publications/mayhew1-1.htm

Hugh Mellor & Brian Parsons, *London Cemeteries: An Illustrated Guide and Gazetteer*, Stroud, Gloucestershire: The History Press, 2011

Thomas Middleton & Thomas Dekker, *The Roaring Girl* (editor Elizabeth Cook), London: A&C Black, 1997

Charlotte Mullins, *A Festival on the River: The Story of Southbank Centre*, London: Penguin Books, 2007

Douglas Murphy, *Last Futures: Nature, Technology and the End of Architecture*, London: Verso, 2016

Rick Myers, *Faraday's Synaptic Gap* exhibition, London: Southbank Centre and The Courtauld Institute of Art, 2015

Patrick O'Donovan (writer) & Hugh Casson (narrator), *Brief City: The Story of London's Festival Buildings on London in the Festival Year 1951*, London: BFI, 1952

Michael Paterson, *Voices from Dickens's London*; Cincinnati, OH: David & Charles, 2006

Roy Porter, *London: A Social History*, London: Hamish Hamilton, 1994

Stephen Porter, *Shakespeare's London: Everyday Life in London 1580-1616*, Stroud: Amberley Publishing, 2011

Samuel Pepys, *Diary of Samuel Pepys – Complete Edition*, ebookworms.co.uk, 2001

William Rendle & Philip Norman (1888). 'XIII'. *The Inns of Old Southwark And Their Associations*. London: Longman, Green & Co., 1888

Arthur Rimbaud, *Complete Works, Selected Letters* (translated by Wallace Fowlie), London: The University of Chicago Press, 1970

Graham Robb, *Rimbaud*, London: Picador, 2001

Chris Roberts, *Cross River Traffic: A History of London's Bridges*; London: Granta Books, 2005

Howard Roberts & Walter H. Godfrey (editors), 'Carlisle House and Carlisle Lane', in *Survey of London: Volume 23, Lambeth: South Bank and Vauxhall*, ed. London, 1951, online at http://www.british-history.ac.uk/survey-london/vol23/pp75-76

Daniel Rosenthal, *The National Theatre Story*; London: Oberon Books, 2013

Royal Festival Hall foyer exhibition, last visited 19 May 2015

David Rule, ↑, ← and →, privately printed for *On Reading and Walking and Thinking* exhibition at The Poetry Library, Southbank Centre, 2015

Fiona Rule, *London's Docklands: A History of the Lost Quarter*, Surrey: Ian Allan Publishing, 2009

John Rennie Short, *Urban Theory: a Critical Asessment*, 2nd Edition, London: Palgrave, 2014

Francis Sheppard, *London: A History*, New York: Oxford University Press, 1998

Iain Sinclair, *Blake's London: The Topographic Sublime*, London: The Swedenborg Society, 2011

Iain Sinclair, *Lights Out for the Territory: 9 Excursions in the Secret History of*

London, London: Granta Books, 1997

Iain Sinclair, *London Orbital: A Walk Around the M25*, Penguin: London, 2002

Iain Sinclair, *Swimming to Heaven: The Lost Rivers of London*, London: The Swedenborg Society, 2013

Edmund Spenser, *Delphi Complete Works of Edmund Spenser*, Kindle Edition, 2012

Gwen Southgate, *Coin Street Chronicles: Memoirs of an Evacuee from London's Old South Bank*, Bloomington, IN: iUniverse, 2011

Stephen Smith, *Underground London: Travels Beneath the City Streets*, London: Abacus, 2005

Francis Steegmuller, *Apollinaire: Poet Among the Painters*, London: Penguin Books, 1973

John Stow, *A Survey of London Written in the Year 1598* (with an introduction by Antonia Fraser); Stroud, Gloucestershire: The History Press, 2009

Craig Taylor, *Londoners: The Days and Nights of London Now – As Told by Those Who Love It, Hate It, Live It, Left It and Long for It*, London: Granta Publications, 2012

Dylan Thomas, *Collected Poems 1934-1953*, edited by Professor Walford Davies and Professor Ralph Maud, London: J.M. Dent & Sons, 1988

Dylan Thomas, 'The Festival Exhibition, 1951', from *The Dylan Thomas Omnibus: Under Milk Wood, Poems, Stories, Broadcasts*; London: Phoenix: 1995

Walter Thornbury and Edward Walford, *Old and New London: Volume 6*, London, 1878, http://www.british-history.ac.uk/old-new-london/vol6/pp45-57

John Webster, *The White Devil*, London: Methuen, 2008

Henry Benjamin Wheatley, *London, Past and Present: Its History, Associations, and Traditions*, 3 Volumes, London: Scribner & Welford, 1891

Edmund White, *Rimbaud: The Double Life of a Rebel*, London: Atlantic Books, 2009

Jerry White, *London in the Nineteenth Century*, London: Jonathan Cape, 2007

Jerry White, *London in the Twentieth Century: A City and its People*, London: Penguin Books, 2002

Simon Winchester, *The Surgeon of Crowthorne: A Tale of Murder, Madness and the Oxford English Dictionary*, London: Penguin Books, 1999

Virginia Woolf, *The London Scene*, London: The Hogarth Press, 1982

William Wordsworth, *The Collected Poems of William Wordsworth*, London: Wordsworth Editions, 1994

ONLINE SOURCES

Alembic House facts: www.skyscrapernews.com
Blackfriars Road photographs:
nickelinthemachine.com/2009/06/Blackfriars-road-the-ring-and-the-death-of-al-bowlly/
Blake Mosaics article: http://www.bbc.co.uk/london/content/articles/2009/03/19/blake_mosaics_video_feature.shtml
British History Online, http://www.british-history.ac.uk/
Roberto Calvi facts: https://en.wikipedia.org/wiki/Roberto_Calvi
David Cameron goes jogging story:
http://www.mirror.co.uk/tv/tv-news/morning-interrupts-food-segment-sweaty-6011840
James Campbell, 'To London, for love' published in *The Guardian*, Saturday 20th November, 2004,
http://www.theguardian.com/books/2004/nov/20/featuresreviews.guardianreview35
Garden Bridge website: www.gardenbridge.london
London Mental Health: The Invisible Costs of Mental Ill Health. Available online as a PDF, with an introduction by Boris Johnson, here:
https://www.london.gov.uk/sites/default/files/Mental%20health%20report.pdf
Maps of the South Bank through history Southwark Council website at
www.southwark.gov.uk/info/200212/egovernment/1370/southwark_maps
Millbank Prison: Wikipedia page for Millbank Prison:
https://en.wikipedia.org/wiki/Millbank_Prison
Night workers in the UK article: http://www.independent.co.uk/life-style/health-and-families/health-news/three-million-britons-working-night-shifts-and-end angering-their-health-10438592.html
Port of London Authority website: pla.ac.uk/Environment/Metal-Detecting-and-Digging-on-the-Thames-Foreshore
Report about Princess Diana visiting the Royal Vauxhall Tavern:
http://www.telegraph.co.uk/news/newstopics/diana/9963557/Freddie-Mercury-smuggled-Princess-Diana-into-gay-bar-disguised-as-a-man.html
John Rocque's map of 1746, online at wwwportcities.org.uk
James Runcie's website: www.jamesruncie.com
Jude Kelly article, Susanna Rustin, 'Health, Education and the Arts Should be Sacrosanct, Says Kelly', The Guardian, 12 March 2016.
http://www.theguardian.com/culture/2016/mar/12/southbank-centre-director-jude-kelly-health-education-and-arts-funding-sacrosanct]
Ruth Siddall, Waterloo & City: Urban Geology Across the Thames,
www.ucl.uk/Waterloo&City.pdf

The Thirsty Bear website at wwwthethirstybear.com
southbanklondon.com
The Vaults website: http://www.the-vaults.org/
'Walk This Way South Bank: London Eye to the Imperial War Museum'
http://www.southbanklondon.com/walkthisway/TheGuides.html
Michael Wood on Shakespeare:
http.bbc.co.uk/history/tudors/Shakespeare_later_01.shtml

THE PHOTOGRAPHS

ACKNOWLEDGEMENTS

An early version of 'Apollinaire's Stockwell' appeared in *Brittle Star* magazine.

I would like to thank all of the people who have talked with me during the writing of this book, sharing their stories about the South Bank. In particular I'd like to thank Bea Colley, Joanne Donovan, Sophie Herxheimer, Shân Maclennan, Pascal O'Loughlin and Anna Selby. Many thanks to Tom Chivers for allowing me to hear his audio guide and thoughts on the River Neckinger and for organising our Jacobean walk in the winter of 2014. Thanks also to Sarah Dustagheer for her knowledge of Jacobean London – the chapter on Shakespeare's Globe couldn't have been written withouther. Thanks go to Peter Finch for keeping this book on track. As always, the past and present poets of the South Bank remain my inspiration: Rimbaud, Blake and Ivor Cutler – as well as those who continually inspire with their living presence, and on the shelves, at The Poetry Library at Southbank Centre.

INDEX

THE AUTHOR

Chris McCabe's poetry collections are *The Hutton Inquiry, Zeppelins, THE RESTRUCTURE* (all Salt Publishing) and, most recently, *Speculatrix* (Penned in the Margins). He has recorded his poems for the Poetry Archive was shortlisted for The Ted Hughes Award in 2013 for his collaborative book with Maria Vlotides, *Pharmapoetica*. His plays *Shad Thames, Broken Wharf* and *Mudflats* have been performed in London and Liverpool and he has read his work at venues including Southbank Centre, the British Library, the BFI, the Whitechapel Gallery and the Wellcome as well as performing at festivals such as Latitude and Ledbury. His poems have appeared in *Best British Poetry* 2011, 2013, 2014 and 2015.

His creative non-fiction book *In the Catacombs: a Summer Among the Dead Poets of West Norwood Cemetery* was an LRB Bookshop book of the year. This is the first part of an epic project that aims to discover a great lost poet in one of London's Magnificent Seven cemeteries. The next publication in the series is *Cenotaph South: Mapping the Lost Poets of Nunhead Cemetery* and will be published by Penned in the Margins in November 2016.

With Victoria Bean he is the co-editor of *The New Concrete: Visual Poetry in the 21st Century* (Hayward Publishing, 2015) and his short story 'Mud' has been published in the Galley Beggary Digital Singles series.

Also in the Real series
Editor: Peter Finch